# The Crown Is Mine

By

Berlinda Wall

This book was printed in the U.S.A.

IBSN 978-1541015128

Second edition, April 2017

For my
family and friends.

\*\*\*~~~\*\*\*

# PROLOGUE

All I wanted was the crown. Nothing more. Nothing less. It was my end all and be all. The bright, sparkling, rhinestone diamonds over the silver metal frame forming my cylindrical satellite dish fantasy, and it was going to rest on my head. But I digress.

.

# CHAPTER 1

Clayton, Georgia is a good place to grow up if you want to serve the Lord or some spoiled, pampered ass wipes. Why is it that people with money can only talk about their money? I always thought that was rude to all of us who lived from paycheck to pay check. I don't care what you bought, where you're going on vacation, or where your spoiled child is going to school. A part of my anger, I'm sure, is just jealousy because I couldn't live the life they had so the little green monster kept popping up his ugly little head. Money in their life was their way of life so I guess you would spend all day talking about it.

Located in the northeast corner of Georgia, Clayton is a tourist mountain town that I couldn't wait to escape. It was a simple town with a lake, Lake Rabun that my family could never afford to live on. These were the homes of the spoiled rich who I had to serve while I slaved away at the Lake Rabun Inn. You could say it was karma the year the tornado came through and chewed up a bunch of their houses. I know I shouldn't be hateful, but you can only eat so much crow from these people. Plus, they didn't tip well.

The Lake Rabun Inn overlooked Lake Rabun and had a scenic wall of glass so that every view of the lake was maximized. It originally had been a quaint, little hotel, but as the tourist traffic increased for the lake, Tallulah Falls, and the changing of the leaves each fall, the owner went ahead and did a massive renovation. The inn got Wi-Fi, flat screens in every room, a spa, and banquet space. It had become a big fish in a very small pond, especially when your closest competition is a Motel 6. All this was courtesy of the new highway from the Georgia Department of Transportation.

I worked in the dining room at first where I started as a bus-boy and slowly progressed through every job you could have at a hotel. By the time I was 22, I was the front desk clerk, and all I had was a badge that read Tyler. I never felt more trapped.

# CHAPTER 2

My stupidly expensive iPhone rang. It was my friend Marjorie who had escaped to the emerald city of Atlanta.

"Pumpkin, I keep telling you to move down here with me. You know I have the extra room, and it would be good for your heart. I know how stifling it can get up there."

"I know, sweetie. If Daisy Mae doesn't stop rattling that Bible in my face, I'm going to jump onto the next man I see and ride him all the way to Atlanta."

"How is your mother?"

"She's fine. She keeps asking me if I'm going back to church. I tell her I'll think about it, and all she says is that she will pray for my soul."

"So will you really finally chuck it all and move here?" Marjorie asked. "What is keeping you there when there is so much more you could be doing here?" She knew she was right, and I knew it too.

"I don't really know. Don't have a boyfriend, and I've got a dead-end job that isn't going to take me anywhere." These words sounded strangely bitter as they rolled off my tongue. Fear of change is a terrible thing, and it paralyzes me something awful.

"I can help you with getting a job here, but the boyfriend problem is all yours. There is tons of work here. I miss my boo. It has been way to long," as she turned on her sad puppy dog voice.

I could never resist it. It reminded me of warm puppies

playing on a sunny day and all was good with the world. "I promise I will seriously think about it, and I'm not just pulling your leg on this."

"You just want someone to pull on your third leg. There are plenty of boys down here for that, but they're mostly bottoms so you will have a lot of competition. But with your double-bubble butt, you will have a field day," she insisted. I blushed, and luckily, she couldn't see that through the phone.

"Okay already. I will get back to you with an answer soon." But I wasn't sure how soon that was going to be. She was right that I had become stagnant and complacent in my little corner of the world. What a horrible place to be in.

At moments like this, I prayed which is ironic because I shut down Daisy Mae every time she brought it up. It's not that I am anti-organized religion, but more so anti-supposed to be Christians shoving their beliefs down my throat every chance they get. Yes, I may be gay, but I'm not stupid. I truly believe in all my heart that if you are a good person and treat everyone with respect and love, then you will achieve the next level in life after we depart, whatever that is.

I pray to God to help guide me in making the right decisions. I hear all these athletes and pop stars thank God when they win something, and it makes me wonder, do they really believe it, or is it a great PR stunt? OMG, I just came across as the same pompous asses I hate. "God give me the strength to do what is right and bless the people I meet whose hearts are full. Amen. Love, Tyler. P.S. A boyfriend would be nice."

# CHAPTER 3

The front desk was quiet now that the leaf season was over here in the mountains, and it was time to get some paperwork finished. Mr. Eddie, the owner, was chatting up guests in the gracious front lobby beside the roaring stone fireplace. The heat radiated all the way over to the desk and the dancing shadows meshed with the Mazak pouring out over the lobby speakers.

As the last guest parted to their rooms, Mr. Eddie strolled over to the desk. "Tyler, you have been a valued employee here for the past three years."

"It's been five Mr. Eddie."

"Well, you've been a valued employee for the past five years," he continued, "and in those five years, my niece Chelsea has finally come of age. Chelsea, can you come out here?" he bellowed.

From Mr. Eddie's office, a blond bombshell emerged flicking the long, blond strands of hair off her face. If I hadn't seen her with my own eyes, I would have sworn she came out in slow motion. It had been several years since I had seen Chelsea. When I last saw her she was a sullen, thin, little girl with glasses and dark pigtails. This vision walking out of the office would have put any street walker to shame. The pigtails were gone and replaced with a flowing blond mane. I'm pretty sure several hair extensions are involved. And her stick figure was replaced by a curvy, voluptuousness that overflowed from her push up bra. As a gay man a woman's breasts don't excite me, but I still can appreciate a great rack when I see one. I had a friend once who let me touch hers. They were very large and felt like a bowl full of jelly.

After my stupor wore off, I finally realized that on her large right breast was a name tag that read "Chelsea - Front Desk." There were only enough hours a week for two of us on the front desk, and the day front desk clerk was Annie, who was also related to Mr. Eddie.

Crap. This can't be good.

"Tyler," Mr. Eddie said, "Chelsea is going to be taking over the night spot on the front desk. Now that leaf season is over, it gets a little quiet around here. Maybe I can find you some hours helping out back in the kitchen."

"I've already worked the kitchen, and that is a step backwards." My heart was pounding, and every time I got the least flustered, my voice tended to rise. I must have sounded like a canary in a cage. "You can't do this to me. What happened to all that talk about me beginning training to become a manager?"

"I meant every word I said, but little Chelsea here let me know how much she wanted to go into hotel management. I just couldn't let my niece down," he said as he smiled like a wolf at Chelsea, who was twirling a piece of her hair and staring into the ceiling. "She is getting the position in our management training program. Family comes first. I'll have to ask you for your Front Desk badge." And with that he was finished.

There was no arguing on this, and with that I was finished. I couldn't go back to the kitchen. I had scrubbed enough dishes, pots, and pans to work my way out of there. How could I go back? Most of the kitchen staff are lifers who aren't going anywhere. I was going to make something of myself and get a little bit ahead for once.

I took my name tag off and tossed it on the desk. It made that plastic sound as it bounced and landed facedown. Kind of like a face down in a pillow. It seems like you end up getting screwed one way or another. Now to go home to Daisy Mae.

# CHAPTER 4

Daisy Mae was sitting at the kitchen table with her Bible open sipping a glass of sweet tea when I got home. "Viola called me and let me know you quit," she spit out. Viola was her good friend who worked in the kitchen at the hotel and never really liked me. As she put it, my "homosexual tendencies" could be fixed.

"It's not like I had a choice, mom."

"You need to go back there and beg Mr. Eddie for your job back," she insisted. "How are we going to survive?"

"I'll find something else. There is plenty of work up here." But even I didn't believe that. The job market was very limited, especially since we were heading into the winter months and the tourists were no longer driving through.

"I prayed that God would watch over you, but look what happened," she said as she clutched her Bible to her bosom. "Mr. Eddie is a righteous man, and your homosexual ways just don't sit right with such a good Christian man." She was almost crying at this point.

"Momma, please don't cry. It breaks my heart when you do." I gently took her hand. She looked at me for a second, and then I could see the redness rise from her neck and quickly sweep over her face as her blood pressure shot through the roof.

"It breaks your heart?" she screamed. "My heart has been broken ever since you told me you were gay. I've prayed that God would help you find a nice woman so that you could settle down and give me some grand-children."

"Momma, we have had this discussion way too much, and I don't want to go down that road again," I said very plainly. We've been to crazy town over this topic more than I ever wanted to. That's the problem living in a Republican-leaning small town where there is a church every mile.

"Pray with me, sweetie. Pray that God will help us at this hour of need. Get on your knees and pray," she said with a resolute look in her eyes.

I finally broke. "The only reason I would get on my knees is if some big dick man were standing in front of me stroking his hard dick."

Daisy Mae grabbed her sweet tea and threw it in my face. "I taught you better than that," she said as she pointed that accusing finger at me. And we were off to crazy town.

I reached over and grabbed a fluffy dish cloth with a picture of Jesus on it that read, "Idle hands are the devil's work". Before I even had a chance to wipe the dripping tea off my face, Daisy Mae snatched that towel right out of my hands.

"This towel is sacred to me. It was a gift from your father. How dare you blaspheme him by wiping off your potty mouth with our sweet Lord?"

Instead, I was forced to grab a paper towel from the Indian-themed paper towel holder. It was one of those wood posts in the middle of the metal base, except in this case, the wood post was carved to look like a totem pole. Daisy Mae had gotten it in Cherokee, North Carolina at the casino. "So I can use a paper towel inspired by your casino trip? Didn't God have a lot to say about gambling?" I shot back.

"Don't throw all this back on me. I did everything I could to raise you right," Daisy Mae said as she began to cry again.

"Momma, I love you very much, but I need to go and clean up." The sugar from the tea was getting sticky and it dried in my underwear.

"I know you're going to leave me," she said with a whimper and a trail of mini sobs.

"Maybe this is a sign from God that I need to do something else in my life," I said. "I just had this conversation earlier in the day with Marjorie about moving down to Atlanta. As you say, God moves in mysterious ways."

"So you're going to abandon me too?" Daisy Mae looked like a whipped horse. "Your father did it first and now you."

"Dad did not abandon you. He died." My father had passed away when I was five of a sudden heart attack, so I don't have a lot of memories of my father. What I do remember is he was a very loving and kind man. In my heart, I believe that he would have been okay with me being gay.

"He promised we would be together forever. He's gone, and I'm left here alone. What did I do to deserve this?" she asked.

"You didn't do anything to deserve this. Bad things happen all the time, momma, and heaven knows we have had our fair share. The good thing is we have gotten through it together, and this will be no different. You have always said you wanted to see me happy, and a move will make me happy."

"I didn't mean to disrespect you earlier, and for that I am truly sorry." I meant it.

"I love you, baby boy. I just don't want you to struggle the way I had to struggle to keep food on the table. It makes your heart very heavy worrying about where the money is coming from. It gets very stressful, and I don't want that to happen to you. At least my pills keep the blood pressure in check." She got up from her chair and hugged me. "Now go get cleaned up. You can't go to Atlanta looking like a slob."

# CHAPTER 5

Marjorie spent the next days scurrying around getting the apartment ready for her new roommate. The apartment was located at the corner of Piedmont and 14th Street and was a third floor walk-up with a spacious sunroom looking directly into Piedmont Park. The views from here were great all year long as the boys, straight and gay, walked, jogged and strutted their dogs into one of the main park entrances. It was a veritable smorgasbord of men just gliding by all day long.

Every day at 5:30 pm, her favorite object of affection- a tall, muscular dark haired jogger that she called "The Package"-would come running by. She looked at her watch. It was 5:29 pm and I was due at any minute, but she didn't want to miss her daily show. Some days "The Package" wore underwear and some days he didn't, so his kibbles and bits bounced as freely as he did. Unfortunately, she had never had the pleasure of meeting him and her affection remained unreturned. "Once day I'm going to grab those tight buns and just squeeze," she would say to herself.

As she looked out the window, I appeared on the sidewalk carrying an armful of junk and was heading up the sidewalk to the corner turn. Everything was stacked so high she doubted I could even see where I was going. She slid the window open and yelled, "Welcome, baby boy! Watch where you're going!" At that same moment, "The Package" came bounding up from the other side of the building and was heading for the same corner. Marjorie's attention immediately focused on the buns-of-steel as they went bouncing by. It was a non-underwear day. Unfortunately, I turned the corner too soon and didn't see the low brick retaining wall on his right. As my leg crumpled under the obstacle of the skyscraper of junk I carried, I tumbled like the Leaning Tower of Pisa and buried "The Package."

Marjorie looked in horror as "The Package" was pummeled and dropped to the ground. He was buried in a pile of underwear and other assorted sundries as he hit the ground. Marjorie fled from the window and sprinted down the three flights of stairs and bust out the door. As she was running across the grass courtyard "The Package" started pushing the pile of items off of him. All he could say was, "What the hell?"

I was starting to recover from this inopportune moment of clumsiness, and only realized that someone was under this pile of shit when I heard him speak. I quickly scrambled to my feet and started digging through the pile to uncover the person I buried, only to reveal a strange penis among my underwear.

Marjorie quickly hugged me. "I am so glad you are here! Now let's get him out of there."

We pulled each piece away and started throwing it over our shoulders. "Are you hurt?" Marjorie kept repeating as she flung more items out of the way. Slowly but surely, a profile started to emerge from below. She could see his long flowing hair and tanned body parts start to appear. It made her moist, as this was the closest she had ever been to her dream. "Let me help you up," she said as she stroked the uncovered hairy arm.

"That would be great," "The Package" said as he removed a jockstrap from his face. "My name is Roger."

"I'm Marjorie and this ever-so-apologetic person is my friend Tyler."

"Sorry, Roger. I didn't see the wall there."

As Roger strained to stand up straight, it was apparent

that he couldn't put any weight on his left ankle. He hobbled around grimacing in pain. Marjorie could only stare at his tight, tanned body with her mouth hanging open. Finally, I was able to pull her out of the clouds. "Marjorie do you have some ice? Roger, grab a squat here on the wall. We'll get you some ice for your ankle. What's the door code? I'll go get some ice while you keep Roger company."

"Ice would be great," Roger said and he slowly lowered himself down on the wall. When he sat down you could see that his right knee had been scrapped up and was bleeding a little.

As I headed to the door, Marjorie shouted, "You know which one it is, but just in case, third floor unit 10. The door is open. There are some Band-Aids in the bath vanity which is down the hall. Grab those too!" Marjorie's heart was racing, and she was at a loss for words sitting next to this Italian God she had only admired from afar.

"So how long have you lived here?" Roger asked.

"Almost two years now. I was renting a one bedroom while I was at Georgia Tech, but with a new job, I could afford more. I just love the fact that its right by the park and the view is killer." Marjorie started blushing as she caught herself staring into Roger's crystal blue eyes and realized he was staring back at her.

"Yeah, I run by here almost every day. I just live up the block in the Mediterranean-looking complex next to the M Hotel. I think I've seen you out here a time or two."

"Our parking lot is located half a block behind the building on a side street. Our paths may have crossed once or twice." Marjorie reached into her pants pocket and pulled out a tissue. "Here, at least let me try to clean that up for you," she said as she gently wiped at the blood drip on his right knee.

At that moment, I yelled out from the sun-room window, "Where are the Band-Aids? They're not in the vanity."

"Look in the hall closet. There should be a full box." And with that, I disappeared again. "I'm really sorry all this

13

happened," Marjorie said apologetically.

"Don't worry. I'm not. I wouldn't have met you otherwise. Would you like to go to dinner sometime?" Roger asked.

Marjorie swooned for a second and then regained her composure. "That would be lovely."

# CHAPTER 6

For my first night in town, Marjorie took me out to Club Cabaret with three of her gay friends. Who knew that Marjorie was not just my fag hag, but had her own posse?

Club Cabaret was a glittering palace on the outside with spotlights and a large neon sign spelling out Club Cabaret in a Moulin Rouge script. It looked so glamorous.

The inside was divided into several spaces. There was the interior courtyard with several palm trees, a Tiki bar, wicker furniture, low lighting, and low music blowing through like a summer breeze. The main bar was a large gathering space with a lit up glass cubed bar with stainless steel top and stainless, spinning bar stools. This was the main cruising room for anyone looking for their hook up for the night. The dance space had thumping music and many sweaty men with their shirts off in this tight, darker space capped at the end by another bar. There was also a billiards room if you preferred a little quieter entertainment.

The crowning jewel of the club was the Cabaret Room. The room had three levels of seating for the patrons divided by metal railings. The lower level had hardwood floors and your basic two-top round tables and chairs. The second level had cushy chairs and tables for four. This is where we sat. The final level had a row of comfy looking couches with table tops that swung back and forth so you could move your drinks out of the way if you had to go pee. The final space behind was standing room only. If you were here, you had to make sure you didn't block the bar service area and the way to the restrooms. All of this focused your attention to the red, satin curtain that was hiding the stage where the Club Cabaret Girls would perform their feats of talent for the drunk crowd.

The leader of Marjorie's pack was Chas, who was tall and slender and extremely funny. He could crack a joke or tell a story that would have you rolling. He could also be very catty, so I learned you had to watch what you said to him. He was dressed flamboyantly with a very loud print shirt and red pleather pants and shoes that complemented his short blond hair and glasses. It seems he never met any attention that was unwanted. His drink of choice was a dirty vodka martini, which never seemed to leave his hand.

Next was Albert, who was an early-20's conservative gay. He was trim, dressed in a button-down light blue Oxford, khaki pants, and dusty bucks. He was the quiet one of the group, but when he had something to say, he would chime right in with the rest of them. His eyes kept darting around the room on a regular basis as he slowly sipped his Cape Cod, so I finally had to ask, "Albert what are you looking for?"

"One of the drag queens here is in love with me," he said, "So I have to keep an eye out for her."

"Don't you mean him?" I replied.

"Not in this case," Marjorie responded. "This one is so fishy she leaves a stench and a snail trail behind her everywhere she goes. Her name is Miss Gigi."

At that moment, Albert sprang from the table, "Got to go pee." And with that he bolted to the bathroom.

Chas snapped his head and then pointed, "There she is by the door." Standing at the door was Miss Gigi in all her glory hole with her tight, one-piece, red, beaded bodice with red feathers for shoulders showing off her ample cleavage and curves. Her neck was covered in a multi-tiered rhinestone necklace with matching dangling earrings. Her makeup was flawless and she had a jacked-up "The Rachel" blonde wig that framed her face exquisitely. She had legs for days and obviously was tucked extremely well because there wasn't a bulge to be seen in that outfit. To finish out the outfit was a pair of rhinestone shoes with five inch spikes for heels. She looked around the room briefly and then strutted back to the dressing room.

Paul, the third member of the posse, grabbed his phone. "I'll text him the all clear." Paul was a furry bear who liked his beer. He was of medium build with big meaty hands and arms and a full beard and dark hair hidden under a Bud Light ball cap. He had a deep gravelly voice that just turned me on. "Have you ever been to a drag show?" he asked.

"No, this is my first one. We don't have this type of entertainment up in the mountains."

"What type of entertainment did you have in the mountains?" he asked.

"Let's say that if you didn't like the outdoors, you were pretty much screwed. There was bingo at the VFW hall every Thursday if you didn't mind playing with the grey hair crowd."

"That sounds like the Colonnade Restaurant here. You're either gay or grey if you go there," Chas said. "We'll have to take you there one day."

Albert finally slunk back into his seat. "I saw the crazy one go into the dressing room. I need another drink. Waiter! Another round here."

The waiter looked and nodded.

"I hope this round is on you. We can't be crazy patrol 24/7," Marjorie said.

"Yes, yes. It's on me. I know I need to do something about it," Albert acquiesced. "I'll talk to her after the show."

"Thank God for that," Chas quipped. "Because we don't need no drama before the show starts. I am not Mary J Blige. Miss Gigi is just a little high strung."

"If she is so crazy, why do y'all come here?" I asked very naively.

"Because we know the staff, and the staff takes care of

us. Plus, where else can you go and get fucked up this cheaply in this city?" Paul stated.

"Yes, there's that," Marjorie jumped in. "But I also like the entertainment. They do some wonderful group numbers here that none of the other shows in town do. I get tired of the pretty girls standing there pulling cabbage."

"What is pulling cabbage?" I asked.

"Pulling cabbage," Chas started, "Is when the pretty bitch is too tired to do something except stand there and model. All she does is a slow ballad and collect the coins that these low-brow patrons tip because they think this is high entertainment. She looks from left to right collecting the dollars. They need to get off their ass and do something different for once."

Marjorie jumped to their defense, "I like the slow diva ballads. And low-brow Paul here is one of their biggest tippers."

"Yes, I do enjoy a slow diva ballad, and if it is done right I will tip them. Not everyone deserves a tip," Paul clarified.

Finally DJ Scott came over the PA, "Five minutes to show time. Five minutes to show time."

"Looks like they are starting on drag time," Chas said.

"What is drag time?" I had to ask.

"The show was supposed to start at 9:00 pm, and here it is 9:30, so that is drag time. They just seem to start whenever their nelly little asses are ready." Chas finished.

"I'm excited. I don't know what to expect," I said.

"Just sit back, relax, and enjoy the show." Albert said. "And duck if Miss Gigi comes our way."

And when it started, I was not prepared. It was all a coordinated masterpiece in my eyes from DJ Scott to the queen with a clipboard to the entertainers. The show MC, Kit N Kaboodle, masterfully controlled the show's tempo and entertained the crowd. She made everyone feel welcome.

It was one queen after another. Some were the stand and model girls doing the power ballads from Celine Dion to Whitney Houston, but there were some incredible dancers who shook and shook. It was hard to believe that all these girls in crinoline, wigs, high heels, panty hose and sequins were men in dresses. Some you would have never guessed that they were men in a million years. There is an art to female impersonation, and they made it look so easy.

I was in awe of their talent.

# CHAPTER 7

It was a brisk night as Marjorie and I left the bar. We were starving after the show, so we walked to Peachtree Street and strolled down to Mama Ninfas, the late-night Mexican restaurant. "You'll love this place," she said, "It's the melting pot once everybody is good and drunk. You'll see everything from twinks, leather daddies, bikers, skin heads, drag queens, and straight people and the bar staffs as they get off coming here to hopefully get off." And she laughed.

"What's the nightlife like here?" I asked since I had never been down to visit.

"It was really hopping until the city of Atlanta, in its infinite wisdom, decided to eliminate the 24-hour liquor licenses," she sighed. "There were a couple of bars that were just fucking off the chain at night. They would have loved you there, baby."

"You're so kind to me."

"You deserve it," she said and then yelled, "Hey Wendy!" and waved to a gaggle of girls. The girls all waved back and came running over and started a hug fest.

"Ladies, this is my new roommate I was telling you about. Tyler this is Shelby, Wendy, Glady, Mary, and Terry. Ladies, Tyler."

"You didn't tell us he was this cute," Wendy said.

"And such a fine ass," Glady said. "Turn around and shake it for us."

With a couple of cocktails in me I couldn't resist and I started twerking for the girls until they all squealed. When I was finished, I slapped my ass.

"You go, sex kitten," Mary said.

"Come on sex kitten," Marjorie said as she pulled me to a table followed by the whole gaggle. "Slide around, Tyler. We girls like to be close to the bathroom." So I slid all the way to the back of our brown, leather, curved booth. I felt like a trapped animal surrounded by a bunch of cackling hyenas as the volume went up as the drinks kept flowing. It was hard to get a word in edge wise, so I sat there observing and eating the chips and salsa. The chips were warm and crunchy, which is the sign of a good Mexican restaurant, and the salsa was fresh and had just the right kick. I hate it when restaurants try to pass off store-bought chips as fresh made because you can tell all they did was open a bag of Tostitos and dump them in the baskets.

At least the girls had the sense to order some appetizers. When the nachos and taquitos arrived, it brought the table conversation down to a dull roar from the screaming pitch that it had been. I was almost afraid to reach out for any of the food because hands were grabbing at it so quickly. I was afraid to stick out my hand and pull back a bloody stump.

"So Tyler, what type of underwear do you wear?" Shelby asked. "Tighty whities or boxers?"

"Leave the boy alone," Terry said, "He looks like he is shy."

"He's not that shy. Once he gets to know you he can't shut up," Marjorie said.

"Thanks, mom," I responded.

"Well I prefer silk panties," Shelby followed up. "But tonight I'm wearing a thong."

"Ever wear a thong, Tyler?" Terry asked.

"It would really accentuate your ass," Mary said. "And frame it just right."

"I've never worn a thong, but I do prefer colored boxer briefs because they hold my goodies and give it that little push out front," I said proudly.

"Honey, you never use your goodies. You just need to work those hot buns of steel of yours," Marjorie said.

At that moment, all you could hear was a banging pot. It was the shooter girl wearing a sombrero and what looked like a native costume you would see Miss Mexico wear at the Miss Universe Pageant. "Shots only three dollars," she said with a very heavy Mexican accent. "We got two flavors, strawberry and lime," as she held up the two bottles that looked like they were just coated in dripping sugar.

Little did I know these girls were in it for the long haul on my initiation night to Atlanta. The next thing I knew, there were seven shots, a salt shaker and lime wedges on the table with each girl reaching for their favorite flavor. I was left with the lime tequila shot. It smelled just like a margarita. I never had any experience at doing shots, but I was learning quickly. Each girl grabbed a lime wedge and held it between their thumb and forefinger, then filled the cup formed at the base of the thumb and forefinger with salt. Then they held the shot in their other hand.

"Alright girls," Wendy said. "Let's all say welcome to our new friend. Tyler, may you find a pole in every port. Cheers!" And with that, each of the girls licked the salt, chugged the shot, and sucked the lime wedge.

I followed suit only to find another round of shots already on the table. Our shooter girl was earning her money tonight.

"Why don't you try on Shelby's thong?" Wendy said.

"Yeah. Come on, Tyler. It will really show off your ass," Shelby said.

"I don't know. I've never worn women's clothes before," I said.

"Well there is always a first time for everything," Glady said.

With that, Shelby stood up and made the other girls move out of the way in the booth. She then grabbed my hand and dragged me through the restaurant. I felt like everyone's eyes were on me, but I'm sure that was just the tequila talking. She stuck her head into the women's room and then pulled me in. We immediately went into one of the stalls and she started unbuttoning her pants.

"Whoa, I'm not into girls," I said, frightened at this point.

"I know that, silly. Now unbutton your pants," Shelby said as she grabbed my zipper and pulled it down. "If I'm going to give you my thong, I need your undies, because I don't go commando." And next thing I knew, my belt was undone.

By this point Shelby, had already removed her pants and her hot pink thong. "Hurry up, honey."

So in the next minute, I was naked from the waist down and then slipping on a hot pink thong. She was right that it really did show off my butt. As I pulled up my jeans, it was a strange sensation because I had never felt the rough material on my bare cheeks before. It sent a tingle down my spine and into my penis.

As we stepped out of the stall, there was a line of women waiting to use the restroom. We both immediately went to the mirror where we fixed our hair and washed our hands. There were a lot of nasty looks as we slipped by the waiting line and exited.

"So how does it feel?" was the first question from Glady.

"Is pink your color?" was the second question from Mary.

Finally Shelby interrupted and said, "These feel great. There is so much room here! My pussy finally has a chance to breath."

"Honey, your pussy is always breathing over every Tom, Dick, and Harry it sees," Glady said.

I finally did give them the answers, "Pink is not my color, but these make my ass look great. Unfortunately they cut off the circulation upfront."

"If that's the case, then you need to push your balls up into the cavity where they descended from," said Marjorie. "Just like the girls we saw tonight."

"Ewwww. That would hurt. What if they never fell back out?" I asked.

"Don't worry. You can grow another pair," Wendy said as they all started to laugh.

And with that, the party was over. We all had to head out and get some sleep. This was a very interesting evening for my first night in town.

# CHAPTER 8

I had to find some gainful employment because the little money I brought with me wouldn't last forever. Plus, I could only live off the generosity of Marjorie for so long before I felt like a parasitic leach. I do have some skills, so I am employable, but it's hard to break into a city where you don't know anyone. Thankfully, Paul had a lead at the M Hotel, which was just up the block from our apartment. A friend of his was the HR director at the hotel, and they had an opening for a front desk agent.

Before my interview, Paul gave me a brief history of the M Hotel from what he could remember. I just hope he wasn't pulling my leg. Here is what he told me.

The M used to be a Sheraton Hotel until it was sold, and they came in and did a massive renovation. From what I understand, the Sheraton Hotel used to be a very popular destination during what used to be called the Hotlanta Raft Race, which ended many years before my time here. The raft race would bring in hot, hunky men from around the country for a weekend of parties and sex all based around the Mr. Hotlanta contest and the Raft Race, which was just an excuse to float down the Chattahoochee River and party. And the hotel hosted the Miss Hotlanta Pageant, which was for female impersonators. People who lived in the August Tower across the street used to spend many hours that weekend watching the hot, horny men fuck in their rooms with the curtains open. I guess if you are on the tenth floor of a hotel, you don't think anyone is watching, but there are eyes everywhere. Once it became the swanky M Hotel, it was a much more upscale crowd. His final bit of history was that the M Hotel is actually the hotel they used when American Idol came to town for auditions. Even though the contestants used to perform in front of Miss Lopez and crew with a view of Olympic Park in the background about three miles away, somehow they manage to pop out of the ballroom of the hotel and into the motor lobby. The grass wall is a pretty dead giveaway.

So I had an interview with Kristoff at 10:00 AM on Monday morning, and I put on my best grey suit that I think I last wore for Christmas Eve services at Daisy Mae's church. I was as nervous as a cat on a front porch full of rocking chairs.

Kristoff, the HR director, was all business from his black-rimmed glasses and quaffed hair to his black wing-tip shoes. He was very friendly and he made me feel welcome as we headed to his office. "So I hear you are new to Atlanta. How long have you been here?"

"I just recently moved here from North Georgia," I let him know. "And I'm just around the corner from the hotel."

"I've looked over your resume, and you have a lot of experience for what we are looking for," he continued, "Let me take you on a tour of the hotel."

We started by heading up an elevator to the sky party space. It was a large banquet room with windows on three walls offering great views of Piedmont Park and Midtown. This was followed by a tour of the gym, spa, and the pool. He let me know that the Virginia Circle condos, which are attached to the hotel, did have use of the pool.

"I never understood why you would pay so much for one of those condos if you didn't even have your own pool. They even have to pay for their parking because it's not included in the monthly fee," Kristoff spelled out. "Excuse me for sounding bitter. I just can't afford that building and would give my left nut to live there."

Our final stop was the lobby, which was all tile, warm woods, reception, concierge and bar. The hotel guests were milling about, and behind the reception desk were two men and a woman. The two men were polar opposites, with one gentleman in his fifties who was already grey-headed and rail thin and the other in his thirties and very bear-like. This city seems like it is full of bears. Maybe I'm just a cub and don't know it yet. The woman was a tall red head with long, straight hair. Her feet had to be killing her because her heels were really high. Kristoff introduced me to the staff and everyone looked to be in a panic.

"The computer is locked again," Braxton the cute teddy bear said.

"We've tried every trick we could, but it's not working," Sheila added.

"It's this damn system," Germaine continued. "There is a bug in here that we keep asking IT to get resolved." The first thing you noticed about Germaine was the number of rings on his fingers. There were some very big shiny rocks there.

"What type of system are you using?" I asked.

"It's the Front Desk T200 system that's supposed to be the top of the line, but it keeps giving us fits," Kristoff let me know.

Braxton informed me, "It keeps locking up on the room assignments so it slows us down from getting the guests put in their rooms."

"This is the same system that I used at the hotel I just came from," I said, "We may have been small, but our owner believed in sparing no expense when it came to the equipment. Here's the fix we used."

I showed them a couple of key strokes that bypassed the bad part of the program, and let them do their jobs without the glitch. The company was issuing an upgrade to fix the issue, but I never saw it at the old hotel and obviously not here. "That should do it." And with that, the problem was solved.

"You're a miracle worker!" Germaine yelled, "Water Helen! Water!"

I didn't get the reference, but everyone else did because they laughed. I didn't want to feel left out so I laughed along.

"Okay, young man," Kristoff interjected, "You've got the job. Let's get your paperwork started."

And with that, I was gainfully employed.

# CHAPTER 9

So I had a cool apartment to share with Marjorie, who was getting along well with "The Package," and I had a job. It was great to be settling in and getting into a routine, but I was a little lonely. It was hard to see them cuddling up on the couch and watching movies all the time. I guess it made me a little moody. After all, I had been here for two months and still didn't have a single date.

"Boo, you seem a little down," Marjorie said. "Is there something that I can do for you?

"No. You have been so great already letting me play with your friends, but I want a boyfriend," I responded.

"Why don't you go onto one of those apps and order some delivery?" "The Package" asked.

"I'm not hungry, just lonely," I said again.

"No, not a food app. Go on one of those hook up sites and order yourself a fuck buddy," he said.

"Yeah, you should," Marjorie reinforced. "You could have some great, meaningless sex in the meantime until you find that special person."

"What apps are you talking about? There weren't many men to choose from in the mountains so I'm not sure what you are talking about," I said.

"You know. Grindr. Scruff. Growlr, Bear411," Marjorie listed off. "I'm sure there are more. You go on and post pictures of yourself and then message the boys you think are hot. If it works out, you end up riding their disco stick."

"You can either host or travel. Since you're new to town I would say you might want to host for safety reasons," "The Package" said.

"How do you know so much about these?" Marjorie asked.

"Some limited experience. How do you know the names of all the gay ones?" "The Package" asked Marjorie.

"I like looking at hot pictures of men, plus with being this close to the park it's great to recognize some of these men as they head into the park. It's like a game," she finished.

"Where do I start?"

"We need to get some sexy photos of you. You have to have a face shot. You get more traffic that way. Plus you're cute, so the boys will eat you up," she said.

I didn't really know what to think of the hook up apps. It would be nice to release some of this built-up tension, but at the same time, I want someone who is going to care for me and not just think of me as some hot bottom to fuck.

I needed to remind myself of what Daisy Mae said. "Sex is sex, but love is much more intimate. Never forget the difference between the two, otherwise it will screw with your head."

I guess I never had the opportunity to experience the difference between the two, but I do now as she's not here stalking over me.

"Where is your phone?" Marjorie asked. "Time to get this show on the road and take some pictures."

"Wear something sexy and low cut," "The Package" said.

"Sexy and low cut is for a straight site," Marjorie scolded him. "You need just to be you. Now hop on the bed and make puppy eyes. I'm tired of all these photos with their phone in the picture."

"I really appreciate this," I said honestly.

So we took some bedroom shots with me making puppy eyes. I tried to be as serious as possible, but sometimes it struck me as funny how I'm trying to look all sexy only to find someone to take my clothes off with. Marjorie also made me do a costume change for a different look. There were some good shots to use.

"Now if you want private naked shots to send to these boys, you will have to do those on your own," Marjorie said. "Those I won't take for you."

"Now all you have to do is pick a name and set up your account," "The Package" said. "Since you seem to like bears, I would suggest Growlr."

So I found the app on my phone and downloaded it. It was pretty self-explanatory, and I picked the name Spankybtm. I filled in my info as honestly as possible, since I believed that was the best policy, and picked a photo that I thought was the most flattering. Once I completed it, I was online.

In that instant, a whole new world opened up before my eyes. Here was a list of horny men all looking for the same thing, and the best part was it let me know how far away they were.

"If you click on their profile, you get a better look at their picture," Marjorie pointed out. "So you can see them close up. For the ones you like, just click on message and type away."

Within a minute I had a message pop up. It was from someone named Beartuff. It read "Hi." I clicked his picture to get a better look. He was five foot nine and weighed 180 with a six- pack and a great furry chest. He even had the beard. Everything I loved in a man.

Where do I go from here? I liked his picture so I typed back, "Hey, like your fur."

It made my heart rush and my penis throb a little. It has been a long time since I had the pleasure of a man's company, and I really needed it.

"What you into?" was the next message.

It didn't take me long to type back, "I love to have my ass pounded."

Within a second he typed back, "Your place or mine?"

"Marjorie, would it be ok if I have some company over?"

I asked.

"Honey, this is your place too. You don't have to ask me for permission," she said.

"Here goes." I messaged him my cell and said send me your number. With that, I was able to text him my address. He only lived about two blocks away. At least I wouldn't be doing the walk of shame.

"The Package" said, "We're going for ice cream. Just make sure you hide your phone in case we come home to your dead body. At least we can track the bastard down. Have fun." And with that, the front door shut, and I was alone waiting on Beartuff.

That freaked me out a little. I'd never done anything like this, and I didn't want to end up dead just for sex.

Within minutes, the door buzzer rang. I pushed the button and listened as the door opened and the footsteps started falling on the stair risers.

My heart was racing as I waited for the knock on the door. Finally, the knocks hit. Knock. Knock. Knock. I grabbed the knob and opened expecting Christmas, but only finding Halloween.

As it turns out Beartuff had put on some weight, and I don't mean just a little weight. If he had been a couple of inches taller he would have formed a perfect circle. I was at a loss for what to say.

"Are you going to invite me in?" he asked.

"No." And with that, I closed the door. I heard the footsteps as he headed down the stairs and out the door.

My longing for male companionship would have to wait for another day.

# CHAPTER 10

"What's your purpose?" Germaine asked.

"What do you mean?" I responded.

"It has to be more than this," he said as his hand made a grand gesture towards the hotel lobby. "What do you want out of life?"

"I'm not sure yet," I said, which was true. I was too young to really know what I wanted to do and what my purpose was. It's like people starting in college trying to determine what they want to do for the rest of their lives. You may like something now, but what happens in a couple of years when your dream job has turned into a nightmare? If you do something because your parents want you to do it will you despise them for the rest of your life once you're stuck doing it? Or do I give Daisy Mae credit for letting me lead my own life and make my own decisions? She didn't push me, and I'm forever thankful for that. I don't think I ever did tell her how much I appreciated her for letting me make those decisions. I made a mental note to call Daisy Mae after work tonight and thank her.

"Are you there sugar? Come back to me," Germaine said, and then he snapped his fingers.

"Sorry, got lost in my own world for a minute. What were we talking about?"

"Your purpose," he said again. "What drives you and how are you going to get there?"

Both of these were good questions. "I can't think past

tomorrow. I get so bogged down in the day-to-day stuff that I can't think past it."

"Well you made the first step by moving here, so take advantage of it. Now make a plan. I believe we all need to give back to our fellow man, so that is why I like to volunteer for different organizations. It is a great way to meet a lot of people, plus it makes you feel better by helping others out."

"By volunteering, aren't you just making yourself feel better by volunteering?"

"That's a little cynical," he said. "I think the people you help are a lot more appreciative for the things you do for them than you think. Something small that you do may have a greater impact on a family than you will ever realize. I collect toys for For the Kid In All of Us. I may never see the end receiver, but that family may have a Christmas because I put a box out at the Starbucks and collected toys."

"I never thought about it that way," I said, which was true. Yes, you may feel better doing volunteer work, but the end receiver feels even more appreciative than you will ever know.

"The younger generation needs to get that in their heads," Germaine finished. With that, he took a step to his left and bent over to pick up something.

"What are you doing?" I asked.

"It's time to get off of my soap box and put it away."

"So what are some good organizations to volunteer for?" I asked.

"Our shifts just about over and it's the weekend. I'll introduce you to Miss Gorme, a regular at the bar here. She is the queen of volunteers here in town. Just a heads up, she is a straight man who cross dresses. Sometimes it is Miss Gorme and other times it will be plain Jim, but you always must call him Miss Gorme."

So our shift was over just as the happy hour crowd was rolling in and filling the lobby bar. Germaine and I took off the hotel pins and sauntered across the lobby. Miss Gorme was seated at her usual corner spot. Today she was wearing a tight, leather, studded blouse and skirt with matching thigh-high boots with a spiked heel. Her hair was perfectly quaffed, and she finished off the outfit with a leather-studded collar. This was one of her evening outfits.

"Miss Gorme, may I introduce you to a very wonderful young man who needs some guidance," Germaine said.

"Germaine, you sweet thang, give me a hug," Miss Gorme responded. She stood up and hugged Germaine very tightly. I didn't realize she was that tall until she stood up. "Any friend of yours is a friend of mine, sweetie. Who is this young thang?"

"May I introduce Tyler from Clayton," Germaine said.

"Why Tyler from Clayton, you are about the cutest thang that my eyes have seen since I saw my grandbaby last week. Please just don't tug on my curls like she did," she said, and with that, she pinched my cheeks. "Sit down and have a drink. Veronica will take care of you."

"Thank you very much," I said. "We would be glad to join you."

"Tyler is looking to do some volunteer work, and I wanted to see if you could match him up with an organization that would be a good fit," Germaine said.

"What are your interests?" Miss Gorme asked. "AIDS charities, children's charities, gay youth, elderly care, homelessness, cancer, feed the hungry, or animal charities?" she rattled off.

"I guess I relate with gay youth since I'm not that far out of that age bracket," I said.

"Good," she said. "Because there are a couple of wonderful charities that are doing incredible things on minimal budgets and can use the help. Let me recommend Atlanta Street Rescue. It is an organization that gives homeless youth a place to stay and gets them off the street. They just bought a new building and need help getting it cleaned up. Would that work for you?" she finished.

"Sounds like a great opportunity," I said. "Just let me

know who I need to call." Miss Gorme was kind enough to give me the phone number of the director, Jerry Mikler, whom she said can sometimes be a little crotchety, but was a very nice person.

"See you're on your way to your purpose," Germaine said.

He was right. The smallest things can give you a sense of direction, and I was just starting that journey.

# CHAPTER 11

The weekend was here and it was time to get wild. I was going to something called an underwear paint party. Albert and Paul were letting me tag along with them when they go to The Forest, the largest dance bar in the city. I was still learning the personalities of all the different clubs, trying to figure out where I fit in. This was going to be my first experience at The Forest, and the boys assured me that I would be safe in their care.

I wasn't sure what to wear, and I'm not sure what you actually do at an underwear paint party. As it was explained to me, it's like the scene from Miss Congeniality where there are drums of paint that you can bang on and splash the paint around, but only here you are wearing your underwear. When you get there, you strip down to your underwear and leave your clothes bagged up at the clothes check. Leave it to a gay bar to have a clothes check.

With it being a little warmer out for once, there already was a line of scantily clad boys waiting to get in. I felt a little overdressed in my shirt and jeans as I tugged at my pants.

"Don't worry," Paul said, "Everyone will be scantily clad once we get in there and the paint washes off with water."

As I mingled in the crowd, I could feel the eyes tracing the outline of my naked flesh. My underwear and certain body parts glowed with the neon paint colors that were applied at the paint tent. I asked Albert if there was an arrow painted on my back aimed at my ass. I swore it felt like the bristles of the brush gently formed the arrow as the hungry painter colored me up. I didn't know whether to be embarrassed or go with it, so I decided just to go with it.

"Yes, honey it's pointed right at your crack. At least it's truth in advertising," Albert said.

I was surprised how tight Albert's body was. I had never seen either of them out of clothes, but Paul was as exactly as I had pictured. Tree-trunk thighs, hairy pumped up chest, and sculpted guns. I always pictured him with more hair than he actually had, but I was fooled by the tufts of hair that always stuck out over his shirt collars.

We entered the main dance floor to witness the hundreds of men and their naked, painted flesh gyrating in a massive throng with reckless abandon. I was still feeling a little self-conscious so I turned to Paul. "I need a drink."

"Whatever you need to buck yourself up," he said. "This round's on me."

I quickly slid to the corner bar station where the dreamy-eyed bartender asked me "What'll you have?" I lost myself momentarily as I was falling in the deep pools of his beautiful blue eyes. It wasn't until Paul pushed my shoulder that I came back to reality.

"His name is Daniel. Order your drink," he commanded.

My butt puckered as I ordered a screwdriver.

"Coming right up," he said, and he worked his magic getting the drink ready. At one point I swear he was rubbing ice cubes on his nipples and six-pack abs as the water trickled down his happy trail and finished in the Promised Land. Again, Paul had to push my shoulder. "Your drink is here."

I looked down and quickly grabbed my drink as my fantasy bartender was already working on the next round of drinks. "I will call you bun bun," I said to myself.

"He has that effect on everyone," Albert said. "But he never gives his number out or goes out with anyone from the bar."

"A man of mystery. I'm feeling a little verklempt," I said

and proceeded to chug my drink. "Let's dance!"

With my confidence booster working its way through my bloodstream, I summoned all my courage as we entered the cluster of sweaty men. We managed to bump and grind our way to the middle of the floor and were surrounded by a swarm of hard, chiseled, muscular men. I usually am not attracted to shaven men, but this much beautiful muscle made me hotter and sweatier.

Paul pulled out a small brown bottle from the pocket of his sport shorts. He placed it under his nose and pinched one nostril closed as he took a deep breath through his nose. There was a look of euphoria over his face. As he came back down, he grabbed my hand and placed the bottle in the palm of my hand. "Give it a try," he screamed over the music.

"I've never done coke in my life," I yelled back to which Paul started laughing.

"It's not coke," he said, "It's only poppers."

"What?" I yelled.

"Poppers!" Paul screamed.

"What are poppers?" I asked.

"It used to be called rush back in the day. It makes you feel warm all over and horny as hell," Albert said. "Just hold it up to your nose and pinch one nostril shut and inhale."

"This won't kill me, will it? If it does, you guys are going to have to deal with Daisy Mae and Marjorie."

They assured me I would be perfectly fine.

I cave into peer pressure so easily. The bottle was at my nose, one nostril pinched closed, and I inhaled. It has a distinctive smell that you can never mistake for something else, just like pot. As I inhaled I felt the wave of warmth rise from my lungs to the top of my head. Every pore of my body was alive, and I had become a cat in heat.

Paul briskly grabbed the bottle, "That's enough for you junior," he said.

A hot, blond muscle boy from the group had been staring intensely at me as his body swayed to the music. He broke from the herd and was immediately face-to-face with me, gyrating his hips against my groin. He must have felt the heat from my body as I started to sweat. He gently tweaked my nipples, which sent shivers down my spine. He grabbed my hand and rubbed it up and down his tight abs and all over his built pecks. He finally cupped my hand over the front of his paint-spattered tighty whities, where I could feel his manhood rising. I quickly spun around and shoved my crack hard against his ever-expanding underwear. I could feel the blood pumping through his cock as it stiffened and straightened up.

He thrust it between my cheeks as he grabbed my chest and pulled himself tighter. All I could do was grind back, thrusting my ass up and down as I felt his cock slip out of his underwear and my underwear pulled down in the back. I couldn't stop myself. Nothing was said between us as his cock kept rubbing over my sweaty hole. His thrust got faster and harder until I felt the spasm from his cock and a warm sensation on my back. I felt the back of my underwear pulled up over my ass.

I turned around to see the blonde muscle boy, but he had already vanished into the crowd. It wasn't until then that I realized the group of muscle boys and Paul and Albert had been watching us, and the front of my underwear were also stretched and stained.

"At least your arrow is washed off," Albert said.

I couldn't get back to the clothes check fast enough.

# CHAPTER 12

"Am I a whore?" I asked Marjorie.

"No, boo. Everyone goes through their slut phase. Enjoy it while you can. Aren't you supposed to be volunteering this morning?"

"Oh my God! I completely forgot. I'm supposed to be at Atlanta Street Rescue already."

"You better hustle," she said. "Luckily it's just around the corner."

She was right. It was right around the corner, and since we were doing junk removal, all I had to do was throw on some sweat pants and hit the road.

It was a short sprint, and I arrived in time to get my gloves so I could help rip out the filthy carpet. Basil, a thin, but very spry gentleman in his sixties was the volunteer coordinator. "Thank you everyone for coming out today to improve the lives of the LGBT youth. Its volunteers like you who give of yourself so that others may start living their lives."

There was a wide variety of people volunteering, but one person stood out to me. He couldn't have been more than fifteen.

"Hi my name is Tyler," I introduced myself.

"My name is Kenny," he said.

"You seem awfully young to be volunteering. Why are you here?"

"Because I'm trying to help the people who are taking

41

care of me."

"I didn't realize that. How old are you?"

"Sixteen. It's okay. I've been living here for a year now."

"How did you end up here, if you don't mind me asking?"

"I don't mind. When I came out to my parents, they threw me out. They are Jehovah Witnesses and couldn't take the fact that I was gay. They had no problems with my sister who does drugs and is constantly in and out of jail, but they couldn't stand the sight of me. They called me an abomination, packed a bag with my clothes, and threw it out the door."

"I'm so sorry."

"Why? You didn't do anything," he responded. "I begged and I cried, but my mother turned her back on me and slammed the door. The look on her face was ice cold."

"What did you do?

"I went over to a friend's house and slept there. I don't have any other family. The next day I hit the road and hitched here from Tifton. On the way, I was raped by a truck driver in the back of his cab. He dumped me on the side of the road, and eventually I made it here, only to hook up with a nice man who pimped me out for money. It was horrible."

"I can't believe you survived all that," I said.

"I'm just kidding you. I googled LGBT youth Georgia at my friend's and found this group. They took me in and probably saved my life."

"I'm glad you made it here."

"But what I told you has happened to other kids I've met. The sex slave business is alive and well in America. I'm one of the truly lucky ones."

"Is there anything else I can do?"

"You are doing what you can, and I appreciate it."

Why did it feel like I should be doing more?

# CHAPTER 13

When I arrived at work, there was a flyer on the desk waiting for me. The flyer read.

"Sign up to be the 1st Miss Club Cabaret. Help raise money for your favorite charity while competing for the crown. Sign up March 1st at 5 pm. Club Cabaret Room. For more information email Marni@clubcabret.com."

On the bottom of the flyer was a note, "Thought this would interest you, Germaine."

A scrumptious, sparkling, diamond photo of a satellite-shaped crown stared back at me from the page. It caught my brain on fire and blinded my eyes because I'd never seen anything so brilliant. This could be mine and should be mine, but it made me wonder if this was a coincidence or was the universe trying to tell me something. I could raise some money for a charity, but I could also get something out of it that I could show off to everyone. I could even build a pedestal to mount it on in the apartment and shine a light on it so that it catches all the diamonds and spreads their prisms around the room.

So I emailed Marni to get all the details. I was shocked that she responded back so quickly.

"Dear Tyler, the Miss Club Cabaret competition is an opportunity for all of us to give back to our community. Each drag queen participant will be partnered with a charity of your choice to raise money for them. The participant who raises the most money by the crowning on December 7th will be named the first Miss Club Cabaret and receive the tiara that is in the display case in the club. It is that simple. I hope to see you on March 1st. Thanks, Marni."

Did I really want to make that big of a commitment? I'd never done anything like this before, but I could get something really shiny. At least people would remember me for the crown.

As Germaine had said to me before, "There can be no reaction unless you take action."

It was my turn for action.

# CHAPTER 14

Panic set in as I realized I had no clue what I was doing. I called the boys to see what they could do to help me especially since one had a drag queen stalker and the other was a drag queen aficionado.

"Help me!" were the last words out of my mouth.

"Slow down," Albert said. "Tell me what you are doing again. I couldn't understand a single word until help me. How much caffeine have you had today?

"Too much. The guy at Coffee Ole must think I want to date him because I've been there like ten times already today. He's really cute in a nerdy kina way, but with such great arms and a perfect bubble butt. I guess that is from lifting all the bags of coffee and putting them in the grinder. Speaking of grinder, I wonder if he is on Grindr. If he is, I can see if he is a top and what he is looking for and what his likes are and hit him up to see if he would be interested in going out. But where would we go? Maybe dinner or a movie or both..."

"Stop!" You're making me crazy!" Albert yelled. "You need to slow down and start at the beginning. What do you need help with?"

I spoke slowly this time. "I am entering a drag queen contest to win a crown and possibly raise money for Atlanta Street Rescue, and I need your help getting ready. I have no clue what I am doing and desperately need some advice."

"You need help from me because I have a drag queen stalker right?" Albert asked.

"No, I need your help because you have impeccable taste," I responded.

"I thought that's what you said," he replied. "So what do you have to do for this show coming up?"

"From what I understand, we are meeting earlier in the day with all the contestants and then performing two numbers at the inaugural Miss Club Cabaret show."

"Do you have any idea what numbers you want to do?" he asked.

"No clue," I said.

"We need a think tank. I'm calling Chas and Paul and letting them know we have a grade-one emergency," Albert said.

"What is a grade-one emergency?" I blindly asked.

"Grade one is a flaccid prick. It is a minor inconvenience that should be easily rectifiable."

So I had to ask, "Are there more levels?"

"Of course there are my dear boy. I'm glad you asked. Grade two is a chubby. It is an excitable state, but with no immediate resolve in sight. Grade three is the Standing Hampton, but the bottom doesn't have a clean bat cave. Grade four is the irritated starfish. That's where the butthole is too swollen to allow anything in. And finally, stage five is the dildo killer. That is where the asshole has grown teeth and chews up the dildo and spits it out. This requires everyone's participation to solve the problem," Albert finished.

"So you all can help right?" I asked.

"Of course we can. It is in our genes." Albert slapped his own ass. "Plus, this one is only a chubby."

# CHAPTER 15

I felt a sense of relief as we stepped through the doors of the Junkman's Daughter in Little Five Points. L5P is the melting pot of Atlanta. On any day, you can see everyone from skin-heads to Rastas mingling on the street corners and going in and out of the various shops. This is the place to come if you want crystals to skateboards to pizza and a ton of eclectic clothes shops. Hence, the Junkman's Daughter is the best place to start.

The first thing I see as I enter is the giant Jack Skellington from "The Nightmare Before Christmas" propped up in a back corner next to a coffin. I absolutely adore that movie so I knew this was the right place.

Chas, Albert, Paul, and I started strolling through the racks and racks of clothing from vintage to current. Chas grabbed a lovely beaded short dress and held it up. "Honey, you are a size 10. This will fit you beautifully, plus the blue brings out the natural color in your eyes, which are as deep as a Caribbean sink hole in the Bermuda triangle "

I blushed. "How do you know I'm a 10?" I asked.

"After working at the Gap for five years I can tell your size just by looking at you. I can also guess your weight by looking at you, but I'm much more accurate if you sit on my face," Chas said.

"Really?" Paul said, "I'm trying to keep breakfast down here."

"Well there is nothing like a good tossed salad, I say,"

Albert chimed in.

"Can we please get back on point? Do I have to remind you why we are here?" I asked. And with that the boys became more focused.

It was incredible watching Paul peruse through the racks. He was laser-focused as he studied each blouse, skirt, and pants as he pushed it down the rack. He would methodically study each piece, trying to get a feel for the song that would go with the outfit. His concentration was broken when he popped his head up to ask, "What songs are you doing?"

"I don't know," I said.

"You got us down here, and you don't even know the numbers you are doing? No. No. No. This is just not right. I can't use my expertise and be expected to pull a rabbit out of my ass if you don't know your music!" Paul exclaimed. "You need to know the songs you are going to do, otherwise you can't get your outfit. You are trying to do this ass backwards. The music is important because it tells your story and you need to feel it. I had an ex who had a mountain house outside of Boone, North Carolina and every time I play 'Bloodletting' by Concrete Blond, it takes me back to that moment in time. That is what your music should be doing for you," he finished exasperated.

"When is the show?" Chas asked.

"It is next weekend," Albert responded. "So we don't have much time to get him ready."

"No music. No makeup. No accessories. This is going to be a disaster," Paul whimpered as he thoroughly looked disgusted. "If you are going to do this, you need to do it the right way."

"Be nice to our little girl," Chas said. "This is her first time, and it is for charity."

"My God! Let's just find the three outfits and get out of here," Paul said.

"Three outfits? I only need two."

"No, no, my dear. You will need three. Two are for the show, but you need a walk about outfit for when you get there," Albert said. "Just like when that crazy bitch Miss Gigi shows up for her shows. You never see her perform in the outfit she wears when she gets there. It would be unseemly. Plus, it will help you get friendly with the patrons, which in turn will get you more tips."

"If the patrons feel like they know you, then they will truly be more generous. I speak from experience on this," Paul said.

"Here are three perfectly acceptable outfits," Chas said as he held up his arms, which were draped in one red satin mini dress, a vintage 60's outfit, and a yellow and white pin stripped shirt and pants combo from the 70's. "This will get you through the first show. Shoes are over here, so come over and slide that petite size 9 into these flats. I don't think you are ready for heels yet. Remember when you buy women's shoes, they will be two sizes larger than your foot size, so that means you need size 11 in women's shoes."

"Marjorie said she can do my make up for the show, so I'm set there. I just need some wigs."

"So the chubby is on its way to being solved. Get these, Desiree, and we can go to the costume store for the wigs," Albert said.

"Why did you call me Desiree?"

"I don't know. It just felt right," Albert responded.

So Desiree was born.

# CHAPTER 16

It was time to transform myself. I shaved very closely to make sure none of what little facial hair I had would show up, and I did as Marjorie said and sat in front of her Hollywood mirror without my shirt on. The lights surrounding the mirror frame were very bright.

"The better to see you with, my dear," Marjorie said as she pulled out her bag of tricks. "It's time to beat your face."

"What do you mean beat my face?"

"Time to paint you, honey. No harm will come your way unless you don't do as I tell you. Now sit straight up and face forward."

"Knock Knock," "The Package" said. "Sounds like something you said to me in bed last night."

"And you enjoyed it," Marjorie replied.

"Can I watch?" he asked.

"Only if you keep bringing me cocktails," I said.

"Anything in particular?" he asked.

"Something fresh and fruity. I don't want to feel bloated," I said.

"I'll just have a Fresca," Marjorie said. "I want to keep my skills sharp."

With that, she put a head band on me to hold my hair back and started to work her magic. She took her hands and rubbed my eyebrows. Next I knew, she had grabbed a pair of tweezers and was plucking and tweaking my eyebrows. "They're a little bushy for a woman," she said. She stared at me intently to make sure they were even and shaped up. "One final thing," And with that, she plucked some stray nose hairs that made my eyes water. "You have to remember that a lot of people will be looking up at you."

Next, she applied some base to cover up my stubble and spread it around with a sponge. I don't have a lot of facial hair to begin with, so it covered up pretty easily. It evened out my entire face, but boy was I pale. "We have to start with a clean palate and then add to it," she said. I started seeing Tyler disappear and Desiree appear. It was an odd feeling to see yourself become someone else. Who was Desiree and what kind of person was she? I guess I would find out when I hit the stage.

From there, it was time to start with the eyes. She went with a deep sea green color for the eyelids. It really made my blue eyes pop. It was amazing how much I was starting to disappear in the mirror. She put a little bit of white eye powder in the corner of my eyes, which really opened everything. The mascara was applied next to make my eye lashes look fuller. Top lashes and bottom lashes. She finished the eyes by putting a little black eyeliner on the bottom lid. She then took a step back to study my eyes. "I've got to make sure they are even and you don't have wonky eye."

"Wonky eye?" I asked.

"When your eyes don't match and it looks like one eye is lower than the other."

I don't know how women do this every day. It felt like I had been sitting here for hours, but only forty-five minutes had gone by. At least "The Package" kept the drinks flowing.

"Smile," she said. "Like you mean it."

I smiled and held it like one of the contestants from Miss America, but the difference was I didn't have Vaseline on my lips to make it easier to hold that face. Marjorie took the candy-red lipstick and started to fill in my lips. It really gave me a lot of color.

The final touches were blush to bring out my cheekbones

and more powder to tone down the glare from the base makeup. I really did make a pretty woman.

With makeup done, it was time to slip into my red satin dress, which was going to be my sign-up dress and walk-around dress. I felt it showed off my sexy calves. And the cherry on top was a long red wig with tight spiral curls we found at the costume store. The lady behind the counter was nice enough to style it before we left the store and she pinned it to the wig head I purchased. The other wigs were brunette and blond since I really didn't know in which direction I wanted to go yet. They were styled and also pinned to the wig heads. No one told me how expensive drag can get.

I slipped on the pair of heels that were four inches high to complete the look. I had spent a lot of time practicing vacuuming the floors with them on so I didn't land on my face. That would not have been a pretty look to become drag queen road kill during my first performance.

I looked at my drag bags, which were all neatly packed by "The Package" and ready by the door. It was time to introduce Desiree to the world.

# CHAPTER 17

I was the first to arrive in the club room. The only person there was the queen with the clipboard. He came up and introduced himself, "I'm Marni the club manager. You here to sign up for the contest?"

"Yes, I'm Tyler, but you can call me Desiree."

"It's a pleasure to meet you. Please fill out this form, and you can put all your things in the dressing room. We are expecting more people, so go grab a drink from the bar while we're waiting." He then pointed to the corner bar where Alfred was waiting to serve cocktails.

I could use some strength, so a screwdriver sounded good. I went to the bar, but it wasn't till I got right up on Alfred that I realized how handsome he was. I was feeling nervous being here and the first words out of my mouth were, "You're beautiful."

"Thanks," he replied. He was five foot ten, with blond blonde hair and the body of an Abercrombie and Fitch model. Just so dreamy. "What can I get you?"

I laughed like a little school girl and then said, "Your phone number and a screwdriver."

"I can get you the drink, but I've got a boyfriend who doesn't appreciate strange men calling me. Thank you for asking, though. I always take that as the best compliment I can get," he said and handed me my cocktail.

I'm sure I was a bright shade of red as I got my cocktail and grabbed a chair at one of the high-top tables. It was the perfect vantage point to watch everyone else strut in. and strut they did.

The next to arrive was a diva bitch and her crew. Those are the only words to describe a raven-haired, tall, thin bitch with long legs and the fiercest face I've ever seen. Her crew carried her bags because she seemed too busy to be bothered, and then they brushed off her chair and she slid into place. Marni strolled over to her and gave her the entry form. "Good afternoon, Athena. Please fill this out," as he dropped it on the table. You could tell there was no love lost there.

A small Chihuahua walked in wearing a pink tutu and dragging a very thin drag queen in a baggy sequined dress. The dog pulled her to a table where she flopped down and finally caught her breath. A minute later, the little dog vomited onto the floor.

"Like mama like daughter," Athena said.

"Athena, play nice. The competition hasn't even started," Marni said.

"Yes, ma'am," Athena replied.

"Ladies, I'm Desiree. It is a pleasure to meet you," I said.

They both looked at me like I had cum dripping out of my hair and turned away.

A country girl came strolling in. She looked like a cross between Patsy Cline and Mae West. All big-bosomed, cowboy hat, and cowgirl fringe. She took her application and grabbed a seat at the corner bar. She pulled her six shooter from her belt and practiced shooting it into the air.

A rather perky-breasted drag queen in her own version of the wonder woman outfit came in next. She was all stars and stripes in her spandex with white boots and headband. She, too, took her application and grabbed a spot at one of the high-top tables.

The next drag queen to sashay in was a petite thing with an impeccable look from head to toe. She looked to be all business.

The final queen to enter was a rather voluptuous, tall,

black drag queen who had a lot of bounce and a great afro wig. "Hey girls," she said to everyone. "It's time to get it on."

"For those who don't know me, I am Marni the club manager. I have a degree in theater and dance, so if you need advice, do not hesitate to ask. Now that we're all here why don't you each introduce yourselves and then we can go over the rules of the competition."

Athena immediately jumped up and started to speak, "My name is Athena Parthenos, and I am prepared for battle. I intend on winning this competition so you all better be ready for a good fight. Thank you." And with that, she sat down.

That was hard to follow, but I stood up and introduced myself. "Hi, I'm Desiree, and I will be taking home the crown, and I will be working to raise funds for my charity of choice, Atlanta Street Rescue. I'm looking forward to getting to know everyone."

Athena again stood up, "And I'll be working to raise funds for the Gay and Lesbian Center. I don't know why the lesbians need a center, but it is what it is." She then looked at me, "And what is your last name? You have to have a last name. You're not Cher, bitch, and the only head that crown is going to rest on is mine. I'm telling you all that now so don't expect to win."

"I don't have a last name," I said.

"Well you better get one," Athena said.

Next up was the country girl. "I'm Miranda Lambadingdong, and I'll be raising funds for Hope Pantry. I do county music so I hope y'all don't invade my territory

The very thin drag queen stood up and introduced herself. "Hi I'm Ana Mia Drunkorexia, and my little pooch is Natasha. I'm looking forward to raising funds for Camp Hypoglycemic, a fat camp for overweight children. It is very near and dear to my heart since I used to be a camper there." She then collapsed back into her seat and tried to catch her breath. I don't know if it was her make up, but she was awfully pale.

"I'm Mary Jane Bazooka," the Wonder Woman said,

"And now that pot is becoming more legal, I'm here to spread the word on its medical uses. Think of me as the Marijuana Avenger, and I will be raising funds for the Atlanta Cancer Initiative. My mom passed away from breast cancer, and thank god for Mary Jane because that was the only thing that made her feel better most of her chemo nights."

Next up was the business-looking drag queen, "I am here to prove a point that I should be the first Club Cabaret Queen. I'm Dixie Monroe. With that crown on my head I will stand head and shoulders above the rest of you."

"Isn't that the shampoo you use on your wigs?" Athena asked.

"My dear ex friend, it is better than the flea and tick shampoo you use on a regular basis. I think it's A-200, if I'm correct?" Dixie said.

"Why you little bitch!" Athena screamed as she rose from her chair. "I'm going to pull that nappy rug off your head you call a wig!"

Marni slammed the clipboard on the floor. "Ladies, none of this. The competition hasn't even started. Please sit down," Marni said as he regained control of the room.

And last, but not least, the tall drag queen in the afro stood up. "Don't worry, everyone, because I will beat you all. I'm Precious Oil, and I'm here to tell you black don't crack, so you can all kiss my big, round ass as I stomp you in this competition. Oh, and I'm raising funds for Stroke Aid." With that, she strutted for a second and then graciously sat back down.

"Alright," Marni said. "Now that we have all been introduced, I want to tell you the rules of the competition. The first Miss Club Cabaret will be the contestant who raises the most money for their charity over the next nine months. Rule one is at the end of each event, all of the collected money must be turned into me to be counted and added to your tally. Rule two is that at each of your events, you cannot ban any other contestant from attending the event. They do not have the right to perform at the event, but they can attend. Rule three is that you must host two shows a month here in the Club Cabaret Room. This way you can become more familiar with our patrons and they can become more familiar with you. We really are a family here, and our owner, Mr. Winston, is a big proponent of giving back so that is why we have started this contest. The regular cast members are more than happy to help you out at your shows, so please ask. They are a good group, and they will be performing with you tonight. Those are the three basic rules. You can raise funds anyway you want, but please remember to keep in mind that all of this is being done for your charities, so keep it fun. Let's have a good show tonight. The doors open in two hours so get ready."

One screwdriver down, but my courage was still not there. Time to see Alfred again.

# CHAPTER 18

As the patrons strolled in, the contestants worked the room introducing themselves to the clientele. Some of the girls had a lot of friends in the audience so they were very comfortable schmoozing around. Luckily, Marjorie and the boys were there to support me. I quickly slid over to them from the dressing room and grabbed a chair.

"I'm so nervous I feel like I could wet myself," I said.

"You will do great," Albert said. "By the way, is Miss Gigi back there?"

"Yes, she came in the back door about a half hour ago, but she's in boy's clothing. She had a family event out of town and just got back," I said.

"Are you ready to run rabbit?" Chas asked.

"No, I'm a big boy, and I can deal with this," Albert replied.

"I hope they start this on time. I hate drag time," Paul said.

"Let's go back and touch you up a little. You're a little shiny," Marjorie said. "Plus, time to get you into your first performance outfit."

So Marjorie and I slipped behind the curtain and into the dressing room.

"Desiree, I need your music," Marni said as he had labels ready to mark out music.

"Here you go. This is my first song and this is the second one."

"The show order is posted on the wall, so please check where your numbers are," Marni said and grabbed his headset to listen to someone. "Got to go. Ice emergency up front." And with that, he was off.

Marjorie turned to me. "I'm so proud of you. It is so great of you to help other people out."

"It feels good," I said.

"People only do charity stuff to make themselves feel better," Miss Gigi said. "They don't do it to help anyone out. They only do it to fulfill their inner need to be liked."

"That's a little cynical," Marjorie said.

"I may never meet anyone who directly benefits from what I do, but I hope it makes their lives a little easier," I said.

"How altruistic," Miss Gigi replied.

"Isn't there someone you should be stalking?" Marjorie asked.

"Why? Is Albert here?" she asked.

"Yes, he's sitting right out front," Marjorie responded. Miss Gigi left the dressing room. "Sometimes she is just off her rocker, and don't ever tell Albert I sicked her on him. Otherwise you will find all your underwear in the freezer."

"I promise I won't."

"Come on over to the mirror so I can apply a little more powder." Marjorie pulled out a very round powder puff and dabbed it into the container. She then gently blotted my face, making sure I no longer glistened. It was heartwarming to have her here.

"Girls, the show starts in ten minutes. Make sure you are ready when it's time for your number," Marni said. "They will start the number whether you are ready or not, and I don't like any dead stage time."

"So where are you in the show?" Marjorie asked.

"I'm sixth, so we have some time," I said.

"Which outfit are we changing you into?" she asked.

"This one," I held up the 60's vintage outfit.

"And what number are you doing to this?"

"Big Boned Gal by k.d. lang."

Miss Miranda screamed out, "Who's doing country? I said that is my wheelhouse."

"I'm sorry. I've already got this one prepared," I said.

"I suggest you change it."

"And I suggest you back your fat ass up, and get out of her face," Marjorie said. She was never one to back down from anything. "Before I snatch that cowgirl fringe of yours and make you eat it. Imagine that coming out of your asshole where you have to wrap it in toilet paper and pull it out just like a big, long tapeworm."

Miss Miranda retreated back to her dressing station and never looked at me again the rest of the night.

"Thank you, my darling," I said and gave Marjorie a big hug.

We slipped off my red satin dress and put on my sixties outfit.

The show started with the overture of some big-band-sounding music for three minutes followed by the introduction of the hostess Miss Kit-N Kaboodle. She strode onto the stage to a thunderous round of applause and killed her opening number, Britney Spears' "Work Bitch." She was extremely well-liked because she was personable and very quick on her feet. She was one of the most naturally funny people that I had ever met and that's why she was a great hostess. She danced her ass off and the tips came down like rain for her. It was amazing that when she grabbed the mic and started speaking, she had already regained her composure.

"It's a little hot in this trailer," she said. "And welcome to the first Miss Club Cabaret competition. This is the brainchild for our owner, Mr. Winston. I know he's here somewhere. Let's all give it up for him." Mr. Winston stood up from his table in the back and waved to everyone. "Now remember, Miss Club Cabaret will be the contestant who raises the most money for their charity, so that means give generously. Now welcome to the stage our first contestant,

Athena Parthenos."

Athena took the stage doing Joan Jett's "I Hate Myself for Loving You." The crowd loved her in her leather from head to toe and her friends were lined up to give her money. By the time she was done, she had racked up quite a bit of money. I couldn't watch from the wing anymore and went back into the dressing room.

I looked around the dressing room and all the other contestants seemed so calm and collected. I could feel my anxiety build up as it got closer to my number, and it must have showed on my face because Kit-N stopped by while one of the other girls was on stage. "Honey, you look like you are about to crap your pants," she said.

"Performance anxiety," I said. "This is my first time on stage, and I'm terrified."

"You need to relax, baby doll. These are all people here who just want to have a good time, and if you raise some money, even better. Remember to enjoy your song. If you believe in it, so will they," she finished. "I've got to get back out there."

It made sense. I liked my songs and I had rehearsed my ass off. Why should I be afraid? So I went to the wing and waited for my name to be called. My chest was pounding and it was hard to catch my breath.

Athena came off the stage and stopped dead in front of me. She pointed to the stage. "That is how it is done, bitch." Then she dumped her tips on my head. "Make it rain. Make it rain," she said and marched over to her dressing station.

That was very cold, and it made me even tenser.

"Athena, you can't keep treating everyone like shit, you dried out slut," Dixie Monroe chimed in.

"All you ever do is ride my dress train. It's time you realized you will never be anything but someone's lackey," Athena shot back at Dixie.

"Knock it off," Ana Mia piped up, "You're disturbing Natasha. She's not very well." The dog hopped out of her tiny pink basket and vomited on the floor again.

"Marni, clean up on aisle 4," Athena exclaimed.

"Times are different, cunty. You can't walk over me anymore. I plan on crushing you in this competition," Dixie responded.

My worst fear was coming true right before my eyes as this was turning into one big cat fight.

Finally, my moment came. "Ladies and gentlemen please welcome to the stage Miss Desiree," Kit-N shouted into the mic.

With that, the music started and I headed onto the stage. The spotlight blinded me, but I could still hear the people clapping. I felt the beat of the music and I started moving my mouth to the words. They came naturally, which felt great, and I started moving around a little bit even thought I still felt a little unsteady on my heels. After my eyes adjusted, I could see the crowd a little better, and they were just sitting there. They weren't coming up to tip me. The whole purpose of doing this was to raise money for my charity, and they were not moving. I didn't feel any love coming back my way like the other entertainers got, and my confidence was crushed. Keep moving and lip-syncing was all I could do. Just get through this. The boys and Marjorie came up and tipped which gave me some drive again. Finally an audience member I didn't know came up and tipped me five dollars. I believe it was a pity tip, as I think he felt bad for me. The number ended, and there was a polite round of clapping. I quickly raced backstage and collapsed onto my dressing room chair.

I felt awful and yet I had a second number to do. Marjorie came back all glowing. "You were great! How did it feel for your first time?" she asked.

"Terrible. I felt like people couldn't wait for me to be over."

"Honey, it wasn't that bad. It was your first time, and you did great for your first time performing in front of this many people. Look, you're competing against some entertainers who do this all the time and perform in shows on a regular basis."

"Really?" I said timidly.

"Hell yes, boo. The more you do this, the better you will get. Come on we have to get you ready for your second number." She started stripping me out of my outfit with wig first, heels second, and dress third. There I was again in pantyhose and a bra. My mother would be so proud.

"Sugar, if it means anything, I think you did a great job," Mary Jane said as she grabbed my arm. "Don't listen to that whore Athena. She never got enough love as a child. Got to go. I'm up."

It was good to get some support from the other contestants. I was still afraid this was going to turn into a big cat fight.

As the night dragged on each girl went up and did her numbers. I did my second number and had more confidence than on the first number. It must have showed because I actually got some real tips. I guess the Captain and Tennille's "Love Will Keep Us Together" was my lucky number even if it didn't keep them together.

The final number of the night was by Precious Oil, who performed Crystal Waters' "100% Pure Love." I watched from the wing, and this girl was a true entertainer. The crowd loved her as she went out into the audience and picked up one of the audience members and spun him around. She was a big girl and she did this with ease. The crowd went off when she finished and the stage floor was littered with dollar bills. It took a minute to get it cleaned up.

After her number, it was time for the cast call back. All the girls were called back onto the stage where we stood in a Miss America line pretending to like each other. I know I did, but Athena managed to get herself positioned in the middle of the line and kept staring down at the other contestants. The final number of the night was the entire cast performing "525,600 Minutes" from "Rent." All the money raised during this number would be evenly split among all the contestants, so here was a chance to make some money.

Once the last bit of the money was collected, Kit-N Kaboodle announced our standings after the first show. "It is my great honor to let you know how well the ladies did this evening. It was a great show, and on behalf of the performers and the staff here at Club Cabaret, I want to thank you for all your generosity." At this point, the contestants grabbed each other's hand. I had the pleasure of holding Athena's and Dixie Monroe's hands. "In 7th place is the youngest performer, Miss Desiree, with $100. In 6th place is Ana Mia Drunkorexia with $212. In 5th place is Mary Jane Bazooka with $259. In 4th place is Miranda Lambadingdong with $278. In 3rd place is Dixie Monroe with $314. In second place is Athena Parthenos with $421. And it is no surprise that in first place is that valuable resource, Miss Precious Oil, with $502. Congratulations ladies on a wonderful evening. Have a great night, everyone."

As Athena's name was called for 2nd place, she squeezed my hand and Mary Jane's hand extremely tightly, almost causing us both to drop to our knees. She was not a happy camper and stormed off stage the minute the curtain was closed.

"She's always so easy to piss off," Precious Oil said as she watched Athena storm off. "This is going to be fun."

Maybe for her, but the jury was still out on how I would do.

# CHAPTER 19

"So how did your first show go?" Sheila asked the next day at work.

"It was a disaster. I'm currently in last place, and I need some ideas on how to raise money. I can always ask Marni because he said he was always there to provide us help."

"At least you know where to start. I'm proud of you for putting yourself out there to help others. It's a good thing. Have you thought any more about coming to my friend's place in Savannah next month? I really could use a friend for the drive."

"Are you sure you wouldn't want to take along a real date?"

"Hell no. I want my best girlfriend with me."

"You make it sound like so much fun that I would be thrilled to go with you. I've never been to Savannah, so it will be a first for me."

"Thank you. You're an angel," she said.

"Hey angel, you need to go to the restroom and get the rest of the mascara off your eyes. It's creeping me out," Braxton said.

"Yes sir." Off I went to the restroom. I looked in the mirror closely and sure enough there were still traces of mascara in the corner of my eyes. I thought I had scrubbed hard enough to remove all of it, but somehow I had still missed some. Chalk that up on my learning curve about drag. Wash your face better after each show. I grabbed the warm wash clothes we kept in there for the guests and proceeded to soap up my eyes. By the time I was done, I looked like I had been smoking pot with my red eyes. I had gone from one extreme to the other.

When I got back to the, desk Sheila shared with me the drama going on at the hotel involving the night manager, Mary Grace Rhineland. "Well, while you were out over the weekend, they found out that Mary Grace had been using the empty rooms to have sex. It turns out she has a furry fetish, so she was sneaking her furry animal lovers in through a side door. Security would never have caught her, but they found the tail of one of the furry outfits stuck in a door of what they thought was an unoccupied room. They opened the door and there was Mary Grace riding a furry hobby horse. All she could say was, 'Ye haw.' Needless to say she was escorted off the property."

"Are they looking to fill that position?"

"Too late, sweetie. The new night manager, Jaime something-or-other, starts tonight. We all get to meet him at the end of our shift," she said.

I liked Mary Grace even though I never had to work with her. She was always nice to me whenever she saw me. I hoped that the new night manager would be just as friendly.

Germaine hadn't made it in yet, which was very surprising. He was never late and didn't look so hot when he finally got to the front desk. He was very pale.

"Honey, what's wrong?" I asked.

He looked up at Sheila and me and his eyes started tearing up. It just broke my heart to see him start to cry.

"I just got news that a former friend committed suicide. We had a falling out and hadn't spoken in a while," he said.

Sheila and I both grabbed him and hugged him. None of us wanted to let go. I finally had to ask, "What happened?"

Germaine took a second to compose himself and pulled his silk pocket handkerchief out to wipe away the tears. "I got a phone call from a friend asking me if I was watching the news. I wasn't, so I quickly turned it on in time to catch the end of the news story. Billie had hanged himself and was discovered by the house-keeper. There was no note. There were all sorts of people trampling over his front yard. It was a disgrace."

"I am so sorry," Sheila said.

"Is there anything we can do?" I asked.

"Thank you for your kindness. I really feel sorry for his family and friends. It is sad that he couldn't reach out to one of them for help. Hell, I would have even gone over if the bastard had only called. Even though it had been some time, it still feels like I had the wind kicked out of me. We used to be so close, and I hated it when that friendship died," he sighed.

"We're not that busy," Sheila said. "Why don't you two go grab a coffee and talk? I've got the desk covered.''

"Are you sure that is okay?" Germaine asked. It was never like him to shirk his responsibilities.

"Please go. You need this time," she said again.

So I grabbed Germaine's arm and we walked over to the small café in City Center, which was connected to the hotel. Germaine was very quiet and still as he sipped his coffee and stared off into space. I was just giving him time to gather his thoughts and then he let it all out.

"Once upon a time, Billie and I were great friends. We did everything together and even lived together, but we were only friends. We used to go to plays, see movies and travel together. We even had a three way once. It was like kissing your sister, and thank God the boy toy was beautiful with a big dick and just wanted to be serviced," he continued. "But everything changed when I started dating someone long distance. At first, nothing seemed to change and everything was status quo, but then he started hanging around with another friend, and they slowly cut me out of everything they were doing. I made every effort to keep involved in his life, but he just kept getting more distant. I would go to New York every eight to ten weeks and then my boyfriend, Iggy, would come here every eight to ten weeks. Long distance dating sucks, and I highly don't recommend it. I think Billie no longer saw me as his playmate and had to move onto someone else. I felt alone every time he and his new friend would go out and leave me alone, and it was hard to get comfort from someone who was six hundred miles away. Eventually, things with Iggy didn't work out, and I was tired of being treated as an outsider, so I decided to move out. Nothing much was said at all the day I packed the moving truck and left. I think the only words out of his mouth were 'See you round.'" He sat quiet again.

"You don't have to get this all out today," I said.

"Yes, I do. I can't hold it in. They say the first thing people do who are mourning is get angry. I don't want to be one of those people. I still think I'm in shock. All I could do after I heard the news was function like I normally do. I finished breakfast, took my shower, and got dressed. I sat on the bed and put on one sock at a time like I normally do, followed by my underwear, pants, dress shirt, shoes, then tie. I don't remember if I turned my oven off or not. I hope I did."

"I'm sure you did. If not, we can always call your neighbor to go over and check."

"You are so sweet to me. My friend let me know that there would be a memorial service, and my first instinct was not to go. We hadn't been close for a long time, but then I remembered memorial services are for the living and not those who have passed on. I need to go and give my support to his friends and family. The last time I think I ran into Billie was at the grocery store. We exchanged pleasantries, but not much else. It is sad when a friendship dies, but I wish he had just called me. I would have been over there in a minute."

I hugged him.

"No more drama. Time to get back to work," he said. He wiped the last of his tears, drank the last of his coffee, and out the door we went. Welcome to Monday.

# CHAPTER 20

As I struggled to get organized, Mary Jane Bazooka got a jump start on her fundraising. Her event was her band, Baked, doing a show and having a "baked sale." I didn't know what that was, but the flyer looked good, and I needed to see what the competition was doing to get my creative juices going. Plus, I liked Mary Jane because she was always nice to me.

The show was held on a Saturday afternoon in the backyard of one of her friends' homes. Albert and I got there a little early to see what the set up was like. They had a stage at the far end of the flat yard with what seemed like decent sound equipment, which was playing classic rock songs of the 70's, and some lighting. They had a couple of bars set up and the "Bake Sale" set up along the fence lines.

"There's not much to the 'Baked Sale,'" I said to Albert. "It's just brownies wrapped in plastic, and they're asking ten dollars a brownie. I would never pay that much for one of those."

"Silly rabbit, tricks are for kids," Albert replied.

"What do you mean?"

"Those are pot brownies, hence the name 'Baked Sale,'" he said as he stressed the words Baked and Sale with bunny ears.

"Ohhhhhhhh," I said.

"Turn off that light bulb over your head. It's blinding me," Albert said. "Everything refers to pot. The band name

69

and the lovely brownies."

"That makes sense since her charity is medical marijuana." I myself am not a big pot smoker because every time I drank and then smoked pot, it made me throw up. And when I smoked pot only, I hated it because I couldn't judge distance, which made driving impossible.

"Hey Desiree," Mary Jane said. "It's good to see you here," and then she air-kissed me so as not to mess up her make up. I was surprised that she recognized me in just my boy clothes. "You make a cute boy."

"Thank you, and yes, we paid the cover charge," I said.

"Go grab a beer. The kegs were donated and the show will start in an hour," she said.

"I sure will," Albert said as he grabbed my arm and pulled me over to the bar. We were able to get a couple of solo cups and top them out before heading to a quiet corner to watch the crowd stroll in.

"This reminds me of high school," I said.

"Why's that?" Albert asked.

"Because when I was in high school, there were three groups and you only belonged to one of them. The first was the stoners who are well-represented here today. I knew a bunch of the stoners, but I wasn't considered one of them. Then there were the socials, who were the popular, mean kids, and again I wasn't them."

"Then what group did you belong too?

"I was in the middle group, who were about as normal as you get, but I mingled with everyone. It wasn't that big of high school since we lived in the north Georgia Mountains, and the girls all loved me."

"Why was that?' Albert asked.

"Because the girls knew I was gay, so I was never going to be more than just a friend. They knew I didn't want anything from them except their friendship."

"Did the boys know you were gay?"

"Most didn't and the ones who did knew not to fuck with me or the girls were never going to go out with them. If the boys were going to get any, they had to play nice with me. I was lucky and it was never an issue. What about you? How was high school for you?"

"Not much to tell. I was very mellow in high school, but I wasn't out either, so pretty much I just drifted through day to day," he replied.

"How many people do you think are here already? I asked.

"Probably fifty, so that means her take is already $500. We need to get some events going for you," he said.

A few refills later, it was show time. The classic rock stopped and the announcer grabbed the mic. "Ladies and gentlemen please welcome to the stage, Baked."

Baked made its way on stage and Mary Jane was now dressed in camouflage shorts and a tank top with a bandana and black boots. The guitarist strummed the opening notes of the Rolling Stones' "Jumping Jack Flash," and next I knew it was a full onslaught from the band with Mary Jane strutting around like Mick Jagger. Then she began to sing live. She had an awesome voice. It was such a change to see her sing live since so many drag queens just lip sync. I guess ever since RuPaul's Drag Race hit the TV, every drag queen on that show is now putting out music and trying to extend her career.

The band rolled through an hour and a half of music, and before their last number, Mary Jane got a chance to say some final words to the crowd.

"I want to thank everyone for coming out. As many of you know, my mother had breast cancer, but she couldn't get access to medical marijuana to help ease her suffering after chemo. I'm not trying to get marijuana legalized, but I do want to get it more available so that cancer patients will be able to ease the effects of chemo. Luckily, my mother is a survivor, and we are looking forward to many more birthdays with her. Thanks for coming. And now for our final number we would like to do something from one of my personal favorites, Queen."

The band ripped through "Tie Your Mother Down," and then it was over. By the end there were two hundred people in the crowd standing and cheering for the band, who were all very sweaty as they left the stage. But Mary Jane's make up didn't run or have a single smudge on it. I wonder how she did that.

She came over, "So what'd you think? I know I'm no Freddie Mercury."

"You did him proud," Albert said. "I didn't realize you were such a big rock fan."

"I love classic rock, but for a drag show, it doesn't go over too well. You have to do the songs on the radio or you don't make any money and the crowd gets bored."

"How much did you make tonight?" I asked.

"Not sure yet. I've got a couple of cash managers who will give me the final numbers once everyone gets out of here. We have an agreement with the neighbors that the music would be over by 9:30 so they don't complain, and they are all invited to the show to see it free. It worked out really well."

Just then one of her cash managers came up to give her the number. "Is this a good time?" he asked.

"Give us a minute," Mary Jane said.

"We've got to get going anyway," Albert said.

"Thank you for a wonderful evening," I said. "I'll see you at the club."

As we were leaving, I could see the cash manager and Mary Jane hugging. "It must have been a good night," I said to Albert.

"Well you figure two hundred people at $10 is $2,000. Plus, who knows how much money they made at the Bake Sale? I think they had a good night. Maybe $2,500 to $3,000."

"I'm jealous," I said. "I don't' know if I can pull something like that off."

"Yes you can. We just got to get you organized, and get things going."

As the night air cooled, we headed home. I tried thinking of events to do to raise money, but I was a blank. Time to seek help.

# CHAPTER 21

Our planning meeting was set. It was the boys, Marjorie and Shelly. Shelly used to work for a non-profit, so I needed to pick her brain for ideas. I was so new to fundraising and I was new to Atlanta, so any help I could get was appreciated.

"Since you don't have an organization behind you, I would like to recommend starting small and building up. There are plenty of things that don't cost you anything to do, but it will get you out there in front of people," Shelly said.

"Like what?" Chas asked.

"You can do the street begging. I believe someone mentioned that the club has some permits for that. There's bowling events, car washes, yard sales, wine tasting, a beer bust, and doing the drag shows at the club. But for the drag shows, try to get some raffle items so you can do a raffle where people buy tickets, and give away prizes that you can ask businesses to donate. Since you work at the hotel, you could ask if they would be willing to donate a weekend at the hotel that you can raffle off or free haircuts or restaurant gift certificates. People would buy tickets for those things," she said. "I knew one charity that volunteered at Georgia A & M home football games by running a booth and made money that way. This is all stuff that is easy to do and doesn't cost anything. Once you have a following, it will get easier."

"If you enjoyed working at the non-profit so much, why did you leave?" I asked.

"It takes a lot of time and commitment to work at one

for a long time plus you usually don't make much money. I don't think most people realize how much need is out there, and I just hit my burnout point," she finished.

"Desiree, you've got nine months to raise the money. I will check with Georgia A & M to see what we can do to get into their charity program," Paul said.

"And I'll check with several of the restaurants we patronize to see what they can donate," Albert said. "I know sometimes they will donate 10% of a day's receipts to a charity."

"And I'll check with the bars to see if they can donate any bar tabs," Marjorie said, "I'll even put "The Package" to work to see what he can come up with."

"This is a great start," I said. "I finally have some hope. Everyone put your hands in the middle." Everyone got up and put their hands over my outstretched hand. "On three, say, 'go team Desiree!' One, two, three." And everyone yelled, "Go Team Desiree!"

# CHAPTER 22

Marni gave me the permit, and I was ready to work the street. His only advice was, "Don't get hit," which made me feel even more uncomfortable.

The permit gave me permission to work the corner of Monroe and Piedmont from 10:00 A.M. to 2:00 P.M on Saturday. I had never worked a corner for money, and I really wasn't good at begging, so this was going to be a challenge. I felt like I was a hooker going out to turn a trick or two if I should be so lucky. My love life was non-existent since all I seemed to be doing was putting on a dress lately. It was nice to be in boys' clothing for once instead of having to worry about the dress, make up, and heels.

It was a beautiful spring day with everything in bloom before the clouds of pollen started coating everything in their layer of yellow green dust. I was supplied with a pink safety vest that made me stick out like a sore thumb, and it was hard to match clothes with the neon pink. So I went with a white t-shirt, blue shorts, and flip-flops.

I got a bucket and made up a little sign to hold up as the cars came by. It was a very busy intersection with a gas station, restaurant, small island park, and a protein shake shop. There were tons of cars and plenty of people walking their dogs because the new entrance to Piedmont Park was just down the block. And I can't forget the joggers. It was like a man smorgasbord with all these sweaty hot men running shirtless in their extremely short shorts. Even though it wasn't hot or humid out, I was getting a little bit warm under the collar and I could feel the heat rising in me. Before I chugged one of the bottles of iced water from my small cooler, I held it up to my forehead to try to cool off. I had to be here for four hours so I couldn't turn into a glistening mess just yet.

Even though I felt a little out of place, I had a new determination to put myself out there and make some money. I always had a hard time putting myself out there, and my mama kept telling me, "Let your light shine." This was some advice I needed to follow to see where it leads me.

So I stood on the northeast corner in front of the small park right at 10 that morning and held up my sign and bucket. As the light turned red, the line of cars in front of me didn't seem to notice me or didn't seem to care. I waved and held up the bucket and sign, but people kept staring back at me like I had two heads or looked away. I even tried walking between some of the cars and holding the bucket up to the window. With the way the people drive in Atlanta, I really needed to heed Marni's advice of not getting hit. I saw more people texting and talking on their phones as I dodged more than one car whose driver wasn't paying attention. I noticed on the license plates that a lot of these careless drivers were from Cobb and Gwinnett counties, which explains a lot since those are the suburbs and these drivers are always lost once they come inside the perimeter.

Finally, one of the drivers gave me a dollar and said, "My heart is full." I said, "Thank you," but I had no idea what that meant. I made a mental note to ask Marjorie. At least that driver seemed to care, and I did have a couple of other drivers ask me what I was raising money for, and they donated once they found out it was for homeless youth. It restored my faith in human kind, even though I wasn't making much money.

A couple of hours and several water bottles later, Mother Nature was calling and I really needed to pee. Thank God this intersection had a plethora of choices, so I weighed my options, since peeing in the little park would have gotten me arrested. I ruled out the gas station because it was only an exterior rest room on the station and those usually smell like an open sewer flowing through India and they are a toxic breeding ground for mold and all sorts of other crap. And when I mean crap. I mean crap. The protein shop was nice and clean, but they had a sign up that said no public restrooms, and I wasn't in the mood for a shake. That left me with the little restaurant from which the smell of fresh grilled burgers started causing my tummy to rumble. I didn't realize I was this hungry because I was trying to focus on raising money.

So I strolled across Monroe Drive, stepped into Bonk, and sashayed my way to the bar so that I could place my order.

"What can I get you, jumpy?" the bartender asked.

I didn't realize I was doing my potty dance, so I quickly ordered a burger, fries and a coke to go.

"We'll have it out to you shortly," she said.

I sprinted to the restroom without a second to lose. After peeing for what seemed like an eternity, I went to the sink to wash my hands. When I looked in the mirror, I was horrified. I didn't realize that in several of my front teeth were poppy seeds from the bagel that I had eaten earlier before taking to the street. No wonder people kept looking at me funny. They must have thought I had gingivitis or that my teeth were rotting. Heaven help me. I grabbed a paper towel and started scrubbing my teeth to get rid of the seeds, followed by a very strong swishing of water in my mouth, followed by a big spit into the sink. I watched as several seeds went down the drain. I smiled and saw that my teeth were now debris-free so I could return to my post.

Back at the bar, the waitress asked, "What are you raising money for? I can see you here through the front door."

"Atlanta Street Rescue which is a program to help homeless youth."

"That's a great cause, and thanks for doing it. Here's your

order. It's on me." And she gave me the boxed-up meal in a to-go box and a large to-go soda.

I reached into my wallet and pulled out three dollars as a tip. After working in the lodge, you wanted to make sure that the staff was taking care of. "Thanks. And my name is Tyler."

"You're welcome, Tyler, and if you ever need anything else, please stop on by. My name is Stephanie, and I'm the manager here."

"I sure will."

As I headed back to my post, I could quickly see that I had been replaced by a homeless person working the same corner. With Atlanta being a warm weather city, we did have a large homeless population and you could see them on several street corners at any time of the day. He looked like he had been through a lot, so I decided to work the corner in front of the gas station and crossed Piedmont. I started getting set up on the new corner, and as I did, I noticed the homeless man started crossing Piedmont and heading to the other corner across from me. He didn't stop there, and he started crossing Monroe and headed straight for me. I didn't know what to expect since I had never done this before.

He stopped right in front of me and looked at me with his old soul eyes. "Sir, I'm sorry to tell you, but this is my corner to work," he said. "I'm here every Saturday afternoon as long as the police don't chase me away."

"I've got a permit from the city to work this corner this weekend," I said, "And it goes until 2 P.M."

"Sir, I'm sure you do, but I'm not going to lie to you. I'm here to get money so that I can eat. I'm not using this money to buy cigarettes or alcohol. I live under the overpass just up the block where the Beltline is going to be built. These pants and shoes were given to me by a Good Samaritan who saw that my old clothes were just worn out. God bless her. I'm just asking you to let me have my time so that I can eat," he finished.

Damn my Catholic guilt started racing through my head.

How could I deny this person an opportunity to eat? "Sir what is your name?"

"My name is Temple, sir," he said.

"My name is Tyler. It is a pleasure to make your acquaintance."

I reached down and grabbed my to-go box from Bonk. "Temple, please have this compliments of Bonk." I stretched out my arm to pass him the box. He looked at me in disbelief. "Take it, please. I hate to see someone go hungry."

"Thank you very much, sir. You don't know what this means to me."

I reached into my bucket and pulled out every bill and all the change that I had collected for the day. "I was collecting this for a homeless charity, but I can actually see who the money benefits this way. It's not much, but it's all yours."

He looked down and started to cry.

# CHAPTER 23

The shows at the club started, and first up was Ana Mia Drunkorexia. She had been performing in Atlanta for over ten years and had quite a following, but to me, most of them looked like sickly twinks. They all brought Easter lilies to give to Ana, but it seemed to me to be a little foreboding since every funeral I had ever gone to had lilies on the casket. It smelled like a floral show in the club.

It was a full house, and I was able to grab a cocktail and a seat in the back. Ana mingled in the crowd. She really looked in good spirits walking from one table to the next hugging and kissing her Mia Army fans. I think I even saw a smile on her face as she slipped behind the curtain for her costume change. Her little dog was nowhere to be seen tonight.

The overture came up and the lights dimmed. It was show time.

The unfamiliar music started and the curtain opened with Ana Mia in all her country glory best surrounded by a bevy of big countrified girls dressed like hookers. I finally leaned to the person standing over my shoulder and asked, "What is this song?"

"Honey, they are going to have to take your gay card. It's Dolly Parton from Best Little Whorehouse in Texas," was his response.

This was the first time I had seen this large of a group, which made me wonder if I should do a big group for my first show.

Ana was actually an excellent performer. She knew her words and music and really sold them to the audience, who were all clapping and singing along with her and the group. It did strike me as odd that she was so pencil-thin while everyone else in her group had to be at least a size 18 or larger. I'm just glad the stage could support all that weight.

When the number finished, Ana took to the mic. "I want to thank the Mia Army for coming out tonight and helping us raise money for Camp Hypoglycemic, a charity that is near and dear to my heart. When I was a little child, I was sent to the camp because I weighed over two hundred pounds and my parents were afraid I would become diabetic. With the camp's help, I am standing in front of you as a model of health!"

The crowd erupted into a thunderous round of applause as Ana raised her thin arms up in a victory stance. I was again surprised that she could raise her non-muscular arms up that high, especially with a mic in one of them, but she did it.

With that, she introduced her next entertainer and slipped off stage. What followed was a constant flow of her larger-than-life entertainers, all performing a variety of dance and pop numbers. The money flowed into the buckets on stage. Every now and then, one of the club employees would come up and empty the buckets into large envelopes and then seal them to count later. The total money raised by each contestant would only be announced on the crowing evening, so it was hard to tell how everyone was doing from these shows at the club.

It was a very pleasant evening until Miranda Lambadingdong showed up a couple of numbers before the end of the show. She had a couple of her spies sitting at the front-row table who graciously gave up their seats so that Miranda could be front and center for Ana Mia's final number. Miranda sat quietly in her "I Beat Anorexia" t-shirt and clapped politely when the final guest entertainer was finished performing. Then all hell broke loose.

Miranda pulled out a red flashing police light and placed it on her table and stood up and yelled, "It's a big girl sandwich emergency!" She then turned on the siren, which was the signal for one of her accomplices to come running to the front of the stage carrying a tray over his head with two extremely large and greasy double-stacked cheeseburgers and what looked like a pound of fries. The smell of grease filled the room immediately, and I thought Miranda was going to be attacked by the Mia Army, who all started salivating at the smell. Miranda grabbed the tray and sat her fat ass down and started devouring the burgers while moaning very loudly like she was in heat. She then took one of the bystanders' arms and wiped her mouth on their sleeve, leaving a big stain of ketchup and mustard. Thank God Miranda turned off the siren before the music started for Ana Mia's closing number.

Ana Mia came on stage looking like a Grecian goddess in a flowing silver char moose-draped dress wearing silver armbands with a wig styled like it came off of one of those Grecian urns you would see at a museum or on TV. Her music started and there was no turning back now. She chose to ignore Miranda, who kept waving the fries and a burger in her face as she performed.

It didn't matter what side of the stage Ana Mia would go to because Miranda started shouting, "What'll you have," which was the greeting at The Varsity, one of the best burger joints in the city.

Finally, some of the Mia Army stepped it up and ran interference as they tipped their Grecian goddess forming a wall between them both. Several of the army started bumping into Miranda and it was like a wall of tissue paper trying to fight off a bull in a china shop. The army mustered up enough courage and shoved Miranda back into her chair, which tipped back, causing her to kick the food tray, sending burger bits and fries into the air. Once she regained her balance, Miranda came back up, swinging landing a punch to face of the army leader, who stood between her and Ana.

From there, the army pounced on Miranda, pulling at her cowboy hat and cowgirl fringed jacket until they all collapsed onto the stage where they were joined by Miranda's accomplice, who started landing punches of his own.

In a moment of clarity, Miranda was able to clear the fray and find an open spot to stand in. This was very short lived, as Ana Mia yelled, "I'm coming for you bitch!" With that, she flung her body, doing a graceful Hamel camel into Miranda, sending them both into the crowd on the floor and spilling the buckets of money. I swear I saw hairpins and sequins flying all over the place.

It was at this point that the bar staff, led by Marni, stepped in and broke up the ruckus. "What the hell is wrong with you two?" Marni asked.

"She started it," Ana Mia said.

"You started it the minute you did Dolly. Dolly is in my wheelhouse, and I told you girls to stay away from the country music. Luckily I have friends who texted me from here and told me about this grave injustice," Miranda said

"I don't care who started this, but I'm going to end it. You have lost the entire purpose of these fundraisers, and we will all have a talk with Mr. Winston in the morning," Marni said. "Miranda, hit the road. You are done here for the night."

Miranda and her accomplice left the building. Marni did speak a little more to Ana Mia in private and calmed her down. Several Mia Army fans slunk around the room waiting for their star to come out of the dressing room. I don't know if this is how a show should end, but overall, it was a good show, and I hope she raised some money.

# CHAPTER 24

Dixie Monroe is going to be a fierce competitor. She got the jump on everyone by attacking Facebook to promote her upcoming show by setting up an event and promoting it to several groups she belonged to. One of the other girls let me know that she sent the invite out to over two thousand people. I can't compete with that since I barely know ten people here in the city.

Her show was called "The Sparkling Diamond Revue." I was clueless what that meant. I was covering for Sheila at the hotel because she was running late, She texted me in a panic begging me to stay a little bit over. She promised she would make it up to me. I really believe she was running late because she couldn't stand to be around the night manager, Jaime. Jaime was a very nice person, but shortly after he started working at the hotel, he started to perspire on a regular basis, and with that, he started to smell. It was getting very difficult to be around him, and we were all trying to find new ways to avoid him. I was just hoping Sheila would get here in time because I wanted to see Dixie's show. I need to learn as much as I can from these girls before I strut my stuff on that stage and run my own show. It terrified me because I didn't want the show to be a turd in a punchbowl.

So I got to the show as the overture was just finishing, and I had to find standing room in the back because the room was packed. It seemed like all her marketing had paid off. I had better learn how to better use the Internet to my advantage.

The curtain opened to reveal a large spinning disco ball hanging from the middle of the stage. Once the spotlight hit it, it lit up the room like sparkling diamonds. The music started - Nicole Kidman from "Moulin Rouge" covering "Diamonds Are A Girls Best Friend" - Dixie came out in a silver-mirrored full-length gown. As the spotlight hit her, she turned into a giant disco ball herself. She had the whole routine down to a "T." The crowd ate it up with dollar bills raining down on the stage. It brought a tear to my eye because I loved the movie and she was killing it. I wished I could pull something off this well.

She grabbed the mic and proved to be a very gracious host as she welcomed her guests to her party. And a party it turned into. "Tonight we are here to raise funds for Meals on Wheels, which is a cause near and dear to my heart. They provide food to those individuals who are confined to home or are not healthy enough to get out and take care of themselves. I've volunteered in their kitchen and helped prepare the meals, and I believe all of us need to give back. So please take this opportunity to get involved and help out. It can make a huge difference in someone's life. Enough preaching bitches! Let's bring out one of the regular cast members here from Club Cabaret. Please welcome to the stage the dynamo in action, Miss Crystal Belvedere."

Crystal was known for her high-energy dancing. I've seen her perform several times. Some days she phones in her performance and just goes through the motions, but tonight she was giving her all to Rihanna's "Only Girl (In the World)." Her legs were everywhere with the high kicks to the splits. It was incredible. She left the stage to a thunderous round of applause.

The next entertainer, Bertha, was a new girl whom I didn't recognize from the regular cast. She was a special entertainer friend of Dixie's. She came out in a red, sparkling, full-length dress with a fiery red wig on top to match and started in on Reba McIntire's "Fancy." All I can say is I was very happy that Miranda wasn't here to see this, because all we needed was another free-for-all at the show. As the chorus of the song kicked in the mix changed and the opening notes of Iggy Azalea's "Fancy" pummeled the crowd with the bass beats as Bertha stripped off the dress and wig to reveal a long, blond wig and a very tight, form-fitting, black and white spandex one piece with cha-cha heels. The crowd went crazy as Bertha changed her whole performing style to match the new song.

How do I put something like this together? I had a hard enough time walking in heels, and here were these girls strutting, jumping, and high-kicking their way across the stage without missing a beat.

The rest of Dixie's show was an endless parade of beautiful beaded and sequined gowns, which is why it was called "The Sparkling Diamond Revue". I was just amazed at how professional these girls were and how flawlessly everything transitioned from one to the next. This was a learning experience. I had to congratulate Dixie after the show.

I went backstage and Dixie was in the process of removing her make up. I was in boy clothes, so I made sure that I introduced myself, since I doubted she would recognize me out of drag. "Dixie, it's me Desiree, I just wanted to tell you how wonderful I thought the show was."

"Hi darling. Yes, I recognized you. You don't look that much different in or out of drag," she said.

All I could do was look for a hole to bury myself in. I was trying to be nice and Dixie decided to pull out the claws.

"Where are my manners?" she said. "My momma always said when someone pays you a compliment, say thank you because compliments are far and few between. Thank you. I'm looking forward to your first show," she finished and let out a small laugh.

At that point, I slunk out of there with my tail between my legs. My nerves were really starting to get the best of me. I was already worried about my first show. I also thought there would be a lot of camaraderie among the contestants, but I guessed that wrong. A nice walk home might help me clear my head. As I thought that it started pouring rain on my head.

# CHAPTER 25

My first show was a week away, and planning for it was a lot more work than I had thought. Between getting entertainers and getting my numbers together I was a little frantic. The stress of putting it together and worrying if anyone would show up was wearing on me. Luckily, my beefy bear muffin, Paul, agreed to organize my show, thank God. He was able to get Kit N Kaboodle to host the show for me, which was a feather in my cap. My show was the first contestant show she agreed to host. She must have really liked me. I am a very nice person, but I don't have the personality to MC a show. I don't even know how to describe the "It factor" it takes to be a great host. I know you have to be quick-witted and think on your feet because you never know what is coming your way. People have to feel that they can relate to you and that you put them at ease. That was Kit N's best quality.

Paul also got a lot of the regular cast members to agree to do my show. "You owe me for this," he said when he gave me the show order list. "I had to call in a lot of favors to get everyone to commit to performing on an off night. These girls work hard for their money, and it was hard for some of them to agree to work for free."

"I understand, and I truly appreciate it. Is there anything I can do to make it up to you? I could get my knee pads out."

"Thanks, but not right now," he said. "But I won't forget about it. Do you have your songs finalized yet? And what are you calling your evening?"

"Yes, and I don't know. I've decided on Britney Spears's 'Toxic' and Kylie Minogue's 'Can't Get You Out of My Head.' "

"Not bad choices, but are you ready to dance your way through both of those? It takes a lot more energy than you think. And do you have the words down?"

"Mostly."

"Mostly? If you can't remember the words, remember peanut butter watermelon. With all those vowels some of them will have to sync up with the song."

At that moment, Chas burst into the apartment. "I've got your show name," he said. "It should be 'Like A Virgin,' since this is your first show, and for the finish, you can end with a pagan sex orgy."

"Ha ha," I said. "There is nothing virgin here."

"That is why it is *Like A Virgin*. From the way you talk, it sounds like it's been a long time since your cookie got poked. It's been so long, your hymen has probably grown back."

"Dildos don't count, do they?"

"No," Paul chimed in. "But it isn't a horrible title. I'm sure Kit N could have some good fun with it through the night."

"Good. I'll go and get the Facebook event set up and invite everyone I know," Chas said. He volunteered to be my social media coordinator since he spent so much time on the computer. It was just natural for him to incorporate that into his daily routine.

"Just make sure you don't get the lube all over the keys again," Paul said.

"I've switched brands," Chas said. "Less sticky, so I don't run into that problem anymore."

"Have you picked your overture music yet?" Paul asked. "If we stick with the theme, then you need a Madonna medley to liven up the crowd."

"I didn't realize that it took so much to put a show together. I'm so used to just showing up and watching."

"That's why you have us to keep you on track," Chas said.

"It would be more work if the club wasn't providing the DJ, the curtain person, and the spotlight person. What raffle items were you able to get?" Paul asked.

"I got a couple of restaurant gift certificates and some free haircuts."

"Not bad. Did you also remember to pick up the raffle tickets?"

"No. I'll add that to my list for this week."

"And flyers?" Paul asked.

"I'll add that to the list too." I've learned it takes a village to put on a show. It's not like in the movies when Judy Garland would say, "Let's put on a show," and Mickey Rooney would say, "I've got a barn." Barn, my ass.

Marni had volunteered to give me some pointers on my performance, so I met him at the club ready to work.

"Which is your first number?" he asked.

"Britney's 'Toxic,'"

Marni went to the DJ booth and fired up the sound system. Next thing I knew, my music was blaring through the speakers.

"Show me how you are going to perform this number."

I was a little apprehensive because no one likes to get critiqued, but I figured I had better learn to grow a thick skin fast, otherwise I would be drag queen road kill.

I got up on the stage and started to work the number. I was shaking and moving my ass until I saw Marni raise a remote control in his hands to pause the music.

"Now you have to think like a woman. Your moves need to be more fluid and gentle. You are a dancer here, not a football linebacker. You need to become graceful, like a ballet dancer, and smoother on your moves. Have you been practicing in your pumps at home like I told you?"

"Yes, I took your advice and wear them every time I vacuum the floors. I have to do it during the day because I kept getting complaints from our downstairs neighbor about the noise from the vacuum and what they also described as an elephant stomping about our apartment."

"That's a good start," he said as he approached me and took my arm. "When you move your arm, do it like this." And he synced his body up to mine and swayed both my arms back and forth in a much more rhythmic pattern than I had ever thought about. "Your movements need to be smoother, since men tend to be a little more jagged and rigged in our moves." He then grabbed my hips and showed me how to roll them more gracefully.

"I'll take your work on that," he said. He next showed me how to walk as a woman to get the best movement out of my body and costumes on stage. "When you walk, you need to cross your feet over in front of the other one, which will cause your hips to sway more and give you a much more natural look." He then did a cat walk for me, showing me how it was done. "Now it is your turn to walk the runway." I took some practice turns, and after several attempts, it still didn't feel natural, but it was what had to be done. He could tell that I understood what he was showing me, but I wasn't comfortable with it yet. So he then said, "Remember, beauty is pain. Very few people are born a natural beauty, so they have to work at it just as much as you will need to. If you just incorporate these into your performances, you will become a stunning performer."

"You really think so?" I asked since I didn't get any support from the other contestants.

"Yes. Now let's practice." Up went the remote and on came the music.

# CHAPTER 26

I worked on becoming a fluid woman as I danced around the apartment every chance I got. Chas left flyers for me at the apartment and a note that said, "Pass these out to everyone you know and post at the club." I ran by the club to post the flyers on the bathroom walls in front of the urinals. This gave you something to look at while you peed. Marni was there, which was a good thing, since I wanted to ask him a couple of more questions.

"I love my friends, but I think they coddle me too much. What else can I do to improve my performance?"

"Do you want the honest truth?" he asked.

"Yes. I'm a big boy and can take it."

"First you need to determine the direction you want to take your character in. What you have to remember is that drag is theater, and you have to give your character a story. Look at the other contestants. They all have well-defined personalities, and that is how people can relate to them," he said. "With you, you're all over the map from your music choices to your costuming, which don't make sense to the audience. Do you understand what I'm saying?"

I let it sink in for a second and then said, "Yes."

"Look at our current cast members. Each one has a definite personality and their music choices go along with that personality. Some are trying to be the glamour diva and emulate being a real woman, while others are a little less serious but want to look like a real woman. Some of these girls want to stand and model and just grab the cabbage. And you have others on the other end of the spectrum who enjoy the campier side of life and want to be the funny entertainers."

"I understand what you are saying, and it is starting to make sense."

"Once you have that figured out, then it makes life much easier for you, because if you know what your character wants, then you can pick your song choices and outfits very quickly. If you're going to be the rock chick, then be a rock chick, but remember a rock chick doesn't do any R & B numbers. If you want to be the pop dance queen then work on your moves. Just keep asking yourself what would your character do?"

"Desiree feels that she could be a pretty woman who wants to be a professional entertainer."

"You could be a great pop diva, but dress like a pop diva. The costuming has to fit the song, and so far, yours have been way off base. This will help you get more tips and raise more money for your charity."

"That is great advice. Is there anything else you would recommend?"

"Well if you are asking, you need to change your make up to be more theatrical. Who does your make up now?"

"Marjorie, my roommate."

"The curse of the straight woman makeup. You need to either have someone who does stage make up for you or start watching YouTube videos to learn how to do it yourself. Stage makeup is much heavier because you are going to be under a spotlight, and regular make up gets washed out under the bright lights. Miss Gigi does a great face, and I'm sure she could sit down with you and show you how it is done."

Miss Gigi? That bitch is crazy! And what would Albert think if I started getting pointers from his stalker?

"I can give you her number if you like?" he said.

It would be like making a deal with Satan, but I again

said, "Yes." Forgive me, Albert. Hopefully it would remain just a little secret.

"Just find some songs that Desiree can relate to so that the emotion of the song comes out while you're performing," he said as he handed me Miss Gigi's number.

"It sounded good to me," Mr. Winston said as he came up and joined us. I didn't even see him come into the Cabaret room.

"How long were you there?" I asked.

"Long enough. Now I've got a question for you. Why did you decide to enter the contest?" he asked.

"For the crown. It is bright and shiny and would let everyone know that I am someone."

"A crown never lets anyone know you're somebody unless you're Queen Elizabeth," Marni said.

"Marni's right," Mr. Winston said. "What charity did you choose?"

"Atlanta Street Rescue."

"And why did you choose that?

"Because my momma and I were very close to being there a couple times in our lives after my dad died. If it weren't for God's intervention, then we would have been on the street."

"Use that," Mr. Winston said. "That is the passion you need to help you succeed. If you keep that in mind, you will always be a winner. There are plenty of other contestants here who only want the crown, and they don't care who they have to step on to get it and wear it on their head. Just understand that you will accomplish more if you are doing this for the right reason, and not just to be somebody."

I thanked them for their advice and went on my rounds of putting the flyers up over the urinals. As I was completing my rounds I pulled out my cell phone and dialed Miss Gigi's number.

# CHAPTER 27

On the day of the show I met Miss Gigi at her apartment several hours before the show. So that they wouldn't blow me any shit about Miss Gigi, I told everyone that Sadie from the bar agreed to do my make up, but I had to meet her at her place. I felt horrible for lying to everyone, but she was doing it for free, and money is tight since drag is expensive. No one had prepared me for that.

Miss Gigi worked her magic on me and seemed less crazy than normal. Her medications must have been working, which was a pleasant surprise.

She was watching one of my favorite cancelled TV shows, "Smash." "Smash" was the story about the creation of a musical, "Bombshell," based on the life of Marilyn Monroe and the lives of the people who were putting it together in New York. It only lasted two seasons, but I have probably re-watched it about a thousand times. "I love this show!" I said. "And the music is incredible."

"I absolutely adore it! I just think they didn't get the dialogue right for the musical," she said.

"I completely agree. I think they should have made Marilyn stronger. You know, we could complete the story since they really didn't put much of "Bombshell" into the TV show."

"That's interesting."

"I can't do drag for the rest of my life, so I've got to get a plan together. I do have hopes and dreams outside of the club," I said.

"Let's get you finished up because you have to hit the road."

She showed me some make up tricks and gave me a list of the items that she used so that I could go out and get them for myself. She even helped me get into my first outfit for the night and made some adjustments to my boobs and the dress. This was the best I had ever looked in drag.

We finished with plenty of time left before the show so I could leisurely take the ten mile drive over to the club and even have time for a couple of pre-show cocktails. Traffic was light for once, which is a rarity in Atlanta.

I was rehearsing my songs in the car until the red dashboard light came on and steam started shooting out from under the hood. I didn't need this right now. So I pulled into the first parking lot I saw, which happened to be a biker bar, Angel's Hideaway. The parking lot was full of motor cycles. The marquee over the door read "Angel Flight Benefit Tonight!"

I grabbed my phone and called Marjorie. It rang several times before she finally answered.

"Hey sweetie, what's going on?" she asked.

"My car has broken down, and I need your help."

"Where are you at?"

"Angel's Hideaway on Glenwood Road."

"Why are you over there? Sadie lives in Midtown."

"I didn't want to tell anyone this, but Miss Gigi did my make up tonight. She came recommended from Marni, and he was right. She beat my face like never before. I hope you are not mad."

"Honey, I'm not mad. You could have told me you wanted some help with your make up. I'm not offended in the slightest. I don't know how to do drag queen makeup."

"Thank God. I didn't want to hurt your feelings, but that is why I need your help. You can't tell the boys Miss Gigi did my makeup or I will never hear the end of it. Especially from Albert. Can you get Riggo, your mechanic friend, and come over here?"

"I will give him a call and get over there as soon as we can. Why don't you go in and have a drink at the bar?"

"Like this? I don't want to get killed."

"Atlanta's a friendly town. I'm sure you will be good, and there are plenty of gay boys in that neighborhood, so I doubt you're the first drag queen to grace the doors of that bar."

"Hurry please. I can't be late for my own show."

I hung up and gathered my courage to push open the door. The hallway was dark, but you could see a make shift stage that was brightly lit up set up on the far wall.

The doorman rushed up to me, "You must be Claudia, the entertainer we have been waiting for."

"No, you have me mistaken for someone else."

"Come on, let me take you to Tony. He's in charge of the show." With that, he grabbed my arm and led me to a backstage dressing room.

Before me in the dressing room stood a God. Tony was wearing a leather vest with the top button open, revealing a tuft of black hair that matched his full beard and short, cropped hair. His naked arms were guns with leather wristbands. His skin-tight blue jeans did nothing to hide the fact that he was only wearing a jock strap as the back strap lines showed through the jeans as he bent over to pick up the show order list. All this was finished off with black combat boots.

"Here's Claudia," the doorman said.

"Who's this pretty lady?" Tony asked. "Claudia cancelled a little bit ago."

"My name is Desiree, and I only stopped in to get a drink while I wait for friends to come and fix my car. I've got a show I have to perform at."

"Lovely lady, you are the answer to my prayers. Our opening act cancelled, and I don't have a filler. We are hosting our annual Angel Flight fundraiser to raise money for hospital flights for families who can't afford it when they need to be transported to a hospital for medical emergencies.

Would you grace us with your talent on our little stage tonight? I would be ever in your debt," Tony finished. "Give me your keys, and I'll have Bobby Rae look your car over."

I obeyed and gave him my keys, "It's the blue Honda Civic. And what time is the show? And what type of music does the crowd like? I don't sing live, I only lip sync."

"Showtime is in fifteen minutes and you would be the first act. The crowd just wants to be entertained, and all the money raised goes to charity."

He grabbed my hands and stared down at me with his big brown puppy dog eyes. I could feel my penis start pressing against the restraints of a layer of tights and two layers of panty hose. It wasn't going anywhere, and for once I was glad no one could see it. I couldn't resist as I felt my temperature start to rise. The only thing that raced through my mind was grabbing his face and sucking on his pouting lips followed by him pinning me to the wall. "Is it warm in here?" I asked. "Please have them bring me a screwdriver. And I would be glad to help you out." I couldn't tell if I was panting or not. Thank God Miss Gigi sprayed my face with a product that sets your face and prevents it from showing sweat.

"You don't know how much I appreciate this. If there is anything I can ever do, please let me know."

"Well there is one thing," I said. "I am competing in a competition at Club Cabaret so that I can win a stunning crown. It is also a charity fundraiser and the final show will be December 7th, and it would be wonderful if you could come." And the other thought going through my head was that I would love to see you cum, but that thought never made it to my mouth.

"I know exactly where the club is. I will put it on my calendar now." He pulled out his iPhone and put it on his calendar. "December 7th. Got it down. Now let's get you that drink."

The waitress brought a tray of drinks for everyone in the dressing room. As I looked around, I noticed most of the other entertainers had a guitar with them, so I was assuming that they were all singing and playing live. I was glad I was on first. I had no idea of how the crowd would respond since this was the first time I'd been glammed up, and this wasn't a gay bar, so no telling how receptive they would be. Plus, of the women entertainers, I was the only one in sequins, and I looked way over the top compared to the rest of them. I grabbed my screwdriver and slammed it down. "One more please," I asked the waitress.

"Sure thing, honey. Drinks are on the house for the entertainers," she said.

"In that case, make it a double."

Tony returned, "Do you have your music?"

"It's right here." I reached into my purse and pulled out my CDs. "I will need those back right after my numbers because I have to get to my other show."

The overture music came up, and it was a country song that I didn't recognize. Tony came on the PA system. "Ladies and Gentlemen welcome to the 10th Annual Angel Flight Charity benefit. We have an incredibly talented line up for you tonight. So please get out your wallets and welcome to the stage a very special lady who agreed last minute to help us out, Miss Desiree."

Oh shit.

My music started. I decided to open with Britney Spears's "Toxic." The spotlight hit me. My lips moved, and the crowd was clapping already and cheering me on. I shook. I danced. I shimmied. I gyrated. If I could have rolled across that stage, I would have, but I didn't want to destroy the dress before the next show. The people lined up to tip me, and others put money straight in the bucket. It was incredible to see so many smiling faces as they came up to tip me. The DJ did a magnificent job blending into Kylie Minogue's "Cant' Get You Out of My Head," and off I went on another three minute joy ride. I strutted across that stage and grabbed my head, just like on the video. It was so invigorating to get this much love back. I only wished that it would carry over to my next show. As the number ended, I was exhausted, but feeling blessed. The crowd was on their feet for me as I took my bow and exited the stage. I slipped back into the dressing room to grab a seat and cool off.

I heard Tony give me props and introduce the next act. Bobby Rae came back stage and let me know, "You need a water pump O-ring and a radiator hose. Let your mechanic friend know, but your car isn't going anywhere until that gets fixed.

I looked at the clock on the wall and panic set in as I realized I was running out of time to get to my own show. I grabbed my phone and texted Marjorie, "911 I need you to pick me up at Angel's Hideaway and take me to the Club."

Marjorie texted back, "Can't get there for another 45 minutes. Picking up Riggo."

By that time, it was going to be too late. So I texted, "Need water pump O-ring and radiator hose. Will get alternate transportation. Meet me at the Club."

Tony walked in and saw the look of distress on my face. "Are you alright?"

"No, my ride won't get her in time. I need to get a cab."

"No need. I'll get you there."

"You can't. You've got your own show going on. I can't let you just leave."

"Don't worry. The act on now is set to play for a while, so I've got plenty of time to drop you off. I wouldn't want to leave my baby doll in distress."

"I've got to unload my car and take everything that's in there. Is that okay?"

"How much stuff do you have?"

"Not too much."

"Bobby Rae grab, your side car!" Tony yelled out. "We have a delivery to make."

Tony grabbed my hand and led me down the hallway and opened the door for me. This was a gentleman. Bobby Rae was already outside with his motorcycle with an empty side car. We quickly unloaded my clunker into the side car, but there wasn't any room for me. Tony could tell by the look on my face what I was thinking.

"Don't worry, your ride is right here." He straddled a supped-up motorcycle and fired it up. He handed me a helmet to put on, which saved me from seeing my wig fly off as we cruised the streets. "Hop on. I'll keep you safe." He extended his hand and helped me onto the seat behind him. He grabbed my hands and pulled them across his chest. "Hold on tight." I was intoxicated by the smell of sweat and leather. All I could do was breathe it in as we tore out of the parking lot with me squeezing him and pulling my body as close to his as possible.

The ride was too short, Waiting outside the club stage entrance were Marjorie and Riggo. I jumped off the motorcycle on very wobbly legs with vibrations still running through my body. The crew started unloading the side car and slinging everything though the stage door. The DJ was already spinning in the room, so every time the door opened, a blast of dance music erupted.

"Thank you for everything. I know you have to get back to your show," I said hugging Tony and kissing him on the cheek.

"It was all my pleasure," he said.

I didn't want to let go of him, and I think he felt the same way. Suddenly, we were interrupted by Riggo. "I have a ring for you," he said.

I let go of Tony and hugged and kissed Riggo. "I could marry you for that!" The door opened and another blast of dance music drowned out everything.

"Why are all the good ones taken?" Tony said to himself under his breath.

I looked from Riggo and asked, "Did you say something?"

"No. Have a great show," Tony said.

And with that Marjorie, Riggo and I raced into the club.

# CHAPTER 28

As a treat for completing my first show Sheila took me to a friend of hers in Savannah for a couple of days for some much needed R n' R after our shift was over today. The show went better than expected, and I was able to raise $500 for Atlanta Street Rescue. It wasn't the best and it wasn't the worst show that could be put on. I even survived someone gluing my pumps together. Thank heavens they were only $15.99 from Payless.

For some reason, the night shift crew came in an hour early, which I thought was strange, but it could just be their way of letting us out so we could head out on our trip. Little did I know how wrong I was.

Braxton was the first to speak, "We need a favor from you."

"Sure, what can I do for you?"

"You are well aware that Jaime has a serious hygiene problem, and we can't take it anymore," he said.

"Yes, Jamie smells," Sheila chimed in.

"And since he likes you, we were wondering if you could have a talk with him," Germaine said.

"What do you want me to say to him?" I asked.

"I don't care what you say to him, but something has got to be done because the smell is making us all sick," Braxton said.

As I looked around, everyone was nodding their heads in agreement. I guess I was lucky because I worked the early shift and didn't have to directly interact with Jaime most of the time. He was always nice to me whenever he saw me, and I didn't want to do anything to hurt his feelings. "Can't you ask Kristoff to do something about it?"

"We thought about that, but we would rather not make this a personnel issue," Germaine said.

"And since you don't have to work with him night after night, you don't have to worry about him retaliating against you," Braxton said.

"Guys, I just can't do it. I don't want to start any drama here."

"Honey, this is a hotel. There is always drama here whether you like it or not," Germaine said.

"Plus, we have you covered, so you both can take off immediately afterwards," Braxton said. "We are begging you here."

After several more minutes of cajoling, I finally caved in. I didn't know what I should do. I finally settled on the direct approach.

Jamie was working in his office. I knocked on the open door. "Is it okay to come in for a minute?"

Jamie looked up from his paperwork. I could already see the sweat stains building up on his shirt.

"Sure, come on in. What's on your mind?" he said.

I walked in and closed the door behind me. I swear I saw everyone grouped down the hallway watching me with their arms in church prayer mode as I pulled the door shut. "I don't know how to say this, so I will just say this. You smell."

He looked at me dumbfounded for a second, and then finally asked, "Like cigarettes?"

"No, like BO."

He didn't say anything again for another minute. "Does everyone think I smell?"

"Yes. It has gotten more noticeable over time."

"Do I need a stronger deodorant?" he asked.

"I don't think that will help because it smells like you are rotting from the inside out. It might be something medical that you need to get checked out."

He looked shocked and embarrassed. I didn't have anything else to say. "I've got to go. Have a great weekend." I turned the door handle and pulled the door open to make my escape.

"Thanks," he said.

And I was out of there. All I could do was race down the hallway and head to the parking lot where I was meeting Sheila. I got to her car, but she wasn't there. She finally arrived a few minutes later laughing. "Jamie stopped me and told me that you told him he smelled. I just had to laugh. Let's hit the road."

# CHAPTER 29

It was a beautiful evening as we hit the expressway and headed south. Sheila had a very large portable cooler with a spout on the bottom and filled with screwdrivers so we could partake on the road.

Sheila drove an old white Lebaron convertible with burgundy interior. We put the top down so we could feel the slight chill in the air as we headed first to Macon and then to Savannah.

"So why are you really doing this drag thing?" Sheila asked.

"Do you want the honest answer?"

"Yes, of course I do."

"I believe the crown will make me feel like somebody. I know that sounds shallow, but I've never had anything that anyone else wanted. Growing up in the mountains, we never had much. It was a struggle a lot of the time. I just want people to know who I am."

"Honey, your friends already know who you are. That's all that should matter."

"But isn't everyone entitled to their fifteen minutes of fame? I see all these people with their groups of friends, and I feel left out. I don't think I will every make it into the popular group."

"Forget that crap. Those boys are a bunch of stuck-up assholes who don't know their heads from a hole in the ground and all they can talk about is their things, and their hair, and how wonderful their lives are. I call bullshit on that. You think those people's lives are any better than yours?"

"Well they seem to have it all."

"That's all show. How many of these boys' credit cards have been declined at the front desk? If you got to see behind the curtain, you would see their life ain't no better than yours and a lot of the time it's more fucked up than yours."

"Tell me how you really feel."

"They think they are the celebrities of the city, but they remind me of the attention-grubbing whores that Access Hollywood talks about all the time. Most of the so-called celebrities they cover don't produce anything and won't leave anything behind. The so called popular boys are the same way. They don't do anything and don't produce anything. They will be as forgotten as this year's sweaters. I don't watch Access Hollywood anymore, and I don't pay attention to them either."

I respected Sheila because she always said what was on her mind. I needed to soak up what she was saying. I did enjoy the attention I was getting from the crowd, which was great since I wasn't getting any attention in the bedroom. The truth was that I was a little lonely even with people around me all the time. I know I shouldn't put that much pressure on myself to find a boyfriend, but it would really rock to have someone I could kiss and hug on.

# CHAPTER 30

I-16 ended in Savannah, so we rolled into the city. The air felt different than Atlanta's. This is what the south should smell like - a mix of salt air, magnolia blossoms, and Spanish moss.

Sheila took me on a quick drive down to the river walk where an ocean tanker was navigating the river and then around the squares that made up the main part of Downtown Savannah. I didn't know what to expect of the city, but it was absolutely charming.

We pulled up to Dick Knights' home in the historic district. Our host was waiting for us on his rocking chair front porch with a tray of mint juleps. The house was a brick mansion with a gracious front porch, double chimneys, windows everywhere, and of course, the required magnolia tree in the front yard.

"Why Sheila, my darling, how is my favorite Yankee?" Dick said. "And you must be Tyler, Sheila's young traveling companion. It is a pleasure to meet you, sir."

Sheila didn't tell me anything about Dick before we got here. I found him to be the perfect picture of a Southern gentleman. He was impeccably dressed from his trousers to his pressed Brooks Brothers shirt with a gleaming black belt and shoes and a sweater casually thrown over his shoulders. He smelled of old money, but only casually.

"The pleasure is all mine," I said. "Thank you for letting me stay in your wonderful home."

"This old place? She has been in the family for over one hundred years and has every modern convenience you can hope for. Here, drink up!" And with that, our evening of party began.

As we settled in, more people kept showing up at the house. "I forgot to tell you that my neighbor is getting married this weekend, and I am hosting some of the overflow of her relatives here. I hope you don't mind."

Who could mind? I was out of town and out of drag for one of the first weekends in a long time. I was ready to let loose.

After fluffing up, we were all ready to head out. It was a beautiful night with a full moon and a slight breeze blowing as we took the short stroll to the river walk, which was full of shops, restaurants, bars, and tourists. It was such a different atmosphere from what I was used to that I was just trying to soak in all the sights and sounds. "You should be here during St. Patrick's Weekend," Dick said. "You can't get down this promenade without some horrible drunk person spilling their beer all over you. It is the largest party in the South, and Savannah loves a good party."

We slipped into one of the bars, Cocky's, grabbed a table, and immediately ordered drinks and two baskets of chicken wings. Sheila and I hadn't eaten anything since we grabbed snacks at the Pick N Pay on the expressway. It was good just to sit and talk without having to worry about being on stage. It gets hard when you are competing because after a while, people recognize who you are and want to talk with you. I didn't get this until after the first show. You have to be nice to everyone if you want them to support you. I mean support your charity, but I guess the two are really intertwined now.

A half hour after being here, I noticed some go-go boys start hopping on the bar and start dancing around in their underwear. "I forgot to mention that the entertainment for this evening is the lovely individuals working their wares for our enjoyment. Tip if you must. My favorite is Andrew. He will be out shortly."

As we sat and watched, a herd of scantily clad go-go boys worked the bar and worked table to table. Dick was very popular with the boys, as everyone came over to say "hi" and rub on Dick's body. Dick kept slipping dollar bills into their underwear, and each time he would pull the underwear further out to get a good look at the boy's penis or stick his hand in to feel up his junk. He was always polite and would introduce the dancer to Sheila and me. There were several who were absolutely gorgeous and caused a stirring in my own pants. Finally, Andrew came over.

The first thing you notice about Andrew is his smile. His teeth just shined whenever he smiled and spoke. It was mesmerizing. And it didn't hurt that he was built like a brick shithouse. He was twenty-five and had an incredible chest with a little bit of fur and several tattoos, great legs, great arms, and a personality. He could actually carry on a conversation.

"Andrew, how would you like to take our little traveling companion back for a private dance?" Dick slipped Andrew sixty dollars.

Andrew took me by the hand and led me to the back where there was a row of private curtained-off booths. We slipped into one of the booths and immediately Andrew started rubbing his bubble ass against my crotch. I could feel the rise in my dick as it strained against my jeans. He spun around. I couldn't resist pinching his nipples, rubbing my hands all over his chest and licking his pecs. He even let me pull out his dick and start stroking it. He was kissing my neck and slightly moaning as I felt his dick keep getting harder. He took his hand and started rubbing the front of my jeans, which caused me to squirm more on my bench seat.

"Unzip your pants," Andrew said.

Whatever he said, I was going to do. So I slipped the zipper down, revealing my underwear-covered bulge, which started pushing out the zipper. He took his hand and grabbed my bulge and started rubbing. As he did, I could feel myself starting to sweat.

"Undo your belt and open your pants," he said.

Again, I complied. I opened my jeans. He pulled down the back of his underwear and started grinding his hole against my underwear. Up and down, pushing his hole against me and tightening his ass cheeks as he did. The pleasure was exquisite, which was strange, since being a bottom, I never had someone tighten their ass on my dick. But he was the hottest man I had ever played around with. Next thing I knew he pulled down my underwear and stuck my throbbing dick into his hole and began to ride it up and down. His ass muscles were incredible, as I could feel him tighten on the down stroke. Unfortunately, this was short-lived, as his name was called to get up and start working the bar.

"Heading to the bar, my man," he said as he unmounted himself and then grabbed my underwear and pulled them back up over my still hard dick.

All I could do was say, "Thank you" as I pulled up my zipper and buttoned and belted my jeans back up.

"I'll come over to your table later," he said.

"That would be lovely," I said.

And we both slipped back out of the booth. There was already a line of dancers and their patrons waiting for a booth space to open up so it was quickly filled.

"Are you okay?" Sheila asked as I got back to the table.

"I think I just topped someone," was my reply. "I've never done that before."

"Andrew is a great dancer. He will do just about anything you ask. Next time, tell him you would like to sit on his dick," Dick said. "He's definitely worth the money."

"I'm just extremely horny now," was all I could say. "Excuse me while I go to the restroom to wash my face."

"Are you sure you shouldn't wash your dick?" Sheila said.

She had a good point there. The bathroom was empty, so I grabbed a handful of paper towels, wet them down, and then went into a stall. There I was able to rinse my dick off and dispose of the evidence.

I stepped out to wash my face and all I heard was, "Did you have some trouble in there?" I turned to see a hot, bearded ginger man leaning on one of the sinks.

"What do you mean?" was my response.

"Take a look," he said.

As I took a look, I finally saw what he was talking about. The towels were definitely wet and had dripped causing my jeans to look like I had wet myself. "It's not what you think it is," I said.

"It usually isn't. My name is Sammy," he said.

"I'm Tyler."

"It is a pleasure to meet you. Can I buy you a drink?" he offered.

"I'm with friends, but I think that would be okay."

"Come over here," he said. He then grabbed my shoulders and turned me around to face the wall. I didn't realize the men here were so forward, and I'm not the type of person to have sex in a public bathroom. I'm looking for love, but not in public. He reached around me and pushed the button. Next thing I felt was the warm air from the hand dryer blowing on my pants to dry them out. Thank God I didn't open my big mouth.

"That looks better," he said. "How about that drink now?"

We shuffled back to the table, and I introduced Sammy to Sheila and Dick.

"No introduction needed," Dick said. "How are you this evening?"

As it turns out, Sammy worked at one of Dick's favorite restaurants, so they already knew each other.

"I was wondering if I could join you and buy a round of drinks for the table." Sammy asked.

"Honey, you can do what-ever you want you sexy, young thing," Sheila said.

And with that the drink fest began. It first started with more cocktails and quickly led to shots. There was a group selling Jell-O shots to raise money for their softball team. Of course, this gave me an idea, but this was a night to forget the crown and just have fun. Dick plopped down a $20 bill, and next thing I knew there was a giant stack of Jell-O shots and we are all swilling our tongues around the plastic cups. These were really strong shots, but that didn't stop any of us from consuming.

The entire time, Sammy and I were playing handsies under the table. He had such strong thighs and arms that my mouth began to water.

As the evening progressed, my manhole kept puckering and it started calling the shots. I wanted to go home with Sammy so bad, but I thought it would be poor form to do so since Dick was kind enough to let us come and stay with him. It was pretty obvious that he felt the same way, but I don't think he wanted to bring it up in front of my friends.

"Boys why don't you go to Sammy's and fuck like animals. It's obvious you both have the hots for each other, and you will be in good hands. Just remember my address 2115 Bull St," Dick said.

"Really?" I asked.

"Go have some fun, but be safe," Sheila said.

"Are you sure? I don't want to run off and leave you," I said.

"I will be fine. Plus, I'm here with my old friend and we have more catching up to do. You boys go have some fun," Sheila said.

I couldn't believe they were being so gracious, but I guess that was just Savannah rubbing off on us. Or at least hopefully rubbing off on me.

As I got up from the table, I stumbled a little bit. I didn't realize how wasted I had become. Sammy wasn't in much better shape.

"It is a very short walk to my apartment. My roommate works at another club and won't be home until much later," he said. I hadn't looked at my watch for a while, so I was surprised it was 1:30 already.

So we stepped out into the cool night and headed up the cobblestone street to the dangerously-angled stone stairs back up to the main street level. I think Sammy had his hands on my ass to balance me the entire time up the stairs to make sure I didn't take a digger and crack open my head. Once we were at the top, he took me by the hand and kissed me on the mouth. His lips were warm as he put his massive arms around me and pulled me tighter. I got weak in the knees. "Come on," he said as he led me the couple of blocks to the basement apartment in an old house. It was rather charming and cozy, and as he said, we had the place to ourselves.

"Would you like a drink?" he asked.

"Just water. I need to sober up a bit."

He handed me a bottle of water and we settled onto the living room couch in front of the TV. For some reason "Honey I Shrunk The Kids" was on, but we paid very little attention to the movie.

He immediately began to unbutton my shirt and started kissing and sucking on my neck. It sent chills down my spine as he slowly removed my shirt. I couldn't wait and I started pulling his shirt off over his head, revealing a wash board stomach and bulging pecs with a forest of red fur. He pushed me down on the couch and started sucking on my nipples, which usually made my dick get hard immediately. Something was wrong because I didn't feel anything down there. My penis was dead. I had whiskey dick and there was no getting an erection. Panic set in.

Here I was with this extremely hot man and couldn't get it up. How can I explain that I was turned on even though my penis wasn't cooperating? Think. Think. It really doesn't matter because I am a bottom, and as long as his dick works, this shouldn't be a problem. Relax now.

I could feel the heat from his naked torso as he bumped and ground his body all over mine. He pulled off my shoes and ripped open my pants and tugged them off as quickly as he could, causing us to tumble onto the blanket-covered floor. He got to his knees and unzipped his jeans and began to roll them down, revealing a tattoo just below the waist line. It was a Winnie the Pooh Bear. It blended well with the start of his red bush peering out of his Andrew Christian underwear. The jeans kept sliding down, revealing more and more as they slid past his tree trunk thighs and fell to the floor. The only thing it didn't reveal was a package in those Andrew Christian tighty whities. It lay there like a lump of Play-Doh, and no amount of kneading was going to get this dough to rise. He kicked the jeans off the rest of the way, and there we were, two drunks with dead dicks. We continued to make out, but the thrill of the evening was lost. He finally fell asleep with one arm wrapped around me, so I pushed it to one side, grabbed the pillows off the couch, and pulled the blanket over the both of us. It was chilly on the floor, but at least I had my own red-headed nuclear reactor to keep me warm as I finally dosed off to sleep, only to wait for another day to find the perfect man.

# CHAPTER 31

The sun came through the basement windows and landed directly on my face. It became impossible to sleep at this point, plus I had to pee. I slipped out from under the blanket and headed down the hall to the bathroom. I was trying to remember my ginger's name and was drawing a complete blank. Did I really have that much to drink last night?

"Did you and Sammy have fun last night?" came out of the second bedroom door as the roommate pushed open the door.

Sammy, that's it.

"There's coffee in the kitchen if you need some," the roommate said.

It was good to pee. It seemed like I peed forever. I kept trying to remember Dick's address. I was still a little fuzzy. As I looked at myself in the mirror, all I could think about was that I needed a haircut. With the competition going on, I didn't have as much time to myself as I used to.

I woke my giant ginger gently. "Hey, I got to go. I had a great time."

"Me too," Sammy said. "Hope you can come back to Savannah soon."

"How do I get to Bull Street?"

"Just take a left out the door and head down two blocks," he said.

By the time I grabbed a disposable cup of coffee, Sammy was already back sound asleep as I headed out the door.

It was a beautiful, cool day and still a little early. There was very little traffic out and I had the street to myself. I walked a block, and to my surprise, there was a beauty salon open. I pushed open the door and the only one there was the person behind the check- in desk reading a magazine.

"May I help you, sugar?" she asked. "My name is Char."

"I would love a haircut, please."

"Come over here, baby boy, and I will get you taken care of."

She sat me down in the chair and put on the giant plastic cloth with the name of the salon – Hair Today Gone Tomorrow Salon - in pink letters.

"Is that a birthmark?" Char asked.

I had no idea of what she was talking about, and I didn't really want to know so I said, "Yes."

She got my hair cleaned up and we finished with a shampoo. At least my hair was clean, since I didn't know how the rest of me smelled. I paid her out and tipped her. I was back on the street again and heading to Dick's doing the walk of shame.

It was nice to have some time to myself since I never got any private time. I turned on Bull Street and started paying attention to the street numbers. It wasn't that far up the street before I spotted the house. Thank God it was so distinctive, otherwise I would have been totally lost.

There was a lot of activity out front next door as the wedding party was trying to get everyone into the cars and off to the church. I didn't meet the bride, but she looked stunning in her wedding gown as they got her into her chauffeur-driven limo and sent her off. The groom came out of the door a minute later. He was hot in his tuxedo. Next, I'm assuming, were his parents, who were a little older, but were beaming at their pride and joy. They all hopped into an SUV and off they went.

I strolled up the front walk-way and was greeted by the guests staying at Dick's house as they were heading out the door. We exchanged small talk and off they went.

I closed the door behind me and let out a sigh. To my surprise, Sheila was already up running around in her pink robe.

The same clothes as the night before, I see," she said. "Didn't have time to change into anything else?"

"Honey, you know I didn't have any time," I responded.

"So how was he?"

"My giant ginger was a fantastic kisser, but WD40 kicked in for both of us and nothing happened past that."

"What is WD40?" she asked.

"Whiskey dick," I replied.

"So sorry to hear that. Oh my God. What is that on your neck?"

"What do you mean?"

She pulled out her reading glasses to get a better look as she pulled my shirt collar down. "You better take a look in the mirror. Cute hair-cut, by the way."

I ran over to the mirror and pulled down my shirt collar. To my surprise there was a huge hickey. When I say huge, I mean it looked like a leach had hooked on and tried to drain me dry. I touched it, and it hurt a little. "Holy crap Batman." That is what Char was asking about.

"Holy crap is right. It looks like you hooked up a vacuum cleaner and went to town." She started laughing.

"Stop it. It's not that funny."

"Sweetie, yes it is," she said. "I've got some cover up we can use to hide it for the rest of the day. You don't want these good town folks thinking you're a slut.

I could feel the burn on my face as I started turning a bright shade of red. "Is it warm in here or is the last of my dignity going up in flames?"

"You have nothing to worry about. No one here knows who you are, so just relax," she said.

So I finally went to the bathroom and slid off my evening rags and stepped into the hot, steaming shower. It was good to relax in the steam. Sheila also told me to let the heat from the water pulse on the bruise to see if it would loosen it up any. I let the water get into every crevice to wash away the man funk from last night. It felt good to be clean again.

As I stepped from the bathroom wrapped only in a towel, Dick was coming out of his bedroom.

"Well hello, my weary traveler. Did you get any sleep last night?" he asked.

"We got a little," I said. That's what happens when you leave a bar late.

"Put on some comfortable clothes because we are heading to brunch, and then I'm taking you on a tour of downtown."

It had warmed up nicely, so shorts and a t-shirt were in order.

The three of us strolled several blocks and headed over to Lady and Sons, which is the restaurant owned by Paula Deen located right downtown. There was a waitlist, so we put our name in and headed to the bar. The next thing I knew, there were three mimosas sitting in front of us.

"It is a tradition to drink here in Savannah. You need to become a part of it," Dick said.

Who was I to argue with tradition? We each grabbed our glasses and toasted to each other. What I didn't know was this was just the start of the drinking for the day, because after brunch, our day out turned into a bar crawl of the downtown. The downtown was constructed of squares, which were to help encourage people to socialize back in the day. It was a dreamy downtown brought back to life by the Savannah College of Art and Design, better known as SCAD. As Dick informed us the city center was shutting down as the malls were built further out in the suburbs. The only thing left downtown was the river district and a Woolworths. The local theater was shuttered and became an eyesore. But SCAD had the vision and started renovating downtown, and with that came the condos and restaurants. Even the old theater was done and is now owned by the school as their performing arts center.

Dick took us over to the large park, Forsyth Park, and I

marveled at the fountains. They were gorgeous, and amazingly, they were ordered out of a store catalogue and shipped to Savannah. I pulled out some change and went over to the fountain, which had tons of change lying in the bottom. I threw in a quarter, hoping that it would improve my luck.

"To the almighty powers that be, please let me meet the right man for me. I hope I'm not asking for too much." The quarter splashed into the water.

"What did you wish for?" Sheila asked.

"If I told you, it won't come true."

"You wished for a man again, didn't you."

"Yes."

"Baby boy, it will happen. It happens when you least expect it. It's when you go looking for it that it won't happen."

"You really think so?"

"She's right, you know," Dick said. "I had the love of my life and even though our time was short, I know that it will happen again."

"I'm so sorry to hear that."

"Don't be. Love will find me again. Let's go get a drink. I'm thirsty and there is a great bar just around the corner."

As we left the park, there was a plaque that read "Here in 1857, James Pierpoint, organist and music director of the Unitarian Church first performed his composition 'The One Horse Open Sleigh,' or as it became better known "Jingle Bells" on Thanksgiving Day."

"It was performed right here in this church. Unfortunately the Yankees in Medford, Massachusetts are trying to claim that the song was written there," Dick said. "Stupid carpet baggers trying to steal something else from the South."

We went to Manny's, which was the place where all the politicos went when they came to town to stump up votes. They had a great mini shuffleboard game that we got to play. The next thing I knew shots were sliding down my way. So I consumed and consumed.

Our bar tour continued. With each stop I became even more inebriated and disoriented. My day turned into a beautiful fog bank as we strolled the streets of Savannah.

The next thing I remembered was Sheila waking me up. "Time to wake up, sweetie. We have dinner reservations to make."

"What time is it?"

"Seven. Our reservations are for 8:00."

Where had most of my day gone and why do people here eat so late?

The house was in a flurry with wedding guests running up and down the stairs.

"Look, the only way we can do this is if we share the bath," Sheila said.

The fog was lifting, and I could pull myself together to say, "That's okay. You don't have anything I want and what I've got you've already seen before, so we are good." Next thing, we were both naked, giggling up a storm in the bath. One hopped out of the shower as the other hopped in. We managed to process and make it downstairs in time.

"I don't know what was going on upstairs," Dick said, "But the other guests said there was a lot of laughing coming out of the bathroom."

"Just having some fun," I said.

The rest of the evening was very tame, which was much appreciated after two days of binge drinking. The people in Savannah really take their drinking seriously.

In the morning we said goodbye and thanked Dick for all of his hospitality. We then started our long, quiet drive home to Atlanta. The only thing that broke the silence was a text from Braxton. "Jamie decided to take some time off and discover his true self. He has left the hotel."

I hope he didn't do it over what I said.

# CHAPTER 32

My break was over and it was time to get more competitive. I needed some advice from someone who's been around for a while, so I set up another meeting with Marni. As I sat at the bar waiting for Marni, I was listening to "Smash" on my iPod. It was one of my favorite songs, "Let Me Be Your Star." I couldn't help but to sing along with it. This had become my unofficial anthem as I could relate to the TV characters and what they were going through. It's about the love of a man and them wanting to be chosen. That's what I want and that's why I love the build up to the moment where they crescendo to "Let me be your star," and with that, the song was over. They were singing about the desire to become something better. This contest was my star-making moment. Suddenly, I felt a tap on my shoulder.

"Hey girl," Marni said.

"Sorry. I got lost in my own world there."

"So you want some ideas?"

"Yes. How do you think I'm doing? I have no idea where I stand in the rankings."

"No one does. That's the beauty of this. I'll give you a hint. You are not at the top, but you are also not last."

"That's good to know."

"Look, you can keep doing all these small fundraisers, which will wear you out and kill your support staff, but you have to come up with something bigger. Less effort for more money. Here is a list of everything that has been done here at the club in the past to raise money."

I took the list and scanned it over. A lot of the ideas I had were already there. The car wash. Jell-O shot nights. I began to panic a little until I saw something that I didn't know what it was. All it said was "Pageant" in quotation marks. I know they held pageants here in the past, but they all had a title like Miss Hotlanta and Miss Barfly, so I asked, "What is 'Pageant'?"

"'Pageant' was a musical about a fictitious Miss America-like beauty contest. Each contestant represented a state. It was hilarious."

"So we could have the Cabaret Room for something else other than a typical drag show?"

"Sure. As long as it doesn't conflict with something else scheduled. What are you thinking about?"

"Miss Gigi and I both have an unnatural love for the cancelled way before it's time TV show 'Smash.' When she was doing my makeup, we were tossing around some ideas of how you could do it as a stage musical. I think I have worn out my DVD because I watch it so much."

"Now you have something. It's new and fresh and it will put butts in the seats. I'm sure it will take you a little bit to work it, but when you're ready, let me know and I'll give you a night. You could easily get a hundred people at ten bucks a head. That's a thousand dollars for the night depending on your costs. Remember to keep doing what you are doing to keep the money coming in, but get your stage show done as soon as possible," he advised.

"You think we really could?"

"I've done enough theater and you need to keep the staging to a minimum to keep your costs down. I've got a copy of 'Pageant' from when it was done here so that it will give you a great idea of what can be done to give you the biggest impact. Let me go get it from my office." Marni was off to get the tape.

I finally felt a renewed sense of energy and lightness that I hadn't felt in a long time. As I waited for Marni's return,

Mr. Winston popped out of his office. I really hadn't spent much time with him, so now was my opportunity. "Hey Mr. Winston I want to say thank you for putting all this together."

"You're welcome. It has been all my pleasure," he said.

"I don't feel like I've ever gotten a chance really to get to know you. Do you have some time now?"

"Not right now. I've got to go visit a friend in hospice."

I didn't want to appear ignorant, but I had to ask. "What's a hospice?"

"When you are too ill to take care of yourself and you are terminal they move you to hospice so that you can die with dignity," he informed me non-judgmentally.

"I'm sorry. I didn't mean to interrupt."

"You didn't. I've been in my own world today. Dying is just part of the human condition. No one gets out of here alive."

"Can I go with you?"

"Really?"

"Yes. No one should be alone at a time like this."

"That's very generous of you. It's just a short walk. Let me grab my cane."

While I waited, Marni brought me the tape for 'Pageant.' I had some homework to do in reviewing the tape.

It was very humid as we headed out the door. You could tell summer was right around the corner.

"How did you end up owning a gay club? You're straight, right?"

"Yes, I am homosexually challenged. The reason I own a gay club is because I got tired of making money for other people. My wife was a manager and I was the DJ. We worked at several places here in town and made the clubs some good money. We were the fixers. If you had a struggling club, you hired us, and we were able to turn your place around. We had plenty of people who were encouraging us to open our own place."

"So you finally did here?"

"This place was open and it was in the heart of Midtown, so we knew the clientele was going to be gay. My wife and I didn't care if it was a straight club or gay club, but just based on the location here, we knew our audience was going to be gay. So we marketed to that audience."

He went silent for a little bit as we walked over the cracked brick sidewalk. He seemed to be lost in his thoughts.

"Things were going great until Marie got sick. My wife's name was Marie. She was so beautiful."

Then he paused at the intersection and looked both ways before we crossed.

"Running a club is a tough business. People don't realize the hours that need to get put into a place so that they can come in and have a great time."

"What happened to Marie?"

"Marie was the love of my life. She was an incredible woman who made my heart jump every time I saw her, even after the years we had been together." He paused for a second. "She kept getting these increasingly painful migraines that would take her down. We finally went to the doctor and they ordered an MRI. It revealed that she had an inoperable brain tumor, and within two weeks of finding out she was gone." He stopped and looked up at the stars.

"I'm so sorry. I didn't mean for you to have to go through it again." I really didn't want for him to have to relive that painful moment in his life.

"It's perfectly alright. I like to talk about Marie. As time passes you forget the bad things and only remember the good things. The other day Queen's 'Bohemian Rhapsody' came on the radio, which was one of Marie's favorite songs. I realized at that moment that I have known that song for forty years already. You see, you will remember the good things no matter how old you get. He stopped and pulled out his wallet to show me a picture of Marie. She was stunning.

"This is the way I will always remember her."

"She was a looker."

"Thank you. She would have liked you," he said. "And while we're at it, let me tell you a couple of things that no one tells you about as you age. Once you're in your fifties, you will start taking naps. I have always hated naps because I wake up grumpy, but you will start taking them whether you want to or not. And your bladder control isn't as good as you get older. Remember to shake it several times before you zip up."

"I will remember that."

"We're here. Thanks for walking with me. Have a great night." He gave me a hug, and then entered the building.

I'm glad we had this time together.

# CHAPTER 33

Germaine called, which was strange because we both had the day off.

"I really need to meet you for coffee," he said.

"Is it something serious?" I asked.

"I need to tell you something, but I want to do it in person," he said.

"Give me an hour and I'll meet you at Java Jive."

"Good," he said. "See you then."

All I could think was that he had some dire health issue that he wanted to talk about, but didn't think he could discuss it at work. I hoped it wasn't cancer.

When I got there, he was already seated at a booth looking all prim and proper. His hand glimmered as the light caught the rings on his fingers. He appeared to be in good health for someone who was sick. I waved and signaled that I was going to the counter to get a water and a donut. I never drank coffee. When I was little, I told my Grandma I wanted to try coffee, but it turned out that I didn't like the taste of it. Grandma put in a bunch of Cool Whip, which in my mind turned it into hot chocolate, and that was the only way I could tolerate it. Since Grandma wasn't around that often, I didn't see the need to drink coffee unless she was there.

"Are you alright?" I asked as I pulled my chair closer to the table. "You sounded so serious."

"Yes, I am fine. I want to share something with you that

is not to be discussed at work. I don't want people to talk about it."

"Is it cancer?"

"Cancer? What are you talking about?" he asked.

"I assumed that you were ill and didn't want people to know."

"Heavens no, my little one. I'm perfectly healthy, and that is not why I asked you here. I want to tell you a story."

"I like stories."

"Once upon a time, there was an ugly duckling who was awkward and uncoordinated and very, very shy. She was having a hard time finding her place in the world. It wasn't until she discovered a very magic world called the club that she was able to find where she belonged. It wasn't easy at first, and the other ducks made fun of her because she wasn't as experienced at performing as they were. They were just nasty and evil to her. But she persevered. Over time, the ugly duckling watched and learned from everyone, and eventually the ugly duckling started turning into a beautiful swan. The other ducklings were jealous, and did everything they could do to tear down the rising swan with their pettiness. The rising swan marched on, and her rising star kept getting brighter drowning out the other ducklings. The rising swan reveled in her new found popularity and lorded it over all the other ducklings, destroying their egos at every opportunity. The rising swan became the most hated person in the magic club and even turned off her legion of followers. She even got into fights with the goose manager who eventually told her to pack her bag of tricks and leave the magic club forever. The rising swan soon became a recluse and faded out of memory realizing how she wasted her opportunity to do something with her brightness. Now no one remembers that once lovely swan."

"That's a lovely story, I guess."

"Do you understand what I am trying to tell you?" he asked.

"Not really. I've never been a swan."

"The story is about me. I have never shared this with anyone here in town, and I want this to go no further because I'm embarrassed by my behavior," he said.

"You could never have been that bad. You are always so eloquent that I can't imagine you ever being petty."

"Believe me, it happened, and I am not very proud of it. I sabotaged gowns, shoes and props. I was horrible."

"It is so hard to imagine that from you."

"I grew up in a small town in Kentucky, and being gay back in my youth was very different from what it is now. You take for granted all the things that we couldn't do back in our day. You couldn't put up a gay flag or put a sticker on your car without being afraid of getting shot. I had a boyfriend who got fired for being gay. One day they were taking him out for his birthday, and the next his boss found out he was gay and fired him on the spot. This generation takes it for granted."

"I thought you grew up here?"

"I just tell people that now. I've been here for so long that people don't know any different. Just listen to what I'm telling you," he implored.

"Go ahead."

"You will become a role model for some of these people who come out to support you. You have the power to do a lot of good, and I want you to realize that."

"Power? How do I have power?" I asked confused.

"You are raising money for a good cause, and those people who benefit from your efforts may not know who you are, but they are grateful for all that they receive. The people who come to see you get the information about the charity, and they in turn may be affected enough to go out and help them or donate more money. You are a force in this world for good. Don't let the attention you will be soon receiving go to your head and destroy everything that you can accomplish. Tyler, you are a lot like me, and your time is coming sooner than you know."

"What was your drag name?"

"It was Glory Swanson," he said.

"And how did you come up with that name?"

"Well, there were two food processing plants in town that I had worked at for a very short period of time. One was Glory Foods, and the other was Swanson Foods. It just made sense, and everyone in town got the joke."

"Shouldn't it have been Gloria?"

"No, Gloria Swanson was a silent movie actress back in the 1920's. Didn't you every see 'Sunset Boulevard'?"

"What is that?"

"I forget that was way before your time. Just remember what I told you. You have the power for good, so don't let the attention go to your head."

I left our meeting feeling good because I had never been told I was a swan before.

# CHAPTER 34

The competition was heating up, and it was time for Precious Oil's show. I was running around getting ready and waiting for Albert to come over. He said he wanted to go, and I had to let him know I was working on a project with Miss Gigi. I was sure how he would take it, so I needed some back up. Marjorie agreed to hang around till he got to our apartment. I had a pit in my stomach.

The buzzer for the door rang. I pushed the button so Albert could come up. I swear I could hear every step he made. Each one got louder and louder. The door knob turned for what seemed like an eternity, and the door swung open very slowly.

"Hey gang," he said cheerily and came over and gave us both a hug. "It feels like I haven't seen you in a while."

"Can I offer you a cocktail?" Marjorie asked.

"I thought you would never ask. I'll have a Chardonnay if you have some."

"I'm almost ready. I wanted to have a little chat with you before we left."

"What about?" he asked.

Luckily Marjorie came back with the wine for Albert, a screwdriver for me, and a beer for herself. She plopped herself next to Albert as if preparing to hold him back.

"As you know, I am working on a higher dollar fundraiser show for the contest. I'm writing the show and then working with an editor who's helping me get the stage version of 'Smash' into a workable show."

"That sounds like a great idea. I thought that show was much underrated," he said. "Do you need any help getting it ready?"

"Not yet and thank you for offering, but I need to let you know that the editor I'm working with is Miss Gigi."

For a minute I thought his head was going to explode, but he just sat there with this blank stare on his face. I could see the gears turning in his head as he connected the dots.

"What the hell do you mean? She is bat-shit crazy. How can you work with her after all the grief she has caused me?"

"It was just a coincidence that we both have a mutual love of the show, and she has some really great ideas," I said trying to explain myself.

"Great ideas? I could shit on a piece of paper too and that would be better than anything that would ever come out of her mouth."

"To give her some credit, she has gotten off the coke, so she is more focused than and not as crazy as she was. You have to admit she has been leaving you alone lately."

"Albert, please hear him out," Marjorie interjected.

"I don't care. I don't want to have anything to do with her and neither should you. I can't believe you are making this decision to choose her over me."

"Albert, I'm not choosing you over her. I need her help and this is an area where she is passionate and has a lot of knowledge about the subject. It's a good fit."

"A good fit was my dick in her ass. This is just ludicrous. I have distanced myself from that nut job, and my life has gotten much calmer. I got tired of all her drama, and mark my words, you will too. She leads you down that primrose path, and the next thing it turns to shit," he finished.

With that, he stood up and chugged his wine. "Marjorie, thank you for the company, but I am out of here. Have a great evening."

He headed for the door and didn't look back. He slammed our door and the door to the building as he left.

"Well that went over wonderfully," Marjorie said. "At least he didn't try to kill you. He'll get over it. Don't you worry, baby boy."

"I didn't mean to get him upset, but I know we have the chance to do something great and actually make a name for myself."

"When you started this journey, you said that the crown was the most important thing. It now sounds like someone is craving attention."

"What's wrong with a little attention?" I asked.

# CHAPTER 35

Since Albert didn't go to Precious Oil's show, Marjorie came instead, and we met Miss Gigi. It gave us some time to toss around ideas for the Smash show before the drag show started. We all sat at a table in the back and Miss Gigi came incognito so that we wouldn't draw attention to ourselves.

"I had a conversation with Albert and let him know that we were working together," I let Miss Gigi know.

"I'm sure that went over like a turd in a punch bowl," she replied.

"You got that right," Marjorie chimed in.

"I promise I will apologize to him. I am a different person now than when we were dating. I'm off the pills that made me crazy, and I am so much calmer now and thinking much clearer."

"I can see it, so I hope he will too," I said. "People have a hard time forgiving people with addictions because it isn't medical, and they think it all should go away with a snap of the fingers."

"Tyler let me know about your 'Smash' show. I'm a huge fan and would love to help," Marjorie said.

"The more the merrier," Miss Gigi replied.

The cabaret room lights dimmed, the overture music started, and the video screen dropped down. What unfolded on screen was Precious Oil in a pill box leopard-spotted hat and matching blouse with a black skirt telling the story of lost love to an R&B song. Again, I'm horrible with song titles, so I sat and watched as the crowd cheered. The scene before us was Precious Oil getting dumped by her boyfriend as he stormed out of the house. She ran to the window where we then saw that it was raining as a tear fell down her face. The story was of love and loss and we felt her pain. The song ended with her on the Baker Street Bridge overlooking downtown. The tempo of the music changed as it picked up with a gospel influenced number from the "Sister Act 2" soundtrack. At least I could recognize music from movies. Precious was now dancing and feeling the joy of the music. She was joined by five back up dancers as they started a dance routine on the Baker Street Bridge. As the dance routine progressed, the screen rose, presenting Precious Oil and her back-up dancers now performing the dance routine live on stage in the same outfits. The crowd immediately jumped to their feet screaming. It was an amazing opening number.

Precious grabbed the mic and said, "Welcome, boys and girls! We have a lot of tricks up our sleeves this evening, and I want to thank all of you for coming out to raise money for my charity, Stroke Aid. I hope you leave here with some valuable information about identifying a stroke because knowledge is power and with that knowledge you can help save a life. Now welcome to the stage one of my dear friends, Evanora!"

Precious slid backstage to take a well-deserved rest and get ready for her next number. As I looked around I could see some of the other contestants in the room. Athena here was a rarity because I had not seen her at any of the other shows. She was in her high whore drag trying to steal as much attention from what was going on stage as she could. She considered Precious competition. Otherwise she wouldn't be here. I'm not sure what she has been doing for fundraising yet because I haven't seen anything publicized for her yet, but I'm sure she has something going on.

Evanora was finished and Precious did an off stage announcement introducing the next performer, Ethel

Vermin. Ethel was also another good friend of Precious. She kept the tempo up doing an Ethel Merman song, "Rose's Turn." The crowd really loved the guest entertainers and kept tipping at a steady rate. I wished the crowd would tip this much at my shows.

Finally, it was time for Precious to come back on. She had changed into a beautiful vibrant red cocktail dress and now was her time to speak about her charity.

"I don't think many of you know, but the reason I have picked Stroke Aid is because my mother suffered a stroke. At the time, there was no one around, so the effects were very devastating and much longer lasting. Even with physical therapy, she will never fully regain the full function on the left side of her body. The key to surviving a stroke is to get medical attention immediately, because with medication, the effects can be reversed if caught quickly enough."

"I wanted to give you some tips on identifying a stroke. If your loved one is experiencing any weakness in their face or legs, especially on one side of the body, they may be having a stroke. If they are suddenly confused, are having trouble seeing out of one eye or both eyes, they may be having a stroke. If they are having problems walking, feel dizzy, or are having a problem with balance or coordination, they may be having a stroke. And if they have a severe headache with no known cause, then they may be having a stroke."

"I want you all to remember FAST. These tests will help you identify if your loved one is having a stroke. First is Face. Ask the person to smile. Does one side of the face droop? Next is Arms. Ask the person to raise both arms. Does one arm droop downward? Next is Speech. Ask the person to repeat a simple phrase. Mary had a little lamb will work. Is their speech slurred or strange? Finally remember Time. If you observe any of these signs call 911 immediately. You just might be saving their lives."

"So what do you need to remember?" she asked.

The crowd shouted back, "'FAST!'"

"Good. Now don't forget it. Hit it, Scotty." And with

that, her next song started.

The evening was going wonderfully until one of Athena's minions started passing out flyers on the tables during the show, which we were not supposed to do at any of our competition's events. Next thing you, knew one of Precious's supporters was grabbing all the flyers from the minion's hands. Athena's minion then pushed Precious's supporter, knocking him up against the railing. You would have hoped it would have ended here, but no such luck. Precious's supporter charged the minion, tackling him onto the stage. Precious bent over, never missing a beat, and grabbed both the wrestlers by the scruff of their shirts, yanking them both off the floor. Precious was a very powerful woman who you didn't want to fuck with. She dragged them both and threw them out the door. It was amazing how she kept her number going even with these distractions. When the song was finished, she received a standing ovation from the crowd.

"Why can't we all just get along? Everybody say 'love!'" she said.

The crowd cheered back, "Love!"

"Miss Athena, I am a very peaceful girl, but if you ever pull this crap again, I will rip that tired Miss America wig off your head and make you eat it," Precious said looking directly in Athena's eyes.

Athena grabbed her purse and promptly left the cabaret room.

"Good. Now let's get back to some fun. Please welcome to the stage Miss Regina."

"Why can't all these shows be this much fun?" Miss Gigi asked.

As the show finished, Precious made a point to stop by our table. "Thank you for coming out tonight. Sorry we had some trouble makers."

"It was a great show and very entertaining," I said.

"You are a true professional, sweetie," Miss Gigi said.

"Thank you all again. Hope y'all have a fabulous night." Off she went pulling her drag bag behind her.

The cabaret room was empty now, which was the perfect time for us to work on the Smash show.

Miss Gigi hopped on stage and we started to block out the scene where Marilyn Monroe meets Joe Dimaggio. This is where Marjorie's expertise came in hand. She had a great understanding of the characters and was able to give us the much-needed woman's touch.

"How are you going to tell Albert you're helping out?"

"Heaven knows," was her only reply.

# CHAPTER 36

"Now all you have to do is lie on the bed and look at the camera," Chas said.

"Are you sure this is a good idea?" I asked.

"Honey, you're young with a great ass. You will clean up doing this and it doesn't take any real work," Chas said.

"So explain to me one more time how I can make money doing this?"

"The website is called 'See Me Now.' You broadcast yourself to the world doing whatever you want. People watch you and chat with you online. You can either speak live back to them or you can type your response."

"But how does this make me money?" I asked again.

So Chas pulled up the page of people live on their webcams so he could show me how it all worked. "So you see, all these squares with the photos represent people who are live on their webcams broadcasting so that everyone can watch. They are in order of who has the most viewers." He clicked on the first square, which was for Boner Buddy. The webcam opened and there was Boner Buddy butt naked on the bed sucking on a guy's dick. "This is a little more advanced than you want to be, but that guy can really suck a good dick. He could give you some pointers."

"Ha ha," I responded.

"So here at the top is a flag of the country they are broadcasting from with a one-liner of info." Boner Buddy's one-liner was "Cum for the fun".

On the right, comments kept popping up one after the other. Chas pointed out that these were the viewers watching live and they were chatting up the performer. This was also where the performer could respond back by typing a response or getting the mic working and just saying their response to the viewers. If you clicked on the Viewers button, it took you to a list of all the people watching. Bonner Buddy had 800 already. You clicked the "Chat" button to take you back to the comment section.

"Right below the video is the "Tip" section," he said. "Here, you could set a tip goal and give people incentives, like every 50 tips you will show your butt, or every 100 tips you will show your dick. Here you could also set a tip total goal and once you got there, you had to perform some act or show some other body part. Here was where you made your money. For every 100 tips, you make $10 as a performer. So you just have to learn to be nice to the viewers," Chas said.

Below that was the description of the performer. It gave you the age, country of origin, sexual preference, weight, and height if you wanted to disclose it. It also gave you the choice of disclosing your relationship status.

"I recommend your relationship status is committed. They don't know you are mentally committed instead of actually dating someone."

"Why don't I want to be single? What if I meet someone who wants to date me?"

"They are not here to date you. If they wanted a hook-up they would be on Grindr or Scruff. Plus, you can feed their fantasy that you are cheating on your husband. Just keep dropping lines like you think you hear him coming so that there is the thrill that you could get caught. It is all about feeding their fantasies, not yours," he said.

"I guess you're right. I just have to remember that I'm here to raise money. What do you suggest my tip goal be?"

"Since it's your first night, I would say go small, like four hundred."

"And what should I do at four hundred?"

"Promise to show your ass. It's very tight and these men will pay to see it. As you feel more comfortable, you can always do more."

Chas got my profile set up and decided that my name should be SpankyBtm, and even took a picture and downloaded it in. He even picked out my outfit, a loose-fitting tank top and mesh gym shorts over underwear. I was nervous putting myself out there since I didn't have my drag protection. This was just going to be me. And what if no one watched? I didn't think I could handle the rejection.

"Let's get you into position. Hop up here," and he patted the bed. "For your first time, I think it would be best if you typed your responses back instead of speaking. It will help you break the ice and give you something to do. And if you get bored, you can also surf the other performers and chat with them. Here, put on this headset." He plugged in the iPod so that I would have some entertainment if it was slow. There was already some dance music playing for my enjoyment.

"I think I'm ready," I said as I lay down on the bed and faced the computer screen. The camera was built in, so all I had to do was stare at the computer screen. I could see myself on the screen so I knew exactly where to be.

"All you need to do is push this button and you will be broadcasting."

It was the start of a new adventure as Chas left the bedroom and I pushed broadcast. I sat there and watched myself on screen for a while with no one chatting. I figured I might as well check out some of the other broadcasters. There was a wide range of men to choose from so I decided to check out someone named Rumbletop. As I clicked his picture, his live video came up. He already had a steady stream of comments coming his way. He was extremely hot with a full beard and hairy chest as he sat there in his chair shirtless staring at the camera with his piercing blue eyes. He made me melt. He was the perfect person to watch because he gave me a better idea of how to respond to any chats since they were coming at him rapid fire. He was always generous and thankful for all the comments as he kept rubbing his chest and nipples. His goal was $2,500. At $500 he would show his cock and at $1,000 he would show his ass and at his goal he was going to cum for everyone to see, which I would have loved to watch. After my little crush, I went back to my broadcast to see if anyone was there to chat.

No one had sent a message yet, so I started looking through one of the gay rags, *The Atlanta Epic*. It had a lot of ads for the local bars, cars, and doctors. All the stuff the gay boys needed to meet someone in a club, drive home and fuck, and then go to the doctor to get treated for a venereal disease. I loved the photo sections from the different events because you always got to look at the hot men. As I flipped the pages and checked out the men, I stopped dead in my tracks. There were photos from a masquerade party at one of the clubs, Rexasaurass, and one of the pictures was a man in a checkered mask and musketeer hat. His brown eyes were so dreamy, warm, and inviting. I could stare into them forever. I had to meet this man. All gay boys are creatures of habit and always hang out at the same places. I made a mental note to go to Rexasaurass to find this man.

Suddenly there was a ding from the computer. There was one chat.

Leatherman25: "How are you doing tonight?"

I froze. I tried not to look like a deer in headlights as I typed back,

"Great. What are you doing this evening?"

Pretty bland, but I felt good about it. I waited for a little bit, but there was no response back. I remembered that Chas said to click on the viewer's button, and it would tell me how many people were watching. I clicked on it and saw that three people were watching. Now if I could just get them to chat.

Sir Baby: "Fucking hot looking"

SpankyBtm: "Thanx"

Leatherman25: "You have beautiful eyes"

Sir Baby: "Where is your boyfriend tonight?"

I need to stick with what Chas said and play along with the boyfriend line. I have to remember that this is all fantasy for the viewers.

SpankyBtm: "He's out with some friends having drinks"

Sir Baby: "What do you like to drink?

SpankyBtm: "Vodka and orange juice is drink of choice"

Sir Baby: "Have you ever tried piss?"

I stopped dead in my tracks on that one, and I'm sure the look on my face wasn't the most pleasant.

Leatherman25: "Be kind to Spanky since this is his first time here"

How did he know that it was my first time here? Did it show?

SpankyBtm: "How do you know this is my 1st time?"

Leatherman25: "Your member since and last broadcast dates are today"

So I looked at the computer screen to see where this was, and sure enough, there it was. Anyone looking at it would know it is my first time. Well, no sense in acting like an amateur. It was time to start mugging for the camera to get some more viewers. I started to bite my lower lip and ran my fingers through my hair. It was time to show my playful side to get the tips coming.

Partyblond: "You look like you have a great ass"

SpankyBtm: "And it's really tight"

Leatherman25: "There is some fire in you after all"

SpankyBtm: "There needs to be more in me than just fire"

Partyblond: "I can take care of that for you"

SpankyBtm: "How big is it?"

Leatherman25: "So what are you looking for?"

I had to think about how to answer this one since I was supposed to be in a relationship. If I said everything great in the relationship, then what reason would I have to be here? It would make more sense if the relationship sucked, but I guess it would be best just to say the truth.

SpankyBtm: "I'm here to raise money for a charity"

Leatherman25: "Which one?

SpankyBtm: "Atlanta Street Rescue"

Leatherman25: "Great charity"

SpankyBtm: "They really are"

Kilgore: "I'm not here for a charity unless it's me. Let's see some ass."

SpankyBtm: "All in good time."

And with that, I got my first tip. Leanterman25 tipped 100 tokens. That was very sweet of him and got me a quarter of the way to my goal. I guess it was time to give the people what they wanted so I slipped off my shorts revealing my snug fitting Andrew Christian underwear.

Partyblond: "Very nice"

Sir Baby: "Great ass. Want to see those cheeks"

You give a little and people seem to get a little demanding. I needed to let them down gently and get control of this conversation.

Leatherman25: "Come on boys be nice to the newbie"

Well I guess I have to, thanks Leatherman25. It was nice to know that someone had my back. Now if I could just meet a person like that in real life.

PartyBlond: "Love your body"

SpankyBtm: "Thanx"

Roberto112: "Hey sexy"

Slowly but surely, I was getting more people here, so it was time to encourage some more tipping.

SpankyBtm: "At 250 I'll take off my tank top"

Sir Baby: "Junior I don't pay for porn so why should I pay here?"

That was harsh, but true. The tip bell went off, and I saw that Letherman25 had tipped another 150, bringing the total to 250, so I guess it was time to take off the shirt.

SpankyBtm: "Thanx Leatherman"

Leatherman25: "You're welcome"

So now was the time to take off my shirt. Every body-conscious thought I ever had came flooding back into my head. Am I too skinny? Am I too fat? Am I too pale? It was time to throw caution to the wind as I sat up and slowly pulled the tank top over my head. I felt like I had a thousand eyes staring at me. I sat there for a minute for people to see before I lied back down and stared into the camera again.

PartyBlond: "Hot motherfucker"

Sir Baby: "Damn baby"

Kilgore: "Do you ever rub your nipples?"

Leatherman25: "Very nice. You have a beautiful soul"

That was an interesting post. What did he mean by that? I've never had anybody say anything about my soul except for my mother when she got on her religious soap box.

SpankyBtm: "Thanx boys"

Sir Baby: "Now let's get that underwear off"

Roberto112: "Show that hot ass"

Leatherman25: "Do you want to make it a short night?"

PartyBlond: "Who said it was short have you seen it before?"

SpankyBtm: "It isn't short and no one here has seen it yet"

Sir Baby: "Want to rub them both"

Kilgore: "And run my finger between the crack"

Leatherman25: "That's it"

I heard the tip bell, and I was now at four hundred. Time to remove the underwear. I never said I would show my dick, so I needed to do this very carefully. I turned my back to the camera and slowly slid my underwear down my legs. I tried to do it with some drama to give the viewers what they wanted. As they came off, I turned my head to the camera, brought my underwear up to my face, and smelled them. I knew they were clean so I wasn't too worried about it. I quickly cupped my dick and balls with my hand and rolled back over onto my stomach.

PartyBlond: "I'm going to cum"

Kilgore: "Very hot"

Roberto112: "Run your hands over your ass"

SpankyBtm: "Thanks for making my first night a pleasant one"

I didn't say how long I would stay on once I hit my goal, but I figured two minutes was plenty so that everyone could get a good look.

Leatherman25: "I would love it if you private messaged me your email"

I was surprised by the request since I wanted to keep everything here as anonymous as possible. Leatherman was the only person who genuinely seemed interested in me and not just for the skin show. I threw caution to the wind and private messaged him my email. It could go either way. And I might never hear from him anyway.

SpanyBtm: "Have a good night everyone"

And with that, I disconnected my broadcast. I was a little turned on because it was kind of thrilling having people look at you. Isn't it horrible that we get our sense of self-worth from what people think about us? And I forgot to thank Leatherman25 for the final tips to get to my goal. It made the night less painful. Why did he mention my soul? Now that is hot.

I heard a knock at the door.

"I and "The Package" are going for ice cream. Do you want to come along?" Marjorie asked.

"Let me put some clothes on and I'll be ready."

# CHAPTER 37

There was one month before our "Smash" show was set to debut, and today was costume fittings. Germaine rolled into the club with a huge rolling rack of outfits. "These should help. I've had them in storage, and you should be able to use a good bunch of them."

I was extremely glad to see Germaine. He understood what we were trying to accomplish, and I felt like we were kindred spirits having gone through some of the same prejudice against the beautiful people. "You are a sight for sore eyes." I went over and hugged him. "We are just waiting on Miss Gigi's friends from the community playhouse to get here with their costumes and their players who are generous enough to be doing the show for free. From my understanding, some of them are just doing it for more experience. Crossing my fingers on this one."

"Hello darlings!" Miss Gigi announced as she came strutting into the room, looking all bubbly and perky. I think she had found her true calling with the play, and I think she was keeping off the pills.

"Are the players with you?" I asked.

"Yes, they are unloading the van right now. Who is your sexy friend?" She said as she extended her hand to Germaine.

"This is my good friend Germaine. We work together at the hotel."

"Isn't that convenient? You don't have to go very far to

find a place to have sex, do you?" she said.

"It is a great pleasure to meet you. Tyler has told me so much about you," Germaine said.

"He didn't tell me anything about you at all. Meow is all I can say," Miss Gigi said as she made a cat paw swipe in the air. "I love your rings. Is anyone a wedding ring?"

"Those are all at home. I haven't had the pleasure of proposing to anyone yet, but this might be my lucky day," Germaine said.

The rest of her crew rolled in the door with another rack of clothes. The players were all so friendly and eager to get everything up and running. They seemed to have a real camaraderie amongst themselves, which was truly lacking in our group of contestants. Miss Gigi stepped up and took charge.

"Alright everyone, as you can see, our staging is going to very minimal, so our blocking should go pretty quickly, and the dance numbers will be really easy. Marjorie will walk you through everything. You've all had the book of the show, so we are going to start at the beginning and just go. I'm going to introduce you all so that you know who you are working with. Tyler is our Marilyn, Edgar is Joe DiMaggio, Sid is Mr. Zanuck, Billy is President Kennedy, and Beatrice is Mama Gladys. We also have several of the club performers here filling the background roles. This will be fabulous, and we can't thank you enough for helping us pull this off."

I pulled Marjorie to the side. "I can't thank you enough for putting up with all the crap surrounding the contest and for helping out choreographing the show. You really don't know how much that means to me."

"Sweetie, you are welcome. I am more than glad to help you out," Marjorie said as she hugged me.

The run-through was a little rough at first as everyone was feeling out each other's character, but after the first hour things got much better and everything was running on all cylinders. Germaine was grabbing each person every chance he got and kept trying costumes on them. He could size someone up and find the right costume for them, and if it didn't fit exactly, he pulled out his sewing kit and made a dart here and there to make it work. I could see why he did so well in the past. I wished I had his sewing skills because he just made it look so easy.

We finally took a break and everyone headed to the main bar to grab a drink. Of course, Athena was there snooping around. She was like the bad penny that kept turning up, and all she wanted to do was cause trouble. I guess I could take the high road, since all these people helping were guests and I didn't want to make anyone feel uncomfortable.

"So are you putting on another tired show?" Athena fired off.

"I've never put on a tired show and this one will be no exception. I've got all these great people helping me out, so it has been lovely having a support network. And speaking of support, I think I saw your underwire support bra back in the dressing room at your station."

"Baby, I don't need any support wire in my bras. I know how to make it look natural, and unfortunately there are several of you who have tits that look like you have loaves of bread shoved under your dress. I'm watching your tired ass as you do your tired boy girl drag. They should give out a prize in this contest for the person with the biggest 5 o'clock shadow. You would win for sure. Ta ta," she said.

The encounter was short and sort of like I thought it would be.

"What did miss thing want?" Miss Gigi asked.

"Nothing. Just the same ole same ole out of her mouth," I said.

"Is Albert still not talking to you?" Gigi asked.

"No. He is really holding a grudge on this. Everyone keeps telling me he will get over it, but he hasn't yet."

"I tried apologizing to him, but he didn't want to hear anything from me. I made the effort, and if he doesn't want to accept it, then he can go fuck himself. I'm a much more positive person now all because of you, and I'm moving forward with my life. It's the first time in many years that I have a positive attitude towards things. I got tired of being a drag, no pun intended," she said.

"You really know what you're doing. You should think about doing theater for real after this," I said.

"Well, to tell you the truth, I've been taking some acting lessons on the side. I think I found my calling, and I'm happy doing it. If it weren't for you pushing me I wouldn't have gotten up the courage. Here's to a great show," she said and raised her glass in a toast. We clinked glasses.

Time to get back to work.

# CHAPTER 38

It was time to work the street for some easy cash, which I planned on keeping no matter what happened on my second beggar's day.

I remembered what everyone kept telling me was I needed to stand out more while working the street and truly be a beautiful person. So I wore black thigh-high boots, a long, red, flat-ironed wig, and a short black, sequined dress, all accented by the pink safety vest. This time there was no being road kill as I made sure that everyone noticed me. I strutted between the cars, chatting up as many people through their open windows as possible.

"Hey baby, you got some change for a working girl," became my mantra for the day. I liked the fact that it had the slutty side behind it, and it made everyone laugh, especially after they read the sign on my bucket about collecting money for Atlanta Street Rescue. It made it a lot easier getting people to pry some coins from their pockets and put it in my bucket. It was amazing how people responded this time.

A very sexy, hot, blond pulled up to the red light in his BMW convertible with the top down. I did my best slow strut right up to him. "Baby, you need to hold your head still so I can check my lips in your sunglasses." His glasses were a reflective mirror and I stared deeply into them as I pushed my lips together and then bit my lip very slowly. I felt like I could see his baby blues through the lenses.

He tilted his head as he reached into his counsel and

pulled out a couple dollar bills. "I always enjoy helping a lady in distress," he said as he dropped the bills into the bucket. The light turned green and he was off.

This was much more fun this time as people would actually chat me up and wanted to hear about my charity. After an hour, Stephanie from Bonk came out and brought me a coke with a very long straw so I didn't mess up my lips.

"I thought you could use some refreshments. Fabulous look," she said and handed me ten dollars. "Good luck, Desiree."

People did like me no matter what some of the bitchy contestants thought.

I kept busy working the corner and working every pose I could possibly do without showing off my business when I noticed a familiar BMW convertible come creeping back up the street. It looked like he was driving slowly just so he could catch the red light. It was the hot, blond and this time the dollar bills were sitting on his crotch.

"Baby, I sure hope you got sticky fingers," he said.

I sucked on two of my fingers as I bent over, leaned into the convertible, and kicked up my heels. "Honey, I'm a pro at this." And with that, I took my hand and rubbed the bills all over his crotch. I could feel his bulge start to grow. "I'm off now if you would like to get off."

"My name is Robert. I live in Vaseline Valley," he said.

"Vaseline Valley" was the pet name for the apartment complex just up the block. It was shabby chic, and mostly inhabited by people in the restaurant and bar industry. It tended to be very rowdy around their pool all summer.

"Hop in," he said.

My feet were killing me in these boots, and I had already made a good haul for the day. I threw caution to the wind and opened the passenger door and slid into the passenger seat.

"You won't be disappointed," he said.

"I better not be," I responded. This was a little more demanding than I ever thought I could be, but it was the power of drag that was coming through me. Germaine had always said it would rear its ugly head, and it was just beginning.

Robert floored it up the block as we pulled into the complex. His apartment was on the top floor overlooking the pool. There was a lot of eye candy out sunning themselves with very little clothing on. I could see why Robert had chosen this apartment, and I could feel the strain against the duct tape in my panties.

Robert's place was nothing like I expected it to be. It was a touch on the feminine side for someone so butch. He must have read my mind. "My mom helped decorate. I can never say no to her," he said. "Would you like a glass of wine?"

"Sure."

Robert went to the kitchen. I could hear him pull the cork out of the bottle as it popped, and he was back shortly with two glasses of white wine. "Baby, you need to relax," he said as he handed me the glass. "Let me help you get those boots off so I can massage your beautiful calves for you." He grabbed the zipper on the left boot and pulled it down with his teeth. He tossed the boot and grabbed the zipper of the right boot with his teeth and pulled it down. He tossed the boot across the room.

He started rubbing my feet, working out the day's boot pain. He followed that by kneading the muscles in my claves like they were fresh dough. His hands kept working their way up my thighs, and I let out a moan as the tension was released. The strain on the duct tape was getting to be too much. "Baby, do you want me to remove the tape?"

"Yes please, you filthy pig," I said.

He proceeded to gently slide my panties down caressing my legs as he removed them. "This might hurt a bit," he said as he started pulling off the tape, which hid all my candy. It is not a glamorous thing, but if you need to hide your dick between your ass crack, duct tape is the way to go.

He flipped me over to pull the tape out of my ass crack. It pulled off gently, as I had moisturized my crack before I put the tape on. He began to rub my ass cheeks in a circular motion. The tension in the muscles was gone, but the tension in my asshole was on high alert. After the tape came of my candy, my dick stood at attention. He slowly worked his fingers around the rim of my asshole, but not penetrating my tight hole. He rubbed some more, and I could feel the heat generated from my asshole. My pussy was tight and ready to receive anything at this point. Robert took his tongue and slowly applied pressure to my rim as he pushed his tongue into my hole. He started moving his wet tongue so that I could feel the full flat part slide up and down the rim. My body was at full attention with every nerve tingling. I couldn't take this anymore. I began to strip off all my clothes so that he could ravage me.

"Baby, what are you doing?" he asked.

"I'm trying to get a little more comfortable."

"Leave your clothes on. I've always had the fantasy of fucking a drag queen, and I want to see your dick bounce up and down as I'm fucking your tight ass," he said.

That was a first for me. I had heard about this situation from some of the other girls, but I didn't expect it to happen to me. As long as he was going to stick that dick in me, I guess I really didn't care. "Let's head to the bedroom. This lady wants you to rock my world with me grabbing your headboard," I said. I could already see the tent in his pants and momma liked what she saw.

He took my hand and led me to the bedroom. Again, it was a little on the feminine side, but it was a beautiful king-size bed with a goose down comforter. I fell onto it and I felt like a fluffy cloud had swallowed me up.

Robert quickly stripped off his clothes. His body was beautiful. The hair that I first saw sticking out of his shirt was covering his entire chest, stomach, legs, and bush. His penis looked like it had a golden glow to it.

He reached into his nightstand and pulled out a condom and a bottle of lube. I was glad he played it safe. He stroked some lube onto his dick and rolled the condom down, covering his mushroom head and shaft.

I was lying on my back and he lay on top of me, working his tongue in and out of my mouth. He slid his tongue down my neck as he took his hand and caressed my breasts. I wish I could have felt this on my nipples, but the bags of bird seed were blocking that. Next, he started lifting up my skirt and put the weight of his arms to raise my legs to the heavens. He took the lube and spritzed my dick and rubbed some onto my hole and his dick. I was waiting for that moment of ecstasy as his dick would push its way into my tight hole.

Suddenly, the bedroom door flew open, and standing there was a very exasperated woman.

"Again! Can't you keep your dick in your pants, you fucked up butt pirate?"

"Mary Anne! I can explain!"

"Explain. Explain what? That you have never been faithful for our entire marriage and that you are really gay?" she said.

"Baby, you know I love you, and I think you are the most beautiful woman in the world," he said.

"Then who is that skank?"

"This skank didn't get the full story from your husband," I said in my defense.

Mary Anne picked up a vase off the dresser and threw it at her husband's head, but instead, it hit the headboard, where it shattered.

"I'm out of here," I said as I un-straddled her husband and picked up my underwear off the floor. "I wish you two the best of things."

I grabbed the rest of my clothes and shoes and ran out of the apartment as fast as I could. I felt the eyes of the people at the pool on me as I climbed down the flight of stairs. To my chagrin, I got a shout out.

"Hey Desiree. How's it hanging?" It was Dixie Monroe hanging at the pool in her boy attire. "You fell for his story?"

I didn't even stop to answer as I ran through the complex

and down Monroe to my parked awaiting car. I hopped in, closed the door, and sat in silence.

# CHAPTER 39

I had been going to Rexasaurass for several weeks now with no luck on meeting the mystery man from the photos. I had even asked the bartenders and none of them knew him or even recognized the photo. They told me the photos were from a charity fundraiser booked in by a group who were not regulars there at the bar, so not a lot of familiar faces that night. Just my luck. So many men and so many crushed fantasies was all I seemed destined for.

Things had been quiet for a couple of weeks, which was a good thing. It gave me some down time to regroup. This competition was more stressful than I thought, but with the support of my friends and co-workers, it was bearable.

I had fallen into my old routine of getting up, eating breakfast, and then walking down the street and into the hotel parking garage. Then it was time to push the elevator button and wait. Depending if the hotel was busy, it could be a long wait some days. The joys of working at a hotel.

We got all types in the hotel day in and day out. Some very attractive, some very freaky, and some down-right sexual. I think I had become a robot at the front desk, repeating the same script day in and day out. "How may I help you?" and "Here is your room key. The elevator is to your right and you are on the tenth floor." Some days it was just too tedious to bear.

"My name is Spencer Jack, and I have a reservation."

Before me stood a beautiful man with the most striking

brown eyes I had ever seen. They were like a deep vat of chocolate that I could just fall into and become sticky and sweet. It took me what seemed like forever to regain my composure.

I looked in the computer and didn't see a reservation for Jack Spencer. "We don't have a reservation for Jack Spencer."

"Ah, a very common mistake. It's Spencer Jack. I'm the person with two first names." And with that, he chuckled.

How adorable was that. "Yes, now I see your reservation in the computer. It says you are checking in with a dog correct?"

"Yes, Thunderball is my assistance dog."

I didn't see Thunderball, but then I heard the bark and looked down over the counter to see the cutest ball of fur staring back up at me. I guess he was a Pomeranian. I couldn't see how Thunderball was much of an assistance dog, and he didn't have the little assistance dog vest on either. "He is absolutely a doll."

"He is a she," Spencer said "And I know she doesn't look like your typical assistance dog, but believe me, I need her services."

The hotel usually didn't allow dogs, but we did allow assistance dogs. "All I need is a credit card."

He handed me his black American Express, which usually has a bazillion dollar limit. For someone so young, how did he have a black American Express card? I swiped it into the computer and handed it back to him. He did something that caught me completely off guard. He grabbed my hand and held it for a second as he took his card back. I fell down the well hole again there for a second, and it took me another second to recover. Was the AC not working? I could feel the blood rush to my face, and I could feel my heartbeat pounding in my chest. "Your room is on the eighteenth floor facing downtown. The elevators are around the corner to the left."

"Thank you very much. When do you get off? I would

love to grab a drink with you. I'm here for a procedure and don't know anyone in the city."

"My shift ends at 8. We could meet in the lobby bar if that works."

"Perfect. I will see you then."

I couldn't take my eyes off of him as he walked away and rounded the corner. If first impressions are correct then I was in for a wonderful evening.

"Girl, get your chin off the counter. You're starting to get drool everywhere," Sheila said.

"Was it that obvious?"

"If it went on any longer, I was getting ready to grab the fire hose and spray you down. You're in heat," she said.

"It's been a while since I've had that instant connection with anyone."

"What about your web cam friend, Leatherman?" she asked.

"I haven't heard anything yet. I hate lying to everyone about having a husband. If they're looking for someone to date, I'm not even available in their eyes. All I am is a piece of meat on the screen."

"Well maybe Leatherman just needs another show from you to pull him out of his shell."

"I was planning on doing another one tomorrow. Its easy money and I don't have to bother everyone else for help. I know it is a drag, pun intended, helping me out all the time, and I really appreciate your help."

"Baby doll, you know I got you," she said. "Now is that a stapler in your pocket or are you happy to see me?"

I didn't realize I was getting a chubby talking about Leatherman, whom I had never even met. I guess the fantasy of the Internet works both ways. I focused on the rest of my shift, and the rest of the time just flew by. I managed to slip away to the back to brush my teeth so that I had fresh breath for my drink date and took off the tie and jacket. I wished I had had another shirt to change into since the hotel shirts made me look more formal than I was hoping to be this evening, and I didn't have time to run down the block and change and get back here on time.

I walked across the lobby and entered the bar and looked around. It was very atmospheric in here, but I was able to see Spencer sitting at a side booth with Thunderball patiently sitting next to him. I saw his face brighten as he saw me wave. We locked eyes as I worked my way through the room. Unfortunately, I didn't see the backpack on the floor behind table five. Next thing I knew, I was face-planted on the floor. It all took place in slow motion. Spencer and Thunderball raced over to help me up.

"Are you alright?" he asked as he took my arm to lift me up.

"Nothing damaged here except my ego," I said. Here I thought I was being Rico Suave and next I know I'm Lindsay Lohan."

"Don't worry," he said. "I do it all the time. Feel this." He took my hand and ran it through his thick, brown hair. "Did you feel it?"

"Feel what?"

"The bump on my head. I fell and wacked myself pretty good a couple of weeks ago, and the bump has been going down very slowly."

His hair was so soft and smelled incredible. I grabbed a seat and the cocktail waitress came over and took my order. Spencer already had a martini in front of him, and I ordered my usual screwdriver.

"Before your drink gets here, I want to answer the questions I know you are dying to ask," he said. "My favorite color is purple. When I was younger, I had a Barney fixation that went on for way too long. I like most music, but I prefer a diva star, so my all-time favorite is Madonna. No one compares to her. My favorite food is Spaghettios. I could eat them morning, noon and night. I am a boxer kind of guy. I don't like the boys to free float, but I also don't like them pressed up against me all day. I think that covers the basics. Did I miss anything?"

I started laughing. None of the questions were in my head, and I was so caught off guard that I immediately dropped my guard and relaxed instantly. How do I top that?

"Here goes nothing. Secretly in another life I was a pirate in the Caribbean. My name was Captain Blueballs, which also happens to be my favorite color. The first car I ever got to drive was a rusted-out AMC Pacer, which happened to belong to the neighbor up the street. The car's nickname was the Guppy because it looked like a giant fishbowl. I bowl left-handed even though I am a natural right-hander, and as a child I almost impaled my own eye with a Jart, which eventually was removed from the market because that happened to several other children."

"And here I thought you had a lot of skeletons in your closet," he said. "But you sound pretty normal to me."

"Normal as the next person, but I'm sitting next to you so that must make me as normal as you."

"Don't judge a book by its cover."

"So what brings you to Atlanta and why do you need Thunderball?" I asked.

"Let's start with Thunderball. Thunderball is my assistance dog because I suffer from seizures and tend to collapse a lot lately. She has a sixth sense about it and starts barking at me when she senses one coming on. The doctors think that right before I have a seizure, my scent changes, and she can detect the change and that sets off her alarm."

"What is causing the seizures?"

"That leads me to why I am here. The doctors don't know, so they sent me to a specialist at Emory Hospital to run some tests. I can't stay out much later because I have to be there early in the morning, but I didn't want to miss the opportunity to get to know you better, Tyler."

"That is extremely nice of you to say that. When you came up I thought you were gorgeous."

"You flatter me," he said.

"The one thing my momma taught me was that when someone pays you a compliment, accept it graciously and say thank you."

"Thank you," he said. "There's more to me than just my looks. I'm extremely hung," and he paused only to continue, "Up on collecting celebrity autographs, but only the ones I can get in person. Not the ones you order off the web."

"Who's the most famous celebrity you got to meet?" I asked.

"Bette Midler. I went to Vegas for a convention, and just by sheer accident ran into her in the hotel lobby as she was heading to her show. All I could say was "'Miss Midler, I enjoy your music, movies, and your incredible talent.'" Then I pulled out a piece of paper and pen and asked for her autograph. She politely obliged and signed. It was a shock meeting her."

"I've never met anyone famous yet, but one day it will happen. We get celebrities in here all the time with all the movie business in Atlanta now, but I'm never working when they come in. The other day Owen Wilson checked into the hotel. To live is to dream."

"That is what the lotto is for," he said. "If you don't play you can never dream about what you would do with the money."

"I know exactly what I would do with it," I said.

"Do tell."

"I would open up a gay bowling alley called Rainbow Lanes, which would have a drag bar and a piano bar."

"And in which part would you work?"

"I would be the talent scout looking for girls to perform in the drag bar. Of course, I would have to seek out talented go-go boys to dance in the cages that would be suspended from the ceiling."

"You've really thought this out haven't you?"

"Just wishful thinking."

"Well my sweet Tyler, I need to go retire for the evening. Travelling wears me out lately. It has been a pleasure meeting you." He handed me a business card with his cell number on it. "I hope to see you again soon."

"You know where I will be."

"I will stop by because I would love to do this again."

And with that, he got up, grabbed my face and gave me a goodnight kiss on the lips. He tasted like apple. "Sleep well." He and Thunderball trotted out of the bar.

Was this really happening? Someone so nice and incredibly hot right in front of me? So why am I thinking of Leatherman?

# CHAPTER 40

Another day, another show. I forgot I was asked to perform at a fundraiser not related to the competition, which meant no pressure. This was a group raising money for Aids Walk, and the people in charge of the show were extremely friendly, so I was looking forward to just doing my numbers with no responsibility for how the show went. It also gave me a great opportunity to push my "Smash" show.

This was going to be a different crowd than the people I normally perform for and at a different bar, so I could do repeat numbers. I don't like to repeat numbers because I'm trying to entertain people, not bore them, and I don't want to get the reputation of being a one-number bitch.

I packed up my shit and headed over to the club. Germaine was my escort for the evening because everyone else already had plans. I loved Germaine because this could truly be a girl's night.

"I've got the last of the 'Smash' costumes finished," he said. "They look exquisite! I couldn't have hoped for better."

"Even the final Marilyn dress?" I asked.

"Yes, honey. You will be the belle of the ball. And when those people give you that standing ovation, just remember you earned it."

"Let's not jump ahead of ourselves here. I just hope people show up for it. I know Chas has been working on promoting it as much as he can on social media, and I've been sending out tweets to drum up as much excitement as possible. It sucks that the club can't include us in their ads."

"Why's that?"

"Because if they promote one charity show in their ads, then they have to promote them all. It's just not feasible because they have to promote their regularly scheduled events and the special DJ's they keep bringing in. Chas has also emailed all the gay rags in town to put it on their calendars, which should help, and it is added to the calendar on Atlanta Street Rescue's page, so just hoping people will come."

"They'll be there, darling. You and Miss Gigi have put so much energy into this that it will pay off. It reminds me of my time on the stage. The lights, the glitz, the glamour. Oh, I do miss those days. Remember what I told you. Once you get good, these girls are going to stab you in the back to bring you down."

"You really think so?"

"Hell yes, honey. They will talk nice to your face, but the next thing you know, these tired drag queens are dialing up their girlfriends on their cheap-ass cell phones and talking smack about you. It really hurts when you think these girls are looking out for your best interest when in reality all they care about is the coin and the attention."

I realized I better change the subject or I was in for an hour lecture on the road to ruin. "How are you and Miss Gigi doing, just out of curiosity?"

"We are doing very well. Miss Gigi is a very generous lover if I must say."

"No, you mustn't say that. Ewww. Now I'll have that image burned into my head all night."

"Don't be a hater."

"I'm not. A fine would have sufficed."

"We are doing fine," he said and laughed. "Where is this show again?"

"The Foxhole. You know the bar on the other side of the park."

"Was that the one raided for illegal gambling or was that

the one that got raided for drugs?"

"Neither. This is the one that had the queen fall off the deck and break her leg a couple of weeks ago."

"Are you sure this isn't the one that had the roach infestation and had to be shut down?" he asked.

"No, that was the sushi restaurant that the health department finally shut down. Their score was so low that the health code display sheet had a negative number on it. Thank God I don't like sushi."

"Me neither. If it smells like a dead pussy, it needs to get thrown back. I've tried it once and that was back in college so never ask me to try it again."

"Was that before or after they invented electricity?"

"Ha ha, young man. Didn't your mother ever tell you to respect your elders?'

"Yes, sir. No more age jokes."

We pulled up to the Foxhole and actually managed to get a parking space. The show started at 6:30, which was good because all the softball players came straight over here after they finished their games in the park. Hopefully there would be a lot of sweaty men here. I was feeling a little randy, and what people don't realize there is a lot of power in drag. You can do things that you would never do in your own life. I've learned that I can go up to any cute man and tell them I want my picture taken with them because I think they are hot. I then hand my phone to someone standing there to get the picture. I've never had a hot man refuse. They like the attention as much as I do.

I didn't know many of the girls in this show. I set up my space next to Vanna, whom I had met at a couple of other shows. She had a great sense of energy about her when she performed which I was trying to get better at. No one wants to watch someone just stand there, and it is even worse when they don't know the words to the song. Come on girls that is the number one rule of drag. Know your words. Peanut butter, watermelon does not cut it.

Vanna was as friendly as ever, but the other girls were

very cliquish. They were all very friendly together, paying each other a ton of compliments that were not deserved, in my opinion. I'm tired of these girls who wear the huge breast-plates and pad their asses for days. They look like a caricature to me. And the sad part is they don't know what to do with it. An over-the-top outfit is only going to get you so far, especially if you do not know what to do with it. I stood in the wings to watch some of them perform and all they did was stand there and wait for someone to come and tip them. What I've learned is that once your initial impression is over, you need to do something to keep the audience entertained. These girls thought they were being entertaining, but they were laying a big egg.

Vanna was up before me. She was doing Blondie's "One Way Or Another," which I had thought about doing in the past, but I could never figure out how to make it work. Vanna had the right outfit, boots, hair, and face for this number. She got up there and she shook those real boobs of hers, and the audience lined up to tip her. I did watch her backstage as she was getting ready. To create the illusion of her cleavage, she squished her boy breast together while her husband put duct tape under it all to hold it in place. I had to ask if it hurt to take the tape off because I would think you would be pulling off some of your skin. She let me know that if you take a shower and let the water soak the tape, it would come off in a gentle pull. Good to know if I ever had enough man breast of my own to pinch together.

It was my turn to perform. I always felt a little anxious as I got up the stairs onto the stage. I stood in the dark in the back while the hostess let the crowd know about the "Smash" show, which was great to hear. I could see the spotlight following the hostess back and forth as she entertained the crowd. She got back to the podium and I finally heard, "Please welcome to the stage, Desiree." I could see the spotlight immediately go to the center of the curtain waiting for my arrival.

I had chosen the Gwenyth Paltrow version of "Do You

Wanna Touch" from "Glee," which was a cover of a Joan Jet song. I heard the driving drum and guitar start and the curtain slowly opened. I was wearing fishnet stockings, a long, black vinyl jacket, a cotton, sequined top, a tight leather skirt, a motorcycle cop leather hat, and black construction boots. Of course, the outfit was accessorized with silver metallic bracelets that I had managed to find at Richard's Variety Store at a checkout counter of all places, and silver hoop earrings. I was feeling fierce. I started moving. The beat on this was a little slower than the dance songs I had been doing, so I felt my way slowly across the stage and then down the stairs. The crowd was bobbing along, so I could tell they liked what they heard.

I worked my way down the stairs and gave the people the heavy metal slut stare. I could really feel this number, and people were lining up to give me tips. The first person was a hot little number, so I grabbed his face and ran my fingers through his hair. There was one person after the next lined up to tip me. This was the high I was looking for. It felt good to be appreciated for what I was doing. I worked for the dollars and by the time I was finished, I was exhausted. I finally got it. This was the feeling I had been searching for, and it was if I had an out-of-body experience. It took me this long to completely understand what it was like to have everything come together at once for that one pinnacle moment where you were the song.

I strutted off stage to the thunderous round of applause and the curtain puller told me, "Good job." Vanna was the first girl backstage to greet me and congratulate me. The rest of the girls were doing their usual gabbing and not paying attention to anything. I know I had accomplished what I had set out to do. Entertain the audience and enjoy the number at the same time. It was great to have both of those come together at the same time.

I had some time before my next number, so I went out front in my outfit and grabbed a cocktail at the bar. There were so many hot men at this show whom I had never seen before, and Desiree was feeling a little frisky. I grabbed my phone out of my purse, went up to the first group of hot men I saw, gave the phone to one of them, and said, "I want my picture taken with a bunch of hot men." They all immediately obliged as I squeezed into the middle and posed. Click went the flash. I thanked the group and proceeded to work my way around the room getting picture after picture with every hot man in the bar. It is amazing what you can get away with when you are in drag. Tonight I was feeling the power as I let Desiree take over for a while. Now it was time to head backstage and slip into my next outfit for my next number. It was time to take on Cyndi Lauper's "Girls Just Want To Have Fun," which was another new number for me. Hopefully it would go over as well as the first one.

For my Cyndi Lauper number, I was wearing a black spandex bicycle jumper covered over with a hot pink icicle dress made of this very sparkly see-through material that looked great when the spot-light hit it, three ruffled skirts, and black pumps. The wig for this was a hot pink bob with a black bow on top all accessorized with black and white bracelets.

I was more relaxed as I waited backstage with Vanna. We chatted, and I was surprised when she volunteered to do one of my shows. It really was a great honor to have someone of her caliber offer to help me out. It made my night. She was on and off she went while I waited behind the curtains to follow her.

"Girls Just Want To Have Fun" went over extremely well, which was a huge relief. This gave me two numbers that I could do back at the club for one of my shows. I don't know if I was more relaxed because I felt like I knew what I was doing or just because I didn't know anyone here so I wasn't as worried about impressing them. I think it was more the latter because I felt so little pressure about doing this show versus doing one of the competition shows. I need to remember this feeling because it will help me in the long run getting over my performance agony. It's not sex, it is just drag.

# CHAPTER 41

I wanted to make some easy money for the contest so it was time to make another appearance on See Me Now. I was secretly hoping that Leatherman would be on. How could I feel this strange attraction to someone whom I had never even met or even seen? Plus, he could be hideous. And since I will stick to Chas' rule about pretending to be married, I will never find out.

I fired up the computer and I was ready. Again, I went with a very clingy pair of sport shorts with a thong on underneath. The girls were right that the thong really showed my ass off well, so why not flaunt what you got? I chose a very loose-fitting tank top, and with that I positioned myself on the bed.

I logged in and SpankyBtm was live on the web, ready for the world to see and criticize. The nice thing with the competition was it made me thicken up my skin, so the bitchy barbs just slid off my back, or at least the ones that I understood did. Otherwise the other ones went over my head.

It didn't take long for the first chat to come in.

HuskyMan: "Hey"

Why do people think that a "Hey" is going to be very enticing for me to respond back? I want someone with whom I can have a conversation and who actually has something to say. But since right now this isn't the real world, I will respond back.

SpankyBtm: "What's up?"

HuskyMan: "Not much. Just looking"

SpanyBtm: "Hope you like what you see"

HuskyMan: "Sure do. Want to see you cream"

Cream, jizz, cum, load, and spunk. I will hear these words over and over tonight, which is okay since I'm not going to be giving them any of it.

TAH: "Cute boy"

SpankyBtm: "Thnx"

Powertp: "Great ass. Can we see it without the shorts?"

I had set a goal of one thousand tips tonight, which was a stretch since I was new on the site. But at least it was a Friday night so all the boys were horny after being at the bars and hopefully they needed a night cap. Plus drunk people tip more since their inhibitions are down. I had set the following tip goals: 200 shirt comes off, 600 shorts come off, and 1000 thong comes off. In all reality, I was probably a cheap date for someone tonight because they get the show and it costs them less than the price of taking someone out for dinner. In all reality, I was a bargain.

SpankyBtm: "Soon enough"

Brazilnut: "Sexy man"

SpankyBtm: "Thnx"

I remembered the rule that anytime someone pays you a compliment you must say thank you.

TAH: "I'm edging here looking at your hot body"

Then the tip bell rang. HuskyMan had tipped 100, which was a good start, and I didn't have to remove any clothing yet.

It was time to turn it up a notch. I stared in the camera and gave my puppy-dog-eye look. It was kind of pouty, but not a full on pout as I pushed my lips out a little and slid my tongue in between. The tip bell rang another 50. So I began to roll my head around slowly followed by running my hands through my hair. I then put my hands under my chin and slowly started grinding my ass into the bed. I went slow and steady, back and forth. The shorts moved ever so effortlessly as they caressed my ass. The tip bell rang another 50 tips, so it was time to remove my tank top. I decided to do it very "Flashdance" style, where I got both arms into the shirt before I pulled it off over my head so I sat up and started.

DjMade: "Hot mother fucker"

Brazilnut: "Give it to me"

Whitestuff: "Grind it baby boy"

I hadn't really been paying attention, but it seemed like the comments were coming in much faster than they were last time. I checked on the chat count and found out that 20 people were actually watching me already. That was more than double what I had for the first show, but still no Leatherman.

I got my arms into the tank top and slowly started pulling it up from the bottom over my head. I stopped half-way up just to look into the camera for a brief moment.

HuskyMan: "Take it off"

MarkyMark: "Don't make us wait"

So I finished pulling it up over my head and stretched my arms all the way up and dropped the tank top to the side of the bed.

Fur Lvr: "Luv the pit hair"

HairyBerry: "Show the fur again"

I'm not a hairy person, and I didn't realize that pit hair was a turn on for so many people. I guess to each to their own. So I raised my arms up behind my head, showing off the pits. Pit hair didn't work for me, but the tip bell rang up another 200 tips. Progress was being made, so I decided to lie on my back for a change, showing off my legs and crotch for the camera. I could still reach the keyboard to respond, since I wasn't ready yet to respond verbally to everyone's chats. I decided to grab my crotch for a second and then rolled onto my side.

DjMade: "Let's see that cock"

Teddybear: "Ass I want to see the ass"

Sparky: "Play with your nipples"

I had to chat back.

173

SpankyBtm: "Be nice, I don't take requests yet"

Sparky: "Rub them just a little please"

DjMade: "Ever tried nipple clamps"

Since Sparky said please, I did rub my right nipple. The only problem with doing that is there is a direct connection between my nipples and my dick. The nipples are very sensitive, and once you start rubbing on them, it starts getting my dick hard. As expected, I started getting a rise in my shorts, which I had never intended on showing on camera. It was time to roll back onto my stomach. I also decided to answer DjMade's question.

SpankyBtm: "I have never tried on nipple clamps in the past because I'm afraid they would hurt too much"

DjMade: "It's a mix of pain and pleasure"

Sparky: "If you don't like the clamps try the magnetic balls"

SpankyBtm: "Magnetic balls?"

Sparky: "They're magnetic balls that pinch your nipple together they stay in place during sex more than the clamps which can come loose from the lube"

SpankyBtm: "You learn something every night"

The tip bell rang up another 150 tips.

Whitestuff: "Grind some more for us hot man"

HuskyMan: "Where's hubby tonight?"

SpankyBtm: "Passed out on the couch"

Whitestuff: "Did you wear him out already"

SpankyBtm: "He had a bar night"

Leatherman25: "And left you all alone?"

He was finally here.

SpankyBtm: "I'm never alone as long as you are here Leatherman"

Leatherman25: "That is very kind of you"

I wasn't being kind, I was just being honest. I really wanted to have a conversation with him, but not in the public forum. I had given him my email previously, but I never heard from him. Maybe this time it would be different.

SpankyBtm: "Leatherman what are you doing tonight?"

Leatherman25: "Just got out of the shower where I was washing all my dirty parts"

I would love to wash his dirty parts. Suddenly, I got a private message from Leatherman25. I opened it and it read, "I was really at the symphony. Didn't want to sound so boring online." So two can play that game online.

I private messaged him back. "So a man with class and culture. I like that." It was nice to find someone who was intelligent for once. I think most men I meet are as deep as a puddle of water.

Next thing I knew the tip bell went off for another 50 tips. That meant it was time for the shorts to come off. With the thong on, I decided I might as well make that a show as well. I got off the bed and started twerking for a minute to get everyone heated up and then I dropped it low. I didn't realize I could be that flexible. It must have been all the new dancing I was doing. I posed with my legs spread apart with my ass at the camera and slowly took by thumbs and inserted them into the waistband and slowly started pushing the shorts down my legs. As they slid down my legs, I brought my legs together, leaned forward sticking my ass out, and dropped the shorts the rest of the way down. This gave everyone a good look at my ass and thong. A minute was long enough so I jumped back onto the bed on my stomach. The only thing separating my cock from the comforter was a thin layer from my thong. It was exciting to feel that bit rub down there.

Whitestuff: "Just came. Thanks for the show"

DjMade: "Yes baby boy"

And a private message from Leatherman25: "You really are the sexiest man I have ever seen. You have one lucky husband."

There was that stupid lie again, but it's better for business. I private messaged back: "Things are not as always as they seem"

Private message from Leatherman25: "Why not?"

Private message from SpankyBtm: "Life is always a little

messy and sometimes people don't appreciate what is right in front of them." How vague could I be? He must have thought I was a complete idiot.

Private message from Leatherman25: "If there is anything I can ever do please let me know.

A lot of good that was going to do me since he thought I was married. At this point I realized I had been ignoring the rest of the chats coming in so I needed to reply.

SpankyBtm: "Sorry boys got lost in my own head for a minute"

FurLvr: "I would like to get lost in that head"

And with that, the tip bell rang for another 400 tips, which meant it was time to take off the thong. Again I never promised them a dick shot, so the removing of the thong was a lot more theatrical and very clinical. Off it went with my dick facing away from the camera and me cupping my dick and balls as I bounced back onto the bed. You are born naked so here I was naked again.

The comments kept flying in, but I wasn't much interested in what they had to say. I was just very happy that I had a chance to chat with Leatherman25. The fantasy lived on.

# CHAPTER 42

The night had finally come. It was the debut of our show "Bombshell," based on the short-lived TV show "Smash." I was starting to freak out a little so, Miss Gigi came over to the apartment to help me get ready. The only opening the club could give me right now was a Tuesday night, which worked out great for the other performers since most of them did community theater and couldn't perform on a Friday or weekend night. My anxiety was building because there were only ten pre-sale tickets, so at $20 apiece the show would at least generate $200 for my charity, since everything for the show was donated and there were no other costs. Hopefully Chas and his Facebook promotions would put some butts in the seats.

Miss Gigi helped me into my walk-about outfit. I was glam from head to toe in my Marilyn Monroe wig all the way down to my silver glitter pumps. "I hope I do Marilyn proud."

"You will, my baby girl," Miss Gigi said.

I noticed "The Package" hadn't made it over, so I finally asked Marjorie, "Honey, where is mister hot stuff?"

"We had a slight disagreement," she said. "He thought he was human, and I told him he was a piece of shit."

"That's rough. Is there anything I can do?" I asked.

"No. It was a stupid argument. I'll call him later, and I'm sure everything will be fine."

As soon as she finished, there was a knock on the door.

Marjorie went to answer. "I hope it's him," she said. She grabbed the knob and opened the door. "I'm so glad you came over."

"I'm so glad I did too," said Daisy Mae.

My mother stood there and we were all in shock. This was not a good time for a visit. "Are you going to invite me in?" she asked. I immediately ran to the bedroom.

"Oh my God, please come in Mrs. Tuttle," Marjorie said.

"Mama, what a pleasant surprise," I yelled down the hall. "What are you doing in town?" I asked.

"A friend had an extra ticket to see Reverend Stan Tidwell at Phillips Arena, and you know how much I love to hear that man preach, so I came down with her. She went to go visit her daughter the slut for a minute so I told her I would stop on by and visit you. Come on out here so I can give a big hug."

I hesitated for a second, and then summoned up some courage to walk down the hall.

"Are you going to a costume party? You're awfully dressed up," she said.

"Oh honey, he is going to be a rising star tonight. He's staring as Marilyn Monroe in our production of 'Bombshell' tonight. You should come and see Desiree perform," Miss Gigi said.

"So let me understand. Not only are you gay, but now you're a drag queen? Where did I go wrong? Your father is rolling over in his grave right now," Daisy Mae said.

"Momma, that is not fair. You know that daddy would be fine with this, or at least I would hope he would," I said defensively.

"Your father would have been ashamed of you for doing this. Where in the Bible does it say a man shall dress up as a woman?" Daisy Mae asked.

"Ma'am, no disrespect, but men have been dressing up like women for centuries to perform the great works by such luminaries from Plato to Shakespeare. It is a time-honored tradition," Miss Gigi interjected.

"It may have been fine for those perverts, but it is not right for my son. I didn't raise a daughter."

"Momma it is all for charity. The show is a benefit for Atlanta Street Rescue. It is a program that gets homeless gay youth off the streets. Remember the times we were close to being on the street, and if it weren't for the generosity of some friends and family, we would have been there too," I said.

"Don't forget the kindness of the church members who came by and brought us all sorts of casseroles to make sure we had enough to eat. Somehow you keep forgetting how important the church is and how important our savior is to us."

"Ma'am, I don't mean to sound judgmental, but you sound like all the Bible thumpers who stand on the street corners during gay pride with the bullhorns spouting off on how we are all going to hell," Miss Gigi said.

I don't know if that was such a good thing. It was true, but momma was so wound tight right now, she could either go one of two ways. She could either see the error in her ways, which would only happen on the day they find the missing Air Malaysia plane off the coast of Australia, or she could start praying at the top of her lungs in her hyper ventilated tongue voice. I was betting on outcome number two. Here it comes in 5, 4, 3, 2, and 1.

"Oh lord, sweet Jesus," she started as she fell to her knees. "Please pray for these sinners to see the error in their ways. I love them all, but cannot forgive them for their sins. Help set them on the path of righteousness so that they can be saved from the eternal damnation of the pits of hell where Beelzebub will torture them to the end of eternity."

"Is she serious?" Miss Gigi asked.

"Unfortunately she is," Marjorie interjected. "Mrs. Tuttle, come on. Get off your knees and come into the kitchen for a glass of tea."

And with that Marjorie whisked my momma into the kitchen. It was a small apartment, so I could hear her praying

179

all the way to the kitchen and in the kitchen. I could also hear Marjorie trying to calm her down.

This was not a good time for drama, as if any time really was, but it was making me perspire, and I didn't want to ruin my make up or get an embarrassing pit stain. I've got to be up in front of people shortly, laying my soul bare.

"Miss Gigi, I'm so sorry you have to get caught up in my family drama."

"Honey, every family has drama. Don't think that any family is perfect. She should be thankful you aren't a serial killer. Try explaining that at the Sunday social. Speaking of serial killers, did I ever tell you I met one once?"

"Really?"

"Yes. I used to belong to a social group, which was wonderful because the group always had these great functions. One day, I met a lovely gentleman by the name of Tim Spencer at one of the potlucks. He was a nurse and absolutely swept me off my feet."

"Go on."

"One day, I am just walking back into my apartment when my cell phone rings, and it was my good friend Rufus. He asks if I was watching the news, which of course, I wasn't. He says turn on Channel 2, so I did, and there was this driver's license on the news. He asks if that was Tim Spencer, and I said it sure looks like him. So we come to find out that Tim was injecting patients in the hospital to cause them to have a heart attack so he could be the hero by bringing them back. Unfortunately, several of them didn't come back."

"What has this to do with me?"

"Honey, what I'm saying is that there are a lot worse things in this world that you could be besides gay and a drag queen. Also, did I ever tell you that I once had a roommate who was a prostitute and had a pet skunk?"

I looked at Miss Gigi exasperated.

"I'll save that story for another day. Look, you are a good kid with a great heart. If your mother doesn't realize that, then she is missing out on so much."

I hugged Miss Gigi for giving me the reassurance I needed. I tried to be a good person, and even though I was not a church-goer, I believed with all my heart that if you lived a good life and treated everyone how you wanted to be treated, then there is no reason why I shouldn't be entitled to whatever comes after we pass on. Let's face the reality that we all have an expiration date.

"Do you think I should try talking to momma?" I asked.

"Let's see what Marjorie thinks? Oh Marjorie, can you come out here for a minute?" Miss Gigi called.

I could hear Marjorie say to momma to stay there and that she would be right back, and she headed out to chat with us.

"Ladies, I suggest you head over to the club. I'm finally getting her calmed down and her friend should be by shortly to pick her up. I will meet you as soon as she is out the door," she said.

"Do I risk another scolding if I stick my head into the kitchen to say goodbye?"

"Yes. Just head on out. I'll keep her busy in the kitchen for a bit while you finish packing up."

"Will you be okay Marjorie?" I asked.

"This isn't the first time I've had to calm your momma down. Remember the first time you went on a date with a boy? I think he name was Steven, wasn't it?"

"Yes, Steven. He was very nice, but a little dull," I said.

"Go. I'll catch up with you shortly."

"Okay." I yelled towards the kitchen, "Momma have a safe drive back to Clayton."

There was dead silence from the kitchen so I yelled again, "I love you momma, and I'll see you soon." Dead silence again.

"Come on sweetie. We've got to get going. I'm sure your adoring fans are waiting for you.

# CHAPTER 43

We got to the club later than I wanted because of the drama. I grabbed a program as I entered the Cabaret Room. There my name was in bold letters just below the "Bombshell" title. I was in print, so I guess that made it official that I had to go through with it.

I was surprised by how many people were in the club room. There were only ten tickets presold, but there were about fifty people in the room, so most of them had to have purchased their tickets at the door. This was more than I could have hoped for. I know we really worked hard on getting this together and promoting it, so I hoped everyone would be happy with what we were about to present. I didn't take rejection well. I guess I shouldn't call it rejection, but instead criticism. Rejection is when your date gives you VD and you make the commitment then and there never to have sex with him again. That is rejection.

All the cast was there backstage and almost totally ready. Germaine had stepped up to make sure everyone was in costume before we even got there. He really was a good friend.

I could feel the excitement among everyone in the cast. This was a great bonding experience for all of us, especially those of us who had not done live theater before. All my cast mates were so complimentary and gave me words of encouragement. This was so different than what I was used to when it came to the drag shows. I was getting a little hyper backstage. My knees started shaking a little, so I had to pull my shit together. This was not a time for a screwdriver, as I had to keep my wits about me so that I could remember my lines, my words, and the choreography. I wished Marjorie would get here. She always knew what to do to calm me down.

"Darling, go and mingle with the crowd," Germaine said as he squeezed my hands. "Remember, they are here to see you tonight and everything is under control. Our once ugly duckling is ready for her swan moment." He hugged me and pushed me into the crowd.

I had never sung live before a large crowd. I didn't count rehearsals because there were only a handful of people around when I hit the stage and belted out my numbers. Since we were on a shoestring budget, the cast was singing to tracks from the show with the vocals taken out. Heaven help us if any of the tracks started skipping. Singing gave me great joy because I could really feel these songs from my heart, which I hoped would translate live. It was funny to think at this moment that most of the queens on Ru Paul's drag race all do music to extend their brand. Maybe this was Desiree's way of extending her brand.

For this show, I had one of the theatre groups positioned at the dressing room door so that none of the shenanigans would happen that happened to me during the drag shows. This was a night to make sure everything went like clockwork. Barry was our door security man. He was just so cute I could have eaten up all his bearness with a spoon. Unfortunately I would probably be picking out the pubic hair from my teeth for a week.

Several of the other contestants I would have expected to come to the show came by to wish me well. "Sweetie, I just wanted to let you know how proud I am of how far you have come. Remember to relax and you will have a great show," Miss Mary Jane Bazooka said. I loved Mary Jane because she had always been the most supportive of me.

"Thank you so much for coming. I hope you enjoy the

show."

Precious Oil was also very kind. "Girl, kill it out there. I know you got it in you."

And of course, Athena showed up, but she didn't stop to say anything to me. I didn't know she was there until Barry called me over. He had prevented her from going into the dressing room. I could see her arms flailing in the air at poor Barry. He was too nice to have to put up with someone like her.

"May I help you, Athena?" I asked as I strolled up to the mayhem.

"Look, bitch, I have every right to go into the dressing room, and you can't stop me," she yelled.

"Why, yes I can. For tonight, Marni gave me permission to bar anyone not involved with the production from going in. Since you have nothing to do with the show, you are not welcome backstage. I don't want anything to go missing or get damaged."

"Are you calling me a thief, you cunt? You better not be. Marni is going to hear about this."

"Marni is going to hear about what?" Marni said as he stood behind Athena.

"This bitch," Athena started and was cut short.

"No names tonight, Athena. Desiree, go ahead and do what you need to. I will take care of it from here." Marni waved me off, but continued to scold Athena. "You are more than welcome to watch the show, but you and all the other contestants are barred from the dressing room tonight," he said.

"I have stuff at my dressing table I need to get," she insisted.

"No you do not," Marni responded. "I did a walk-through of the dressing room earlier today to make sure everything was clear for the show tonight. There is nothing on any of the dressing tables. So, as I said, you are more than welcome to watch the show, but you are not getting in the dressing room."

"I have never been treated so poorly. Mr. Winston is going to hear about this."

"Hear about what?" Mr. Winston asked.

"I give up." Athena finally slunk back to her table where her ruffled feathers were soothed by her band of cronies.

All of a sudden, I felt two meaty arms grab my waist from behind. I turned around and it was Paul and Chas. "Break a leg," Paul said.

"You will be fabulous," Chas said.

"Is Albert coming?" I asked.

"I'm sorry Desiree, but he just couldn't get his heart clear to come out tonight," Paul said, trying to let me down gently.

"I tried talking to him today, but all he said was as long as that crazy bitch was in the room, he would rather have his rectum rammed by a lesbian team of Lacrosse players who were all on their period at the same time with their pointy sticks," Chas said.

"Ouch. I understand. I will try talking to him again. Thanks for coming and grab your seats. We will be starting shortly." We air kissed and they both went to the bar to grab a drink.

Marjorie had still not arrived and we were fifteen minutes from show time. There was no drag time when you were putting on a live show. The latest we were going to start was five minutes after eight, which Germaine said was the proper start time to let people get to their seats.

Sandra got me into my opening number, and of course Miss Gigi and Germaine checked to make sure that everything was in place. We looked over the rest of my costumes, which were lined up on the rolling dress rack. I had five costume changes, so they had to be perfectly timed so that I could get off, strip, get re-outfitted, and get back on stage.

Miss Gigi took her place backstage with the headset on so that she could communicate with Scott the DJ, who agreed to do sound for the show as well. Kandi took her place at the spotlight, so we were all in place

The house lights flashed at the ten minute warning, letting people know it was time to get to their seats. Luckily, Marjorie came running in.

"God loves your mother because I don't think anybody else will put up with her. That woman can drive you guano crazy," were the first words out of her mouth. "I think I got her calmed down, and her friend came and got her. You might want to give her a couple of days before you give her a call," was her only advice.

"I am so glad you made it," I said I gave her a big hug. "Thanks for helping me not become a hot mess."

"You're welcome, boo," she said.

"Time to gather around, everybody," Miss Gigi said as she got the cast and crew into a circle backstage and made everyone hold hands. "We can't thank y'all enough for donating your time to come out and help us raise money for Atlanta Street Rescue. Please bow your heads." She started a prayer. "Dear God, bless these humble, creative players as we attempt something to bring joy into the lives of everyone who has come out to support us tonight. We do this in your name. Amen."

"Amen," the cast responded.

And with that, everyone got into their opening positions.

The clock struck 8:05.

The room went black.

"Ladies and gentlemen, please welcome to the debut performance of 'Bombshell.'"

The music for the opening song, "Let Me Be Your Star," started and the curtain opened. The spotlight blinded me for a second.

I was standing center stage as blonde Marilyn surrounded by several other Marilyns in various poses. The music continued and the words flowed out of my mouth. I think I hit all the right notes, even the high note on the word repertoire. Once I did that, I felt like nothing was going to stop me tonight. We all moved naturally to Marjorie's choreography and everyone hit their mark. The song finished and the crowd clapped very loudly. My heart raced. This was a different feeling than doing a drag number, but I didn't have time to dwell on that.

More words kept coming out of my mouth as the scenes changed and I interacted with the other characters. I even made it through the first two costume changes without any issues.

Miss Gigi and I took some liberty from the original show since they didn't put much dialogue into the actual Broadway show they were putting on, and we eliminated the scene where Marilyn went naked. I don't think a naked drag queen would work for this show.

The story of Marilyn's life has been told so many times, and we wanted to make it a little more light with some more comedy elements since she was a comic genius. The crowd laughed at all the jokes. The final first half number, "Let's Be Bad," was over, and before I knew it we were at intermission. I was flabbergasted that it went by so quickly.

The stage went dark, the curtain closed and the house lights came up. I immediately heard a buzz in the room.

"Oh my God, darlings, that was incredible," Germaine said as he came running in from the wing. He brought me a towel so I could pat down the sweat on my forehead. "Remember to blot," he said. "Blot only."

"Thank you," I said. But I needed to see what Marjorie thought. She had never pulled punches when it came to giving me the truth, and I could see her still in the stage wing.

I came face to face with her, but she didn't want to look me in the eye. The show was a disaster, and she just couldn't say it.

"Boo, you know I love you," she said.

Here it comes. She is getting ready to drop the hammer.

"It was fucking awesome, baby!" Her face lit up brighter than a tree on Christmas. "You are fabulous! Now let's get you changed into your next outfit."

Relief washed over me as I could see the joy on her face.

She grabbed my hand and took me over to the rolling dress rack. "We need to add a few more dance moves in here and there for the next show, but it looks wonderful. Also, we might want to play around a little more with the lighting to create more texture," she finished.

"You think it is good enough for another show?"

"Honey, didn't you hear those people laughing? They got the jokes. They are laughing with you, not at you. Have a little confidence. Wait till they see you in 'Twentieth Century Fox Mambo.'"

This was the opening number for the second act, and it was the biggest dance number of the show. Heels don't fail me now. I got on the next costume and had a chance to have some me quiet time. "Dear God, please let things keep going well, and please help momma to understand that I am just on the path that you have set me on. Amen."

"Sweetie, it's time," Germaine said as he tapped me on the shoulder. The house lights were blinking, which meant get your butts back into your seats.

The second act ran as smoothly as the first half, but now it was time for the most serious part of the show where Marilyn took the pills and died. We decided to use "Beautiful," the Christina Aguilera song that was used in the TV show, but not sung by Marilyn in the show. We felt it would have been appropriate for Marilyn to be singing this as she started popping her pills and tried to reassure herself that she is, indeed, beautiful. I had to practice singing while popping in Tic Tacs so that I didn't choke myself to death on stage while trying to sing the song. No one really knew her mind frame at the time of her death, but we hoped our ending did her justice.

The lights faded and music faded as I lay sprawled out on the bed in a state of repose. The curtain closed. All I could think of was to jump off the bed and get into the wings to get ready for the curtain call. The curtain opened and the rest of the cast came back on stage one by one to the cheers of the crowd. They formed a line with an opening in the middle for me to walk through. When I walked, on stage the volume of the cheering increased dramatically as the crowd jumped to their feet. I curtsied in the middle and then took my fellow cast mates' hands and we bowed in unison. The curtain closed and we all cheered and hugged backstage. The only thing was the crowd didn't stop clapping even when the curtain closed this time. I've been to shows where once the curtain came down, the crowd was out of there as fast as they could be to make sure they didn't get stuck in traffic. I know this was a small show, but I didn't expect this. The rest of the cast pushed me to the middle of the stage and they all exited. The curtain opened again and the crowd was still standing there and clapping for me. I curtsied again, and when I came up, I was presented with two bouquets of flowers. I was overwhelmed and humbled at the same time. Someone gave me a microphone.

"Please, you are all too kind. Thank you for coming out and supporting Atlanta Street Rescue. I want to thank the people who put so much effort into this show. Germaine on costumes, Scott on sound, the entire cast who have donated their time and especially Miss Gigi, without whose inspiration I couldn't have done this. Have a great evening."

The curtain closed and I walked to the wing. The first person I saw was Marjorie, whom I forgot to thank. I felt so bad.

"Who are the flowers from?" she asked.

"OMG I completely blew the thank yous. You should have been first."

"Don't worry, you were caught off guard. Hell, all of us were caught off guard by that reaction. Who are the flowers from?" she asked again.

I hadn't read the cards yet, so I set the bouquets on a chair and grabbed the first card.

"The first is from Spencer Jack from the hotel. He is so thoughtful. Maybe this means we will have that second date sooner than later."

"And the second one?" she asked.

I took the envelope off the bouquet and opened it. The card was blank.

"So who's it from?" she asked.

I don't know. It's blank and there isn't a florist's name on the card, so I can't check with them.

"It wasn't me. Come on Cinderella, we need to get you cleaned up and put to bed."

She was right. The crowd had gone home and I was exhausted. Time to close the shop for the night.

# CHAPTER 44

The reviews of the show started flowing in on Facebook and Twitter. It was really exciting to see the positive response we got. Of course, Athena had to post on what a train wreck the show was until she kept getting shot down by everyone's comments back to her that she wouldn't know art if it had pooped on her face. Art. I had made art.

Memorial Day weekend had arrived, and I was lucky enough to have Saturday, Sunday, and Monday off for a long weekend away from the hotel. I was heading to the North Georgia Mountains. I wasn't heading to Clayton by any means, but instead to the northwest corner of Georgia near the Alabama border.

Paul was heading to his favorite bear lodge and asked me to go. Miranda was hosting for the weekend and he thought it might be good to scope how she did things outside the city to see if I could pick up any pointers. And the complex was clothing optional during the day so I would get a chance to see some bear beef. He had me sold on bear beef before he even told me about Miranda's show. His only comment to me was that I was to pack no drag, upon which I quickly agreed. I needed some time in real boys, clothes, plus this was an opportunity to flirt with some hot men in person and not just on a computer.

It was Saturday morning, so off we went. I hadn't been in this corner of the state before. It looked pretty familiar, like I was heading home into the mountains. We were in Paul's jeep with all the sides off so it was a bit loud in the car, but the wind kept us nice and cool as the day started to warm up. It wasn't like we had a lot of luggage with us. The cooler was tied down to the back seat with bungee cords. This trip was up I-75 into Tennessee to catch I-24 west back into Georgia so that we could get off near the town of Wildwood. From there it was another twenty minutes of two-lane roads as we followed the signs to the Chickamauga and Chattanooga National Military Park, but as we got to the two mile sign to the park, we took a turn and headed south another five minutes. We finally rolled up to the entrance of the Grizzly Bear Lodge and Campground, which was a winding driveway about a mile into the woods. The road was lined with forest on both sides until you came to the clearing, which revealed the rustic three-story cedar lodge with the "Welcome to Bearfest" banner over the covered front porch entrance, where bears a plenty were mingling about.

"Now in the lodge, everyone wears clothes, since that is where the restaurant and bar are. Once you're out by the pool you are free to strip down to your birthday suit," Paul said.

The parking lot was almost full, so it looked like it was going to be a great weekend. We parked and quickly unloaded the jeep and went in and found people already chatting in the leather chairs in the lobby with drinks in their hands. We went up to the check in.

"Welcome back Paul," the desk clerk said. "We have your usual room ready for you." The desk clerk was a hot beefy number.

"Michael this is my friend Tyler who is coming up here for his first visit. And to make it clear, he is just a friend," Paul stressed. "I have a reputation to maintain here," he said as he looked me in the eyes.

"Completely understood. Welcome Mr. Tyler. We hope you will enjoy your stay here with us."

"I'm looking forward to it," I said.

At the front desk were the flyers for Miranda's big show

on Saturday night and her Miss Bearfest amateur contest on Sunday night.

"That's why I didn't want you bringing any drag with you. I didn't want to have to deal with you entering the pageant," Paul said as he saw me eyeing the flyers.

"I could have won, you know," I said back.

"That is not the point. The people who enter are only doing it for fun since the title doesn't really mean much so don't get your panties in a bunch that you can't compete," he finished.

"Don't worry. I have no intention of doing drag this weekend, plus I don't want to step on Miranda's toes. To be honest drag, wears you out!"

"That sounds very grown up of you. And I know you have been working so hard on the contest, so I wanted to make sure you got a weekend away from it," he said.

"Mr. Tyler, your room is on the third floor overlooking the pool. From there, you don't even need binoculars to see all the action that is going on. If you need anything, give the front desk a call, and we will be happy to help you out," Michael said. "I'm here to make your weekend as enjoyable as possible," he said as he stuck his hand out to shake mine.

"That sounds like a proposition, and I never turn down a proposition," I said.

"Aren't you precious? Anything that is either on the menu or on the planned schedule of events I'm more than happy to help you with," he said.

"Come on, cub boy. Let's go freshen up," Paul said as he pulled on my arm and led me over to the elevator.

The lodge was way more rustic than the hotels I worked in while I lived in Clayton. It really was charming. You knew you were in the woods with all the bear and nature scene paintings. There was even a large stone fireplace surrounded by a seating pit and bar cart. The wood was stacked neatly in the circular wood holder in the corner.

"It is really great at night here because they light the fireplace here and they have a fire pit off of the back patio, so just perfect for snuggling up with someone, since the temperature does get chilly here at night," Paul said.

"If I had known that, I would have brought my fur-lined pajamas," I said.

"It's better to cozy up with someone under one of the blankets," he said.

We got to the elevator and I pushed the button. As we waited a gaggle of bears came up and waited.

"Aren't you Desiree?" one of the bears asked.

I was pretty startled to get asked that. "Yes I am."

"I just wanted to let you know your 'Bombshell' show was excellent. My name is Arnold," he said as he stuck his hand out to shake mine. Arnold was a looker, about five foot ten inches, whom I was picturing all over me. "I was lucky enough to catch it."

"Thank you so much. I didn't see you in the crowd," I said. And believe me, if I had seen him there, I would have truly remembered him.

"I got there just as the show started," he said.

The elevator door popped open and we all piled in. Paul pushed three and Arnold pushed two. At least I knew what floor he was on.

"Hope to see you around," Arnold said as he exited on two and the door closed behind him.

"Why didn't you say something back?" Paul asked.

"I'm just not that quick on my feet, and I get tongue-tied."

"I'm sure you want to get tongue tied with that boy," he said. "And there will be plenty of opportunities over the weekend. Come on. Here is our floor."

We exited the elevator and walked about five feet to our door. As it turns out, our room was in the middle of the hotel, directly across from the elevator. "I like it here because you're overlooking the pool and you get to see everyone on your floor on the elevator at some point."

The room was very charming as it was decorated with individual wood-slat walls to give you the feeling you were in an individual cabin and not a lodge. The dresser and side tables were both dark wood and the two queen size beds had hand-carved bedposts and frames. This was all covered by what looked like custom-made quilt bedspreads that I'm sure some mountain hillbilly hand-stitched together. You could find these in several shops in the Clayton area. They were not cheap. It almost made me miss home for a split second, but then I came back to reality. The bathroom was more than adequate for the weekend with a tile walk in shower. I'm sure not many of these bears take baths up here.

"This is the main reason I like this room," Paul said as he flung open the door to the balcony overlooking the pool. As he stepped out on the balcony, you could hear several calls to Paul, "Welcome back!" and "Great to see you again." This wasn't his first time at this rodeo. "Come out here. I want to show you where everything is."

I stepped out. The view was breathtaking. From here you could see the entire pool and patio areas with beach chairs and reclining chairs in front of the fire-pit patio area. Men were already naked by the pool, sunning their fur-covered bodies. You could smell the scent of cocoa butter floating up in the air. One thing for sure is that I did not need to feel self-conscious by the pool this weekend because I think I was the skinniest person here. I guess that's what made me a cub around here. It's like Paul said, after five minutes, all penises look alike. You take a quick look and move on.

"Over there is the volleyball court and croquet field," Paul said as he pointed past the patio area. Now if you go down that path, be careful," he said as he pointed just past the pool.

"Why is that?" I asked.

"Because that leads to the private cabins and many grizzly-bear-virgins tend to get lost down there and don't return till the weekend is over," he said. I'm sure he was kidding, but inquiring minds want to know.

"So what do you mean?"

"Several of the cabin dwellers like to set up bars outside

their cabins and entertain for the weekend. They make very strong drinks and several of the newbie's turn into sweet concubines for the weekend. Remember that the single men here are looking for Mr. Right Now and not Mr. Right," he said.

"I've seen some couples here too," I said.

"Yes, there are several couples here just to relax, and it is a great place to get away and make some new friends. You will find everyone here is very friendly," he said. "That's why I like coming here. I've met many friends here who come back here all the time, so this is like my home away from home."

"Speaking of home, where did you grow up?" I asked because I really have never had a chance just to sit and talk to Paul without everyone around.

"Norfolk, Virginia," he said.

"How did you end up in Atlanta?"

"When I finished my stint in the Navy, I took a job here with an engineering company. Most of my family is still in Norfolk with some of my siblings in Virginia Beach. I grew up my whole life by the water, but I really find my peace and quiet up here in the mountains," he said.

I learned more about Paul in that one answer than I had found out in the several months since I had met him. He is the quiet one of the group, but up here he seems like a much more open man.

"And the path in the middle will take you down to the lake and some hiking trails along the stream that feeds the lake. The property is quite large, so if you go for a hike, please stay on the paths. I don't want to have to call out the National Guard to hunt you down. What do you want to do first?" he asked.

"I'm starving. Can we get something to eat?"

"Sure. The kitchen opens up in about an hour. You can order and take it by the pool if you like."

I didn't know about that because typically if you are at a party, you don't want to be seen as the one eating, since we live in such a body-conscious culture. These gym bunnies will make fun of you if your body isn't just perfect. But as I looked at the pool, these boys didn't seem to care. There were bags of chips and dips and Tostitos and salsa everywhere, so eating at the pool was going to be just fine.

We freshened up after our two-and-a-half hour drive and then went to the restaurant where we grabbed a couple seats at the bar to order our food. As I looked around the restaurant, I could see Arnold sitting in a booth and getting awfully cozy with someone. I assumed it was his boyfriend, since from the way they were acting, they seemed to have known each other for a while already. Oh well. There were plenty of other bears in the woods.

We ordered and went outside by the pool, where they said they would deliver to us. We were lucky to grab a pair of beach recliners as a couple decided to go for a hike around the lake and were vacating just as we got down there. It was good timing on our part because I didn't feel like lying on a blanket on the concrete. I just wanted to soak up the sun and listen to the dance music that wafted through the air. DJ Flying F was set up in the corner, just spinning away in his own world. For some reason, every time a bunch of gay men got together, there had to be dance music. I think that is because everyone feeds off the positive vibes from the songs and it helps everyone chill.

We put down our towels and the cooler, which was full of beer, since that is what Paul likes, and a plastic bottle of vodka with some orange juice for me. They didn't allow glass by the pool, so we made sure we brought some plastic cups with us. Paul immediately stripped down to his birthday suit and handed me the suntan spray. "Will you lube me up?" he asked.

"Sure," I said, but I just thought it was weird spraying him down. I was a little uncomfortable looking at his naked body. The other people didn't bother me that way, but it was just that we were friends, and yes I had imagined him naked before, but it was different with his pecker staring me in the face. I took the sport spray and let it rip all over his body. There was a lot to cover.

"Make sure you get it in my crack," he said. "I don't want to end up with any red marks just yet."

"TMI," I said.

"Relax, cubby, we are all just here for fun," he said.

So I sprayed him down from head to toe, and even in the crack. Thank God it wasn't the rub-on kind.

I, on the other hand, took off my shirt, but did leave my swim trunks on. I hadn't summoned up the courage to do it yet, so maybe a good screwdriver would help me get there. Time for the first round.

Everyone by the pool was just as nice as they could be. Our food arrived, and I got to eat in public while Paul and his friends were telling stories back and forth. It was great to watch him interact in his element, and the boys all seemed to be enamored with him as well.

This was great people watching as I chomped on my club sandwich. There were the serious bears and then there were the care-free bears. For a moment, I was reminded of the old Care Bears TV show I used to watch, except this was excitable bear, gay rainbow bear, hair bear, and a pair of panda bears. Panda bears are a black and white bear couple. They looked hot together.

Time by the pool was interrupted as Miranda rolled out in high-whore country drag with her ugly-as-sin counterparts carrying trays of spiked gummy bears. It was as if a bad Dolly Parton impersonator stumbled into our midst straight out of another plastic surgery procedure, except her face looked like it was melting and dripping down her face. This was her big fundraising weekend so she was starting early selling the chewy, gooey gummy bear shots. The shot cups contained two or three gummy bears and were a dollar apiece or ten dollars for fifteen shot cups. The boys were buying them up as Miranda and her funky bunch worked their way around the pool. She finally made her way over to me.

"Why hello, Desiree. I see you made it out to our little neck of the woods," she said as she took and shook my hand. "I'm so glad you could come and celebrate the weekend with us," she finished.

I didn't know what to say. Normally the first words out of her mouth were either something biting or sarcastic. I didn't know how to respond to this, especially since I had been so catty in my mind just a minute ago.

"Thanks. Here's ten dollars. We'll take some gummy shots," I said.

"Thank you so much for supporting Hope Pantry. Come to the show tonight. It's going to be fun."

She walked off and kept selling and chatting with everyone at the pool. She seemed to know most everyone here.

"She's been doing her shows here for years," Paul said. "They really like her up here."

"Is it just the water up here or the fresh mountain air?" I asked.

"What do you mean?" Paul responded.

"What makes everyone up here so God-damn nice? I even gave the bitch a ten, and she has never been nice to me."

"It's getting away from the city that relieves the stress and puts you at ease," he said.

I could use some release, but it wasn't from the stress of the city.

I split the gummy cups with Paul, and we gave some to the people around us. Next thing I knew my tongue had worked its magic on four of the cups and cleaned out all the gummy bears. They were a multitude of flavors, and they were strong. I didn't think I would need another screwdriver for a while.

"Aren't you the one putting on 'Bombshell' at Club Cabaret?" said the gentleman with whom we had shared a gummy cup asked.

"Yes. We just did the first show this past week."

"I read some good things about it on Facebook and was hoping to go see you sometime soon. When's the next show?" he asked.

"I'm not sure yet. I need to check with the cast when I get back to see what's good for them and also to see if it works with the club's schedule," I said, because to be honest I wasn't sure how well it would go over, so I didn't have anything lined up with the club. "As soon as I know, we will get the word out."

"Don't make it too long. I heard it was great," he said.

"Thanks for the kind words. I hope it lives up to your expectations."

Hard to believe that the show had made an impact so quickly. With work the rest of the week I hadn't checked out all the hype, so I would need to get caught up when I got back.

Paul was holding court, so I decided to go for a walk and explore. I had never seen him so animated. Just past the patio area was a group playing naked volleyball. All I could see was sand in every crevice and crack, and all I could think of was bringing a hose out and spraying everyone down. It was hard seeing some of the men dive for a ball and land flat on their biscuits, but they just got right back up and kept playing.

I went down the middle path to check out the lake. As I went down the path, the sounds from the lodge faded and all I could hear were the sounds of nature. It was a regular chorus of bugs and birds, which was really soothing. You don't get these sounds in the city, and I hadn't heard them since I was up in Clayton which reminded me that I needed to call momma. I hadn't spoken to her yet since she came over for her surprise visit.

The lake was empty except for a couple in a row boat stroking their way out to the middle of the lake. Paul was right that this place covered a lot of land. I could see how you could get lost if you went off the paths, which I had no intention of doing since I was extremely allergic to poison ivy and just looking at it made me break out in a rash. I found a beach chair under a tree and just sat taking in the beauty of it all.

My moment of peace didn't last long, as Arnold and his cozy friend came down the path hand in hand and went off on one of the paths. Luckily their interruption was short-lived as they disappeared into the woods. Good for them.

I sat there for a bit, enjoying the quiet. This place really did remind me of home and being up by the lake. Clayton wasn't a bad place, but it had just become a place I was from. There wasn't much up there anymore for me except momma. I really do miss my dad. His time was short, and I learned a lot from him while he was alive. I didn't realize how stupid I was because it took till just now to realize how much he volunteered and helped people. Maybe it was built into my DNA, and I was just discovering it. Dad, wherever you are, I miss you.

I finally dosed off, but I was awoken when the boys in the boat finally docked. I looked at my watch and saw that I actually got to nap for an hour and a half. It was much needed. I felt my batteries were recharged and ready for the night's excitement.

The excitement started a little early as Arnold came running from the bushes butt naked screaming that he had been bitten by a snake. I really believe it was just a trouser snake from his little friend. I watched as he ran screaming like a little girl up the path to the lodge. It was time to follow him and rejoin Paul.

Paul was still at the pool. He had a little, cute cub lying with him on the beach lounge chair wrapped up in a beach towel. They looked so content that I didn't want to disturb them, so I decided to follow the other path and explore cabin row.

The cabins were spread out a little so you weren't on top of one another even though I'm sure plenty of them would like to top something. Each one had a fire pit in front with chairs around them which would be great at night for entertaining. As I kept walking, I could hear country music pouring out of one of the cabins. It was a number Miranda liked to do. No sooner than I thought that the cabin door flung open, there was Miranda in all her country pride.

"Sugar, come on in for a drink," she said.

"Don't mind if I do," I said as I made my way onto the front porch. As I entered her cabin, I was immediately in awe of how decorated her cabin was. I guess I can't say decorated because it was more a shrine to women in country music. She had pictures of everyone from Patsy Cline to Wynonna Judd on every wall and every table.

"This is the house cocktail," she said as she handed me a Jack and coke which was her drink of choice. "Welcome to my home away from home."

"It's lovely," I said. "I knew you liked country music, but I never realized it was to this extent."

"It's been my passion ever since I was a little boy growing up in Tennessee. My parents loved country music, so that was all I ever heard. As I got older, I even performed in Dollywood in one of their shows. It was very gratifying."

"Did you ever get to meet Dolly?"

"I was not so lucky. She did come to the park one day while I was there, but our paths never crossed. One of these days it will happen," he said.

"You seem so relaxed up here," I said.

"It reminds me of home up here, and I let the tension go. Whenever I get back to Atlanta, the tension builds up and I become very high-strung. Sometimes it doesn't come out the right way. I'm sorry if I've been a cunt to you."

And he hugged me. "I can't promise I won't be a bitch when I get back to Atlanta, but just know that I think you are a great performer and I did hear great things about your show. You need to run with that for a bit."

"Why thank you. That's a great compliment coming from you."

"Don't let that get around too much. I don't want people back home thinking I got soft. You are coming to the show, right?"

"Yes, I will be there."

"Also, I might need your help on Sunday for the amateur show. You do good make up and most of these girls will need your help," he said.

"I would be glad too," I said as I chugged the rest of my drink. "I better let you get finished getting ready and go get cleaned up myself."

"See you tonight sugar," he said as I headed on my way. Did I actually just make friends with Miranda?

# CHAPTER 45

When I got back to the room, Paul was just waking up from his nap. He was alone. "What happened to your little friend?" I asked.

"That's just Stefan. He's adorable, but he is just a good friend. We see each other up here a couple times a year. It's just platonic, but I think he wishes it was more. You want to get something to eat?"

"Sure. What did you have in mind?"

"There is a cute little bistro in Wildwood about ten minutes from here. The owner is a friend of mine and the food is excellent," he said.

"You seem to have a lot of friends everywhere," I said.

"What can I say? I'm a likeable guy."

"Yes you are."

Paul hooked up his iPod and we both jammed out to dance music as we got gussied up for dinner. Paul looked extremely handsome in his white button-down Oxford with tufts of fur sticking out at the top, khaki shorts, and Jesus sandals. I think he even had product in his hair and his beard was trimmed. I, on the other hand, only had a t-shirt and some beat up shorts. I really didn't think we were going to dress up this much, but Paul didn't seem to mind.

We hopped into the jeep and off we went. It had cooled down a little bit, and it was great having the wind blow threw the jeep keeping us cool. Paul definitely had product in his hair because it didn't move one bit. We got to Wildwood, which was about three blocks long with one stop sign in the middle. It was extremely picturesque with the brick sidewalks, gas lanterns, cute shop after cute shop, and of course, an ice cream parlor where the local town folk mingled around chatting and waving to everyone else. With this being a small town, I'm sure everyone knew everyone else's business. Some things never change.

We found a parking space in front of a very cute restaurant, Bistro Milizano. There were people already sitting on the benches out front, so it looked like we were in for a wait. As Paul opened the door, I could already hear his name being called and someone in a chef outfit coming up and hugging him.

"Hello, my friend. It's so good to see you," Paul said as he hugged the chef. "Herman, I want you to meet my friend, Tyler."

"It is a pleasure to meet you, Tyler. Welcome to my bistro. I have a table reserved for you," he said as he led us to a table where you could see everyone and everything that was going on in the bistro. There was a single rose in a small, deep-blue, 1930's-looking vase and candle on the table. The chairs were leather and soft as a baby's bottom. Paul was kind enough to pull the chair out for me. He even ordered a bottle of wine for the table.

As I looked around, I noticed at most every table it was a couple. This must be a huge date-night restaurant, as everyone looked dreamily into the other person's eyes. The dim lighting and the jazz music in the background made this a very romantic spot. Suddenly, a light bulb went off over my head. Was Paul trying to woo my affection? I had the fantasy when we first met, but I didn't think it would ever happen since he usually went for more bear-looking boys than me. I needed to play it cool and see how things progressed.

Herman brought over the bottle of wine and opened it at the table. He poured a thimble-full into the glass for Paul to taste, and of course, Paul approved. He filled both our glasses. "Enjoy," he said. "Your waitress Gertrude will be over shortly."

"How do you know Herman?" I asked.

"We were in the navy together. His family is from here so I guess I just had an affinity for the area."

"If you like everything up here so much, why don't you move up here?"

"Because this is a great vacation spot and not a place to live. Some people get confused when they go on vacation because they fall in love with the place and decide to move there not knowing anyone or anything. Then they wonder why they end up miserable. I like my life in Atlanta, and I like my time here."

Our conversation was interrupted as a very mature waitress came over dressed in a pressed linen shirt and black pants with black apron. "Good evening, gentlemen. My name is Gertrude, and I am your waitress this evening. I see you have your drinks already. May I get you some water or an appetizer?"

It really was a butch moment as Paul asked me, "Do you mind if I order for both of us? There are some things on here that I know you will love."

I said, "Sure, why not? You've been here before, and I haven't." I didn't mind giving control to Paul because I always felt safe and secure when he was around.

So Paul placed out orders like a true gentleman.

We finally got back to our conversation, "Did you ever date Herman?"

"No, we were just really good friends."

"You have a lot of friends, but have you ever had a boyfriend?"

"I've dated around, but I've never met the one person. I had a huge crush back in the day, but it never worked out," he said.

"Why didn't it work out?"

"He was a hot bartender, which was one of the problems. I had a rule that you never date a bartender, bag boy, or a gas station attendant. If we had ever dated I'm sure I would have been jealous when all the drunks hit on him. The second problem was he was married."

"Did you meet him before he was married?"

"No. When we first met, it was just by chance at the grocery store where he was stoking a big zucchini as I was picking though the rest of the fruits. Our eyes met, and I just couldn't look away. He had the same feeling, I could tell."

"Who spoke first?"

"I did, since I had nothing to lose. I don't even remember what I said. It was probably the dumbest pick up line I could think off. He was kind enough and laughed, so I thought everything was going well, and I checked and there was no wedding ring on his finger."

I took a swig of the wine as Paul continued.

"I introduced myself, and he said his name was Matthew. He had a bar t-shirt on for Blizzard, a bar in Norfolk, so I asked if he worked there. He did and he said I should stop by some time on Saturdays because he opened the bar early. This was just the invitation I was looking for. So I would get to the bar just before they opened because he always left the door open when he was prepping the bar. I would come in and we would make out with a lot of heavy petting, but that is as far as it usually went. The bad part was he never really told me much about himself which is never a good sign."

"So he never told you he was married?"

"Never did. It wasn't until I overheard him talking to one of the other patrons one Saturday that I find out. I was crushed. I had already planned out our fantasy life in my head and that's all it really was. Just a fantasy."

"You go on Mariah Carrey."

"Ha ha."

"So what happened next?"

"I realized he was never going to leave his husband. I found out his partner made good money and traveled a lot for work, so he was never around. Matthew had it too cushy with a great house with a pool and a pool boy, yard-man and cleaning lady. He didn't have to do much. As it turns out, he was screwing the pool boy. Working the bar was just to keep him busy and socializing. I finally had to come to the conclusion that the fantasy was dead and I needed to move on."

"That must have been hard," I said. "I've never been there so I don't know what I would do."

"You would do what I did. You make the decision to do what is best for you and you move on. The fantasy is nice, but reality can kick you in the ass. Luckily the job in Atlanta came up, so I moved."

"What ever happened to Matthew?"

"I don't know. Last I heard his husband had dumped him for being a whore, and then he kind of disappeared. The first crush is always the hardest. Why haven't you found anyone yet?" he asked.

I took another swig of the wine to drain the glass before I answered. What I really wanted to say was that people sometimes don't realize what a good thing they have staring them in the face. Instead, I copped out. "I don't really know. I'm a nice guy, but I haven't clicked with the right person yet?"

"What about your online person?"

"How did you know about that?

"Chas. You know he can't keep his big mouth shut.

"Not much is going on there. We chat when I do my webcasts, but he hasn't emailed me yet even though I gave him my private email. I'm sure a lot has to do with the fact that he thinks I'm married."

"And the guy at the hotel?"

"Chas told you about him too?"

"No, that was Marjorie."

"Spencer had to go back to Knoxville. We never had a second date, but he did send flowers to the show."

"That's thoughtful," he said. "I heard you got a second bouquet. Who were they from?"

"Don't know. There was nothing on the card and no

florist name either."

"That's a shame. If I ever send flowers to someone I want to make sure they know they are from me."

So I guess they weren't from Paul. Maybe I'm just reading this all wrong. I had had a lot of wine, and I usually don't drink wine.

Dinner arrive. It was delicious just like Paul said it would be. I could have sat there for hours, but I wanted to get back to the lodge for the show. Paul was even kind enough to pick up the check. We said goodbye to Herman and thanked him for his hospitality, and then we went up the block to get some ice cream for dessert. For a non-date, this was pretty magical.

# CHAPTER 46

We grabbed a couple of stools at the bar to watch the show. The bar was packed with men everywhere. I can't say they were boys because these men all had a little girth on them. It was a very friendly crowd and everyone was primed and ready.

The gummy bear shooter girls came around pushing their gummy cups. Paul bought the first round. He gave them ten dollars, so the next thing I knew, there was a rainbow of gummy bears in front of me. We each had two and gave the rest away to the people around us. They were glad for the free shots. Since these were vodka bears, they mixed well with my screwdrivers. Paul was back to his beer. With the show starting on drag time we had time for another round of gummy bears. I plunked down ten dollars again and we had another rainbow of bears in front of us. This time we each did three rounds and gave away the rest. I'm sure this was just a stall tactic to sell more gummy bear shots since all the money went to charity.

The show only started thirty minutes after the posted time, which wasn't too bad for drag time. It was a total country show with enough Dolly, Tammy, and the Judds to keep the crowd tipping. And at every break between entertainers, the gummy girls were right there selling more gummy shots. It got to a point where I lost count of how many shots I had. Paul was keeping pace, but with his body size, he could handle his liquor better and he was only doing one beer for two of my screwdrivers. By the time the show ended, I finally had hit the point where I was on drunk patrol and couldn't remember anything.

The next thing I knew, I woke up chilly back in the room with no idea of what had happened except that my head was killing me and that I was cold. It wasn't till I looked under the blanket to realize that I was naked. My butt wasn't sore, so I didn't think I had been penetrated by anyone, but you never know. Paul wasn't in the room and his bed hadn't been slept in. Did we sleep together? I think I would have remembered.

There was a jiggle at the door and Paul entered carrying two cups of coffee and some donuts. He tossed me a bottle of aspirin and said, "This should help."

I grabbed the top sheet and wrapped it around myself as I got up and went to the bathroom to get a bottle of water.

"Shy today? You weren't last night?" he said.

"I don't remember a thing."

"Baby, how could you forget a night like last night? It was magical. I don't know how to describe it."

"Did I make an ass of myself?"

"I wouldn't say ass, but you have such a sweet one."

Oh my God, we did sleep together. How was I ever going to live with this and what would our friends think? There was nothing I could do but ask. "Did we sleep together?"

"Sleep? There was no sleeping going on baby. I can't believe you don't remember everything that we did."

"I am so sorry, but last night is a total blur. I remember the show starting, but nothing after that," I said. "I'm sorry if that hurts your feeling."

Paul let out a hearty laugh and kept laughing.

"I don't understand."

"I can't do this any longer. You've suffered enough. We didn't do anything. If you want I can tell you what happened over breakfast. Go get cleaned up."

I immediately felt a sense of relief wash over me. I had

never been that drunk in my life, and I was paying for it this morning. I opened the bottle and took three aspirin hoping it would stop my head from throbbing as I dropped the sheet and hopped into the shower. The hot water felt good and helped clear up some of the fuzziness I was feeling. I dried off and put on some shorts and a t-shirt and we headed downstairs to the restaurant.

We grabbed a private booth and ordered food. I had our waiter keep bringing me glass after glass of water and orange juice. I needed to get my system flooded with something healthy.

I finally asked, "So what did I do last night?"

"The real question is what didn't you do? No, in all honesty you were pretty good for how drunk you were. I knew you were in trouble when you started getting all glassy-eyed and kept telling me how much you thought our dinner was a date at first. It was really charming that you thought of me that much as you kept leaning on me for support as the show was winding up. You just kept repeating it over and over and over."

"I am so sorry," was all I could say.

"Not a big deal. The show ended and you congratulated Miranda for a wonderful evening before she headed out to count the money they made. It looks like they did pretty well. And right after that, one of your adoring fans came up to ask a favor."

"I have adoring fans?"

"Yes, this guy named Rafael who had seen you perform in Atlanta came up to say how much he loved you and to ask if you could help him do his make up for the bear beauty pageant on Sunday. You said yes right away and began to thank him profusely for telling you how much he liked your performances. You had a lot of head bob motion going on while you were talking to him, which I think confused him. At that moment, Stefan came up to chat and I turned my back for a moment. When I turned around you were gone. I really was afraid you were going to fall into the pool and drown, so Stefan and I went out to find you since we couldn't see you in the bar."

"Where did I go?" I asked as I started to really get embarrassed.

"You were like the white rabbit that went down a hole because we couldn't find you anywhere in the lodge, including our room. And I don't want to admit this, but our search got delayed for a little bit."

"What do you mean?"

"Stefan planted a big, wet kiss on my lips and the feel of his beard rubbing against mine turned me on so we sat and made out for a while. That's all it was. We didn't do anything past that. He is a great guy, but I just don't know. I don't want a long-distance relationship, and I figure we might as well enjoy what we have here and leave it at that. He was nice enough to go down to the cabins to help me find you."

"How did you know I was down there?"

"All we had to do was follow the trail of your clothes. There was a shoe here. Another one there. A sock here. Another sock there. We collected them as we went and we knew you might be in trouble when we found your shorts hanging off a bush."

I took a deep breath. "So what happened next?"

"Well, we found your shirt on another bush. When we got to the first cabin, all the bears were dressed in leather by their fire pit, so we figured that cabin was too hard for you. The next cabin had a bunch of chubby bears having a late night buffet out front, which we figured was too soft for you. Finally, we came along a cabin where all the bears were in their underwear having a dance party out front with all these glow sticks. This cabin was just right for you."

"How did I end up there?"

"Your admiring fan, Rafael, brought you down there so that you could meet his friends and party. I could tell you were done at this point as you were staring at your glow wrist-band and starting to stumble around. Stefan and I scooped you up and made you say good night to everyone.

Rafael looked a little crushed that we were taking you away from him."

"What does he look like?"

"Turn to your right."

I turned my head to see a very wide-eyed bear smiling and standing in front of me. "Good morning, Desiree," Rafael said.

"Good morning to you too," I said.

"How was the rest of your evening?" he asked. "It could have been more special if this big brute here hadn't hauled you away last night."

"Just doing my duty," Paul said.

"You're still doing my make up today?" Rafael asked.

"Sure, but I didn't bring any of my supplies with me."

"No problem. I brought plenty. This isn't my first time performing," he said.

"Good. Let's say 4 backstage then."

"Fabulous. I'll see you then," he said as he left to rejoin some of his friends.

"What have I gotten myself into?" I asked.

"It could have been worse. You could have woken up in that cabin this morning without any of your clothes at all, and then you really would have to do the walk of shame."

"Oh my God that would have sucked. Please tell me there isn't anything else to this story," I pleaded at this point.

"There's more. Stefan and I put one of your arms around our necks for support to make sure you didn't tumble. Your mumbling briefly became clear as you stated again how you thought our dinner was a date at first. At least Stefan laughed when he heard that."

"Sorry," I said.

"When we got you back here to the room, we plopped you on your bed. At this point, Stefan had to go, so we shared one last kiss as he left. Great kisser, by the way. Then you said that your head was spinning, so I got you back up and put you on the floor by the toilet. You said you were hot so you removed your underwear and threw it at me to catch.

Needless to say I let it hit the floor. At that moment you turned and projectile vomited into the toilet. I couldn't tell you how glad I was that everything ended up in the toilet because I didn't want to have to clean anything up."

All I could do was hang my blushing face in shame.

"The vomit was colored like a melted box of crayons. You had the yellow from the orange juice and then all the gummy bears. It created a rainbow in the toilet. I got you up and we rinsed your mouth out with some water and got you back into bed, but you wouldn't go to sleep unless I hopped in bed with you and cuddled. I kept telling you no, but you wouldn't take no for an answer, and the only way I was going to get some sleep was to hop in bed with you. You wanted me to strip naked, but I finally got you to agree that I could strip to my underwear before I got in bed, which is fine for me since I sleep in my underwear anyway. I put my arm around you and you pushed back into me to spoon and within thirty seconds you were sound asleep."

"I am so sorry. How can I make it up to you?"

"My little cub, it wasn't so bad. It was nice to actually sleep with someone since it has been a while for me and sleep is all we did. I just happened to wake up at my usual time which let me go down and get the coffee and donuts."

"But how can I make it up to you?"

"Don't worry. I have done much worse so let's leave it at that."

"Thank you."

The rest of the day was pretty uneventful. A couple of drinks, and I was feeling right as rain. And I did my duty and did Rafael's make up for the show. He wasn't kidding when he said he had performed before. He ended up winning the pageant, which was a first for him, and he thanked me from the stage for all my help.

# CHAPTER 47

The real world set back in as the routine of work, sleep, eat, and drag took over. I was beginning to think there was no end in sight. We were getting ready for the second showing of "Bombshell" and the marketing machine had taken over.

Chas had really ramped up the Facebook event and invited everyone he knew. Paul, Marjorie, Miss Gigi, Germaine, and I invited everyone we knew, no matter how near or far. Chas even reached out to all the gay publications in town to make sure they mentioned the show in their calendar section, and even tried to get me interviewed, which would have been very strange. The bar was plastered with flyers, Chas even promoted the show to the alternative straight publication.

Desiree's page was getting more traffic than I ever expected. Every time I posted new pictures, my friend requests went up, and I was up to over 500 friends. I couldn't tell you who half the people were, but I didn't mind that my brand was getting extended. It was nice to have all this attention since I had always been one of those people who faded into the background. Plus, the nice benefit of becoming a celebrity was I kept getting invited to more events and parties. Everyone was starting to want a piece of Desiree.

The phone rang. I could see it was Miss Gigi, so I answered.

"Look sweetie, I have some notes on the show. Do you want to be remembered for something good or for something great?"

"Something great."

"I'm glad to hear that, because the biggest change we need to do is with the choreography," she said. "Right now it is just good, but good isn't going to bust this show wide open. I've got the choreographer from the theater already set up and he is working with the cast members already to make changes on some of the big dance numbers. This will really help the show.

"What about Marjorie? She has worked so hard on the show that I just can't push her aside."

"Don't think of pushing her aside. She has greatly contributed to the show so far, but I think what we need to do is out of her level of expertise. I'm only saying this to make the show better."

"When are you going to tell her?"

"I'm leaving that up to you. She is your friend, and I think it would be easier coming from you." And with that, she said good bye and hung up.

The advance ticket sales for the show were already at one hundred which was making me very nervous. The room packed out at two hundred so we could have a packed house. That would be incredible. Word of mouth must have been working to get people to buy tickets. I wanted as many people to see the show as possible, but how could I tell Marjorie? She is my friend and put so much of her time and energy into it. I needed to tell her before she found out about the other choreographer. There was no time like the present.

Marjorie had been in a great mood lately because she and "The Package" had worked out all their issues and were seeing each other on a regular basis again. It did make me a little jealous that she had a special person in her life and that I had yet to meet that someone.

She was still finishing up her morning coffee. Now was

as good a time as any, so I approached her very cautiously. "Marjorie, you know we are coming up on the second showing of 'Bombshell,' and I know it has been taking up way too much of your time especially since you and 'The Package' are back together."

"Sweetie, it has not been taking up too much of my time. I like helping you guys out. It makes me feel good to get involved in things."

"And I appreciate that very much. I spoke to Miss Gigi a little bit ago, and she had some good notes on ways to improve the show. A little bit of dialogue changes here and there, but his biggest suggestion was to improve the choreography."

"What do you mean 'improve the choreography'?" she asked.

"She thought that some of the big dance numbers needed some more pizzazz to really put the show over the top so she decided to bring in the choreographer from the theater to start reworking some of the numbers." I said.

"Don't you think it would have been appropriate to have spoken to me about this first? I could give the numbers more pizzazz if you want them that way, but since you both wanted them as simple as possible, I made it very easy for everyone to learn the numbers," she said. "If you wanted more jazz hands I am capable of putting them in there.

"I understand."

"No you don't understand. How would you like it if she had gone behind your back and made changes without asking you? You wouldn't have liked that at all. This is your show too, so I would suggest you have a chat with Miss Gigi and tell that bitch I'm pissed," she said.

"I'll see what I can do. She didn't mean to hurt your feelings."

"Yes she did, because she didn't have the courtesy to even tell me this to my face. Albert was right. The bitch is crazy, and I don't want to have a single thing to do with her again. I suggest you man up and get some balls and tell her that she is not the producer God of this show, and that if it weren't for everyone's energy going into this show you would still be just a drag queen doing mediocre shows," she said.

"This show is going to make me a star."

"This show is going to make you a bitch, and I suggest you don't ask me for any help on any of this anymore because I am done. Do you understand me? I am done. I should have known better when you forgot to thank me after the first show. It was a sign of things to come."

"Come on! You can't be serious!"

"I am unbelievably serious. Tyler, I love and respect you, but this drag thing is starting to turn you into this unabashed monster, and you don't even realize it. You aren't in it to raise money for your charity anymore. Instead you are just doing this for attention. We all love attention, but I'm tired of attention whores."

"Wow. I can't believe you think I am like that."

"You don't even realize it. And your friend Germaine isn't doing you any favors either. He just keeps filling your head with all these thoughts when I really think he just wants to relive his glory days through you."

"Germaine is a great talent. He was just misunderstood in his time."

"Well, he isn't getting any younger or prettier. That time has passed him by and he needs to move on instead of getting you to do everything that he can't do anymore. He is a tired old queen who needs to start living his life for himself again instead of living it through you."

"How can you say those things about Germaine? He is one of the most generous and kindest people I have ever met, and he likes me for me, and not because he is trying to be me."

"No, he wants you to be a better version on him. All three of you are made for each other. You all just keep feeding each other's egos. It makes me sick."

"If that is the way you feel about it, then maybe I need to

move out. I may have overstayed my welcome here."

"Yes, maybe it is time for us to go our separate ways," Marjorie said as she put down her coffee cup and walked down the hallway to her bedroom and closed her door.

I couldn't believe her opinion of Miss Gigi and Germaine. They have always been very nice to her and me and tried to make her feel welcome at all the rehearsals as far as I could see. Maybe it was that time of the month or maybe things with "The Package" weren't going as well as I thought they were. Time to make a couple of phone calls if I was going to find a new place to live.

# CHAPTER 48

Germaine met me at the door as I dropped my rolling duffle bag down. He was the first call and he said he, of course, would glad to have me as a roommate.

He lived in a two bedroom/two bath apartment which was decorated exactly how I thought his place would look. Everything was a little over the top, but it all fit together. From the Bette Davis framed print to the overstuffed furniture, it all screamed Germaine.

"Here, let me take that for you," he said as he picked up the duffle bag and started down the hall. "This room is yours," he said as he pushed open the door. "And your bath is right here," he said as he pushed open another door. Neither room looked like they were ever used.

"I was hoping someday to have a boyfriend, but since that never happened, these rooms really don't get much use and would be perfect for you."

"I can't thank you enough. I just don't know where everything went wrong with Marjorie."

"She was jealous of your talent, and your other friends were the same. Albert had already turned his back on you, and it was only a matter of time before the rest of them did."

"I just can't believe it all went down like it did. They were more than friends to me, they were family."

"Baby doll, I am your family now, and you are looking at a very bright future. When 'Bombshell' has its second showing, you are going to become a celebrity here in town.

People will want to be with you, and you will become a member of the A Gays," he said.

"What are A Gays?"

"Not what, but who. The A Gays are the ones who hold the power and the money in our community," he said. "They are the ones who throw the best parties and put on the best charity events. These are the people who will put your campaign over the top and that crown will be resting on your head faster than you know it."

"You really think so?" I asked, since I really had no clue who these people were. I'm used to the people who came out to the shows.

"Yes. You are already getting invited to parties, and that is getting ready to explode once this performance makes you the belle of the ball."

"I don't know about that."

"It is all going to happen for you. Come on, let's get your stuff put away. We have a lot to plan out."

The show was only a couple of days away and it was almost sold out now. Today was dress rehearsal for the new choreography with all of the cast. It was the only time we were going to have to go over the new steps before the show and it had to be perfect. The moves were a step up from what we had been doing, so it was giving the show the extra punch that it needed. I hated to say it, but Miss Gigi was right, and it was the right thing to do.

Germaine and I headed to the club. His apartment was a little further away and we got stuck in traffic. There was only one thing guaranteed about Atlanta and that was traffic. We had to hop on the expressway, which was always a nightmare. Everyone in this city only took the expressway and never learned any of the side roads. It just sucked.

We made it to the club with just moments to spare as everyone was there and waiting for us. I got into my costume, and we were ready to rehearse.

Antonio, the new choreographer, was an affable man and fit in with the rest of the cast and crew. He immediately put everyone through their paces. The steps were not hard to learn and they did make a difference. I was glad Miss Gigi talked me into this.

We managed to get through the dress rehearsal in a relatively short period of time, which was great because now I could get something to eat. It was going to be a little strange because I was used to eating with Marjorie or one of the boys, but since they weren't speaking with me I would have to get used to other arrangements.

"What do you want to do for dinner?" I asked Germaine.

"Well Miss Gigi and I were going to get a bite to eat. You are more than welcome to join us."

I looked in my wallet, and I was low on funds. It would have been better if I grabbed something from the store and just headed home. That would give me leftovers. Home was a new place with a lot of things to get used to. I guess I didn't realize how much I took Marjorie for granted, but Germaine drove so it wasn't like I had much choice.

"Don't worry, I'll pick up the tab," he said noticing I was looking into an empty wallet.

To really cap off the day, I ran into Athena on the way out. She was very subdued for some reason. I didn't say a word as she approached and looked straight ahead.

She didn't say a word until she was dead even with me. "I'm going to get you shut down. Mark my words on that," she said.

"Excuse me?"

"You heard me. Enjoy your last minute in the spotlight."

I let it go at that. I really didn't want to get stuck in another useless conversation with her. I didn't even dignify her last comment with any response. Just best to walk on.

The three of us hopped into Germaine's Cadillac and off we went for Chinese food. Chinese was Miss Gigi's favorite food, so I had better get used to eating where she wanted to go. We ended up at Dim Sums Chinese Food and Bakery. Odd name for a restaurant, but I was told they had the best noodles in town and it was Miss Gigi's favorite restaurant.

We sat down and Germaine and Miss Gigi laid out their plans for me. "This show is your chance to become a star," Miss Gigi said. "This is your moment that will transform your life forever and send you onto the A Gay list. I never had that opportunity, and I don't want you to waste it."

"How do you know it will get me there?" I asked skeptically.

"There is no doubt in our minds that you have that star quality," Germaine said. "I recognize a lot of things in you that I had, but I unfortunately succumbed to the bitchy queens who drove me from my hometown. I don't want to see that happen to you, and we are here to make sure that doesn't happen. Think of me as your Mama Rose."

"Who's that?" I asked.

"My child," Miss Gigi said. "Give me your gay card."

"We just need to educate you on some gay history, which includes Broadway. I'm sure in that backwoods Barbie hole-in-the-wall place you came from, you never had the opportunity to experience the Great White Way."

"Why do I want to be in the A Gay crowd?"

"Sweetie, you just don't get chosen to be in the A Gay crowd. You have to earn it. That's what makes it so great when you achieve it," Germaine said.

"Let's talk about your career path," Miss Gigi bluntly stated. "Where do you see yourself in five years?"

"I don't know. I didn't think this evening was going to turn into a job interview."

"You need to think about these things. You can't be at the hotel five years from now. You have to want better for yourself," Germaine said.

"What about you?" I asked. "You're still at the hotel."

"That was never my intentions, but life was cruel and left I stranded in that cavern of shame. You don't have to be stranded there," Germaine finished.

"Yes, you have so much potential and you need to grab it while you have the chance. Not everyone has people behind them who will help you achieve fame," Miss Gigi said.

I wasn't sure that I wanted to be famous, but if the opportunity was here, who was I to turn it down? A lot of people become famous doing what they like to do so maybe it was just my natural progression. So I sat quietly while they laid out the plans for my world domination. It was a little intoxicating to have people gloat over me for the first time in my life.

# CHAPTER 49

The club let us know the show was sold out, which floored me. These were people who were coming to see me. Suck it, Athena.

As a very last minute surprise congratulatory gift, Germaine got us tickets to go see the hottest insult drag queen comic there was-Torino Del Grand- tonight. She rose to fame on a drag queen reality show, "The Guys as Dolls Show," winning her season quite handily. She was my favorite from the first time I saw her on the show, as she slayed the competition week after week. She was fierce and funny, which made her invincible. They played the show at the club every Thursday, and the boys, Marjorie and I would go out, have drinks, and have a ball watching it. It was off season now so I wasn't missing anything right now.

"We have meet and greet tickets, so we will need to be at the theater no later than 6 to get in line to meet Torino, and we need to pick up Gigi on the way there," he said.

"How were you able to get tickets? The show's been sold out for weeks."

"I had confidence you would sell out, so I bought these when they went on sale. That is how much I believe in you."

"What should I wear?" It was June, but the temperature was already in the 90's, which was way too hot for Atlanta this early. We may have the nick-name Hotlanta, but normally this heat didn't kick in until July.

"And the show is at the Hot House Theatre," Germaine

said.

"Where is that one? I've never heard of it."

"It's the Burgundy Ballroom, but its nick name is the Hot House Theatre because the A/C never works properly in that building."

"What should I wear? I've never been to an event like this," I said which was absolutely true.

"Well, since the people who bought the meet and greet tickets are the A Gays, you need to wear dress pants, a dress shirt, and a nice pair of loafers. No tennis shoes. You need to make a good impression on them, and you need to be dressed properly to meet Tornino."

"Will you pick out my outfit for me?" Should I go in drag?"

"Never go in drag to a show headlined by a drag entertainer. It will appear as if you are trying to upstage her. I've already picked out your outfit. It is hanging on the hook on the back of your closet door. You need to be shaved and showered and ready to go no later than 5:30. Now scoot along and get ready. I don't want to keep Gigi waiting."

I looked in the closet and there was my outfit for the evening. The shirt and black pants were in their dry-cleaning bag, so he had been planning this for a while; the shoes were freshly polished with the pair of socks I was to wear were already in the shoes. The only thing he hadn't picked out was my underwear. At least I knew I could pick out a comfortable pair for the evening.

I looked at my watch, and I still had some time to kill. It was only 4:30, so I decided to check my email. My inbox was a much busier place, but I wish my love life had gotten to this pace. I sat at the computer and opened my Gmail account. It was the usual crap email, but one did catch my eye. The subject was "Hey" and nothing else. I didn't recognize the email address that it came from, so at first I thought it was spam email. I decided to click on it just to see.

"Sorry it took so long to work up the nerve to email you on your private email," it read. "Let me know when your next video session will be. Would love to talk with you again. Leatherman."

I stopped dead and stared at the screen. I had dreamt of this moment for so long, but thought it would never happen. I felt a warm glow from inside. I was terrified of how to respond, so I called Sheila.

"What should I say to him?"

"Look, he obviously has some level of interest in you since he finally responded. Either that or he is a total chicken shit because of the line he had to work up the nerve to email you. Who needs to work up the nerve to email anyone these days? It is the most anonymous thing that you can do. Either that or he really is married," she said.

"I don't think he is married."

"How do you know? The only conversations you have are when he is staring at your hot body on line. He could be a total whack job and you would never know it."

"He doesn't sound like a whack job."

"That's because you only see what he types. All people lie online. If you are going to respond, which I'm sure you will, take baby steps. Just let him know the next time you will be online. That way you can ask him some more questions."

She was right. He could be a nut job, but at least he emailed. He did make some effort. "Thank you, sweetie. I'll see you tomorrow."

I placed my fingers on the keyboard and typed away.

"My next show is tomorrow around 9 pm. I hope you can join me." Very short and to the point. Let's see if he turns up.

I heard a yell from down the hall. "Time is ticking away. I don't hear the shower running," Germaine yelled.

"Yes, mom. I'm hopping into the bathroom right now." He was like a mother. Definitely a mother and not a father.

I slipped of my sweaty clothes from the day and turned on the shower. I was still getting used to the water here taking no time to get hot, versus at Marjorie's place where it seemed like an hour before it even got tepid. All I could think of while I was standing there naked was Leatherman, and I started getting hard. The shear thought of him gorged my dick, and this wasn't even someone I had met in person. He could have been a total troll for all I knew, but the thought of someone wanting me just for me made me hard. I stepped into the shower. The hot water felt good as I shoved my head under the spray and let is wash all over my body.

I had to take care of myself, so I began rubbing my nipples as the water warmed my entire body. Rubbing my nipples made my dick even harder because there is a direct link between the two. If my shirt rubbed them just right it would start to get me aroused wherever I was, so I had to be careful of a good stiff breeze. I stood back a bit so the full force of the water landed directly on my hard cock, causing it to bounce up and down. I finally grabbed my rod and started stroking it slowly. Thoughts of Leatherman flooded my head as I imagined this hot man ravaging my sweaty hole. Fantasy was all I had, and I was going to enjoy every moment of it. I turned the shower head to pulse and positioned one hand on the tile wall and lifted my ass up so the water pounded away at my pink fuck hole. With each pulse, I imagined his dick going in and out of me, slowly at first and then building up speed. I grabbed the shampoo bottle and squirted a load onto my dick so that I could stroke away as the water puckered up my hole. In and out was all I could think about and Leatherman's big hairy arms pulling on my shoulders as he pounded my ass and then pulling and turning my head so that he could shove his tongue into my waiting mouth. I stroked harder and faster as my balls got tighter and tighter until my body shuddered and my load shot out and hit the tile wall. I felt a wave of ecstasy flow through my body and as quickly as it came, it vanished. I wiped the wall down with a wash cloth and turned the shower head back to spray. Now I was going to be totally relaxed for the evening.

I dried off and managed to get myself dressed and ready on time. I took one final look in the mirror to make sure everything was in place. I thought, "I really am a handsome young man."

I didn't know if my rich fantasy life was the best thing for me because sometimes I thought I built up my imaginary sex life too much, which then didn't let me meet a real person. I spent too much time investing myself in someone that I hadn't even met yet, which is never a good thing. If Germaine wanted to introduce me to the A Gay crowd, then maybe I would meet a real live person there who would want to go out.

"Are you ready, sweetie? We've got to get going," Germaine yelled down the hall. I looked at my watch and didn't realize how much time had gone by. We loaded into the car and off we went. Gigi was in her boy clothes and was patiently waiting for us inside her apartment building lobby. She was someone who knew how to dress to impress.

"You look wonderful tonight," she said to me.

"Thank your boyfriend who got me coordinated tonight."

"He has such a good eye for fashion. Thank you, honey. You did a great job," Gigi said as she hugged Germaine. It was very sweet.

We arrived at the Burgundy Ball Room. There was already a line of gay men dressed in long pants and long sleeve dress shirts waiting to get in. God knows why, because the minute I got out of the car's air conditioning, I started to sweat. It was 90 degrees, for heaven's sake. They all had on their fake faces as they greeted everyone who came down the line and hugged and air-kissed. Germaine was no different. He did his sashay down the line until he found his friends, Kit and Biff. They had been holding our spots until we got there.

"It's about time," Kit said. "They are getting ready to open the doors soon. You do have the tickets right? Is this your protégé?"

"Kit and Biff, this is Desiree, also known as Tyler," Germaine said as he introduced me.

"It is a pleasure to meet you," I said.

"You didn't tell us how handsome he was out of drag. I'm Biff," he said as he stuck out his hand to shake. "A firm grip. I like that."

"You two skanks better be nice to him," Gigi said.

"I wouldn't have it any other way," Kit said. "Gigi, I see you have managed to cover up that hump on your back nicely."

"That hump managed to find its way into the front of my pants," Gigi said as she grabbed Kit's hand and pushed it up against her crotch.

"It feels like two rotten cantaloupes down there. That's what that smell must be, and I thought it was the cologne from all the sweaty bears here in line."

"How have you been, darling?" Gigi said as she hugged on Kit.

"Don't forget me," Biff said as he hugged Gigi. "It's been a long time since we've seen you. What have you been doing?"

"I have been working on our 'Bombshell' show at the club," she said.

"I haven't heard anything about the show. And here I didn't think you had a talented bone in your body," Kit said. "Even including that Vienna sausage you call a dick."

"Just for that I'm not putting you on the guest list. Plus it's not just me. Here's your star," Gigi said pointing to me.

"I've been telling you things about the show for weeks," Germaine said.

"But you're not hot like your little friend here," Kit said. "Put us down for two tickets for the next show."

It was very strange that they were talking about me, but not talking to me.

"Germaine, you've really upped your standing there," Biff said.

"Oh look, they're opening the doors. Thank God because I was beginning to melt out here," Kit said.

"Bitter doesn't melt," Gigi said, and they all laughed.

All I knew was I needed a drink.

"Are you guys talking about 'Smash'?" the person in line behind us asked.

"No, we are talking about 'Bombshell,' the show we are doing at Club Cabaret," Germaine said. "You need to come and see it."

"Are you Desiree from the show?" he asked.

"Yes, she is," Germaine said. "This is one talented entertainer."

"I didn't realize that was you. I caught the first performance. You were incredible," he said.

"Thank you," I said remembering my manners. "Tell your friends to come and see it."

"They already have tickets for the next show. I'll have to text them that I met you. Can I get a picture?" he asked.

"Sure you can," Germaine said, grabbing the guy's cell phone to take a picture and pushing me over next to him. I stood there and smiled and Germaine took several shots.

"Got to go, honey. The line is moving," Gigi said. "Give him back the phone and let's move."

"I need to buy you a cocktail when we are inside," the fan boy said.

We entered the theater. Germaine was right- the temperature in the lobby area was just about as bad as it was outside. It seemed like everyone went from one line outside straight into a line inside. This was the meet-and-greet line for Tornio, who was inside the ballroom already waiting to greet everyone.

"Do I have time to grab a drink?" I asked.

"No," was the resounding response from the entire group.

"You can get a drink after we get our photos," Germaine said. "Now remember to be very polite to Torino."

I didn't know what he thought I was going to do. I respected Torino for her talent because she put herself out there and made me laugh. As we entered the ballroom, we could see Tornio in all her glory standing there hugging and mugging for photos with everyone who wanted one. I was kind of surprised how personable she was. She made everyone feel right at home. On the show they never showed how generous a person she really was. It was incredible to learn this about her.

We finally got to the head of the line. We each introduced ourselves, Germaine had to expel my talents to her. "Torino, this is the next up and coming star out of Atlanta."

"What do you do, honey?" she asked.

"I'm currently in a show at Club Cabaret where I get to sing the life of Marilyn Monroe," I said.

"That sounds incredible. You aren't going to be one of those queens who is going to start putting out music, are you? Everyone from the 'Guys as Dolls Show' has a single or an album out."

"No plans for that yet," I said.

"Well keep working on your craft. It will keep you sharp as an entertainer," she said.

We all got a chance to take pictures with her and thank her for her time. Her handlers kept us moving because there was a huge line still waiting to get their turn with the entertainer.

Now that we were done, we could return to the bar in the lobby. I was mighty thirsty, and this was a great opportunity to people watch. I grabbed a drink and a spot on a very comfy couch while the rest of the group went to the restroom. As I looked around everyone was in their own clique. If anyone ever strayed from their group it was only to go over and air-kiss someone in another group. It was very strange behavior that I didn't understand.

The boys finally returned, and I had to ask, "Are these the A Gays?"

"A Gays?" Kit said like I had asked him why his vagina smelled like chicken of the sea.

"Sweetie, if you have to ask you are definitely not one," Biff replied.

"Is that like the Gay mafia?" I asked.

"No, that is completely different because the Gay mafia does not exist," Kit said. "Where did you find this one, Germaine?" he asked.

"They put on all the incredible parties that you will probably not be at," Biff said.

I felt like a shrinking violet at this point. I didn't know why Germaine was even friends with these two.

One of Germaine's former hotel co-workers came over to say hello. He was smartly dressed in a long-sleeve, denim, button-down shirt and a pair of tight pants that cupped his ass exquisitely. He was accessorized with a braided tan belt and sharp tan shoes. His outfit was perfectly put together. After he and Germaine exchanged pleasantries, he went back to his group of friends.

"I didn't know braided belts were back in. Or is he trying to make a fashion statement?" Biff quipped.

After what seemed like several hours of torture listening to these two assholes, the doors of the ballroom opened up for the general admission patrons to come in. As I watched them come in, I recognized several of them from the club who had been to my shows. I felt like these were my people coming in to rescue me. These were the beer drinking, shorts-wearing, rowdy boys and girls who were there for a good time. They weren't there to be seen, but instead to enjoy the show, since isn't that what this really was all about?

I got several shout-outs as Desiree, and I stood up to hug the people who came over to say hi to me. It was nice to be recognized out of drag.

"It seems we have misjudged you, my little princess," Kit said. "What show did you say you were performing in?"

"I'm doing Marilyn Monroe at Club Cabaret as a fundraiser," I said.

"So you're into charity work? That's very good to hear. Germaine, you may have a keeper here," Biff said.

"Gigi and Desiree here put together the show I've been telling you about. You really do need to come and see it," Germaine said.

"Get us tickets and we will be there," Kit said.

"I will put you on the list," Germaine said.

With that, the house lights flickered, telling us to get into our seats. I was glad I didn't have to listen to their whining anymore. It was time to sit back and laugh.

Torino put on an excellent show. I hadn't laughed that hard in a long time. Plus, she showed me what I could accomplish if I put my mind to it.

Once the show was over, I was very grateful to Germaine and thanked him for the tickets. I was glad that I didn't have to speak with those two boys anymore…or at least I thought.

# CHAPTER 50

The sold-out show went exactly as planned. The other contestants even showed up for this one, as word was getting out. Athena sat in a corner and looked like she had sucked on a lemon for the entire evening. It was nice to be congratulated by Miranda, Mary Jane, and Precious, whose words all came from the heart.

After the show Marni reminded me that the Pride Celebration was coming up this weekend and Club Cabaret was entering their float in the parade. It was mandatory for the contestants to participate in the parade, whether on the float or in some other form of transportation, but whatever you did, it had to include the club's name on it. Marni showed me the drawing of the float, which was really basic because it was a flatbed being pulled by an SUV with a sound system on it. It didn't look like there was anywhere to sit on it, and the parade route usually took an hour or more, which meant I would be in my heels and my feet were going to kill me. I guess it was time to consider some sensible shoes.

"Honey, I have a surprise for you," Germaine said. "I had these made up so that you can pass them out during the parade route." He pulled out a fan with my face on it. "On the front it is you and the back promotes the show. You can hand these out from the float because everyone needs a fan during the parade."

And he was right. Pride takes place at the end of June to

coincide with the Stonewall Riots in New York, and it is always extremely hot and humid in Piedmont Park, so these would be good to pass out. And during every Pride I was told to expect a thunderstorm to come ripping through the park at some point. Rain and drag queens don't make a pretty site.

"I can't believe you did this for me," I said as I hugged Germaine.

"You deserve it after all the hard work you have been putting in, and I want to make sure you stand out during the parade. I don't think the other girls are going to be doing anything on the float. I even got Kit and Biff to chip in for the cost."

Yuck. That meant I would have to be nice to the two of them next time I saw them. "That's great news," I said as I slightly vomited into my mouth.

"We already have the dress you should wear on the float to make you stand out even more. It will sparkle in the sun, and it is light enough for you to be comfortable in the heat. I put it in your closet at the apartment before I left for the show. I hope you don't mind. We thought we could get a little more involved in your campaign since you really don't have a manager helping you right now."

"Your help is truly appreciated," which it was since everyone else had abandoned me, and I was feeling overwhelmed by everything that I had to do for the contest. I was surprised that he kept referring to all three of them as we.

"We have a fitting planned for tomorrow morning so all three of us will be there to make sure everything works for the parade. We want to get you ready from head to toe."

"Pookie, it's time to leave Desiree alone. Can't you see she is exhausted from the show? You can talk more shop later," Miss Gigi said.

"You are right, darling. We can discuss this in the morning. Let's all get out of here.

As soon as I got back to the apartment, I went to the

closet to see what they had picked out for me. It was in a zipped-up garment bag which I gently removed from the closet and put on the bed. It was just like Christmas. I closed my eyes as the anticipation washed over me. I pulled the zipper down slowly, and as it parted, I was blinded by the sheer whiteness of the dress. I pulled it out of the bag and was dazzled by the sparkle that lit up my room. It was a white mini dress that was completely covered in plastic pearl shell circles that reflected light everywhere. The material was very light, so it was the perfect dress for the float since I didn't want to sweat like a pig and ruin all my makeup. I didn't see the shoes, so I guess I would get them when we did the fitting in the morning.

I gingerly put the dress back into its protective housing and hung it back in the closet. I was exhausted by this point, so I stripped naked and hopped into bed. I pulled the covers up to my neck and said a prayer. "Dear God, thank you for everyone in my life. I hope I can live up to all their expectations of me. Thank you for giving me the opportunity to help other people. Amen."

I drifted off to sleep. I immediately started having dreams about snowball fights and making snow angels. It was a glorious dream until Daisy Mae popped up yelling, "Be careful what you wish for! And don't eat yellow snow." I shot bolt upright in bed sweating. What did she mean? I lay back down, and eventually, after counting one hundred naked, men I fell back asleep. It was a restless sleep full of sheep and drag queens.

I woke up in the morning to the smell of bacon and coffee and voices coming from down the hallway. I could tell Kit and Biff were already here and chatting with Germaine, so I slipped out of bed, put on a t-shirt, and some sweat shorts, and headed down the hall.

"Ooowww, you look a little rough today," Kit said. "Little princess didn't sleep well last night?"

"But the show was wonderful, darling. I can see why people are taking about you. Germaine, thank you for the tickets," Biff said.

"May I have some orange juice?" I asked. I was still waking up and this was too much too early.

"Here you go. I'm going to get the dress so we can check the fitting," Germaine said.

"Yes, do, because I have places to be and people to do," Kit said.

As Germaine went and got the dress, Biff and Kit chatted privately to themselves, which was fine with me.

"Stand up, sweetie, and strip. I need to slip this over your head," Germaine said.

I followed orders and stood up and got rid of my clothes except for the underwear. Germaine pulled out the dress and slipped it over my head. It fit really well.

"Let me do some adjusting," Kit said as he started pulling on the dress in several places.

While pulling on the dress, Kit decided to pinch my nipples. I thought he was a creep, but this just proved it. Unfortunately, Germaine wasn't looking when it happened so I decided to keep my mouth shut. I didn't know what he saw in these people.

"This dress looks and feels great," Kit said as he ran his hand over my ass. Thank God I had underwear on.

"I want to thank you both for helping to get this and the fans. I'm sure I will be the hit on the float," I said.

"Remember, when you are on the float stand on the right side because as you go down the parade route, there are more people on the right. And as you go by the viewing stand on Tenth Street, wave to the crowd, because we will be sitting there with a bunch of our friends. They want to see the diva we have been telling them about. They all have money and are looking to make some donations to your cause," Biff finished.

"I sure will. Thanks again, but I've got to get ready for work. Hope you both have a great day." I shuffled down the hallway burying all of my disgust.

# CHAPTER 51

The staging area for the floats for Pride was at the Civic Station Marta Station. The road was closed off so that they could be lined up by category. The first group was the Dykes on Bikes, followed by the political groups and then the bar floats. After that, it was the numerous social groups and other organizations in the city. It was great to walk around all the floats and see all the creativity and all the happy faces. These floats put our float to shame. You would think a bunch of drag queens could have come up with something better for our float, which still wasn't here.

Moments later, our float arrived, and I was completely surprised at the presentation. Marni obviously had mislead us all with the float picture from before, because what rolled up in front of us was a multi-level rainbow explosion with Mylar streamers and pictures of each of us over our area of the float, which included a support post and velvet rope to make sure we didn't fall off onto the road. They had even installed a butt post that you could lean on if you got tired. The sound system was at the front right behind the SUV, so we could jam out while we were riding.

It was extremely cool to see my face blown up and blowing in the wind. On the side of the float by our stations, there were banners with our names and our charity names. Luckily, I was on the right side of the float with Miranda and Mary Jane. Anamia, Dixie and Precious were on the left side. But Athena was nowhere to be found listed. I finally asked

Marni where Athena was going to be, and all he had to do was point.

Athena was lying in the back of a stretch, cherry-red Lincoln convertible. That was the only thing that was cherry about that car since Athena had her hole punched more times than a hooker at a prison conjugal visit night. Her chauffer exited the car and opened the door for Athena to step out. She did look radiant in her red sequined dress and her six-inch stacked heels. She slowly sauntered over the rest of the contestants.

"I decided to roll with some grace and class, ladies. And I do use the term ladies loosely," she said. "Giles, where is my cocktail?"

"Coming, madam," he said as he brought over her martini on a silver tray.

Athena reached over with her gloved hand and lifted the drink and put it to her cherry lips. She was soaking in the attention as everyone around stopped to watch. She slowly took a sip and savored the flavor. "Excellent, Giles. Keep them coming." With a wave of her hand Giles was dismissed.

"Keep drinking those, bitch, and I'll be waiting for you to pee yourself during the parade," Precious said.

"No, no, no dear. I have more couth than that. I'm sorry you had to do that in that trailer you were raised in," she said.

Precious took off her earrings and gave them to me. "Hold these, please," she said as she started removing her heels. "Hell no! No one talks to me like that. I'm going to kick your ass."

"Ladies, this is supposed to be a happy day of unity," Marni said. "Athena go back to your vehicle. The rest of you, there is a ladder for you to climb up onto the float. I want everyone to get into their places." Begrudgingly, Precious took her earrings back and carried her heels as she heeded to the float.

"I'm glad that skank isn't riding with us. It will be more

fun for the rest of us with her in her own little world," Mary Jane said. "And isn't she supposed to have the name of the club somewhere on the vehicle?"

"It's coming," I said as Marni rolled out the Athena banner that was being strapped on to the trunk of the car.

"At least they put it in the right place," Miranda said. "On her ass. Oh, I'm sorry, I got that and the trunk of the car confused. They both have a lot of junk going on."

We all kept our sense of humor about the situation and decided to ignore Athena.

Everyone got into their positions, but there was no sign of Anamia. We were all getting a little concerned since she wasn't in the best of health. After several questions on the topic. Marni finally made the announcement that Anamia wasn't going to be on the float. She had accidentally swallowed a breath mint and went into hypoglycemic shock or something else very similar, but was going to be fine. It sucked that she wouldn't be here, but at least she would be well.

"That's more room for me to work this dump," Dixie said. "You girls stay on your side of this floating trash heap and I'll stay on mine."

"Let's get something straight right now, miss thing. You cross this line into my territory, and I will make you fly so fast your head will be spinning by the time Athena's car runs you over," Precious said. "Why do all of you want to get on my last gay nerve this afternoon?"

"Yes ma'am," Dixie said.

It was going to be a fun day, I could already tell. I saw that none of the other contestants had anything to pass out. Germaine was late in getting here with the fans. I knew it was always a bitch trying to find parking in this city, especially when there is a big event like this and the roads are blocked off.

I saw a familiar-looking figure in the distance coming from the Marta Station pulling a wagon. I looked as he got closer and indeed it was Germaine with a little red wagon with boxes. He rolled his way over to the float.

"I thought it would be easier to pass the fans out if I was on the side of the float. Here are a couple of boxes for you and some sun block. Make sure you spray it on, otherwise you will burn to a crisp in the sun," he said as he passed the items up to me. The boxes were already open, so I grabbed one and started fanning myself, since the temperature was rising quickly and we weren't even moving yet. I grabbed the huge sun block spray-can and hosed my arms down, since that was the only exposed skin. Between make-up, hose, and hair, there wasn't much to cover, but it was the thought that counted.

The final passengers for the float arrived. It was a gaggle of the club boys in Speedos and tennis shoes ready to shake their asses for the ride. You could tell they had already been partying, since they were all extremely friendly. Here was my chance to get some helpers for the parade. "Boys, do any of you have any sun-block lotion?" I asked. They all looked at me and shrugged no. "I'll make you a deal. If you help me pass these fans out I will cover you in sun-block spray. Do we have a deal?"

Of course they all said yes and grabbed a handful of fans as I hosed them down from head to toe in sun-block spray. It smelled like a giant Pina Colada party on the float now. It was nice to rub the lotion onto several of the boys' tight, toned bodies. They liked the attention as much as I liked giving it to them. My favorite was Marty, with the big box and furry chest. He had to be about my age and he kept hanging close to me. This could really be a fun ride.

And much to my surprise, in the fan box was a sport drink bottle from Germaine, of course filled with screwdrivers. I was starting to like this. The boys hugged up to me to get their fans. I even had a couple of them fanning me while we were sitting still. Unfortunately, there was no breeze coming down the street, but they were keeping my makeup from melting off.

The parade must have been starting because the Dykes

on Bikes were firing up their motorcycles and started racing up and down Peachtree. It was extremely loud, but very soon they were far enough down the street that you couldn't hear them.

"Alright ladies," Marni said. "This ship is leaving port." We started to ease our way into the parade line. Once we did, the DJ fired up the system. It was appropriate that the first song he played was Jennifer Lopez's "Let's Get Loud." I've always loved that song and it was so fitting for today. It made everyone shake their ass, and I got to bump booty with Marty. He had such a tight ass and I was wondering if he was a shower or a grower.

"Have you ever fucked a drag queen?" I asked.

"Once," he said. "I was extremely drunk, and it was a very weird situation. Once her clothes were off, he was a very sexy man. I'm sure if I got those clothes off of you there probably beats the heart of a tiger under all of that."

"Rawr," I said as a made a cat paw swipe at Marty. He laughed, thank God. I didn't know how serious he was or if it was the cocktails talking, but I wouldn't mind letting him take me out for a ride.

Peachtree Street was lined with the masses who came out to watch and get a glimpse of the participants. A lot of them poured out of the restaurants from brunch, which is every gay person's favorite thing to do on a weekend. Get some drinks. Throw some shade. Heaven.

As we rolled up Peachtree Street, we came to the holy-roller bunch. These supposed Christians were there with their signs saying "God Hates Fags!" and "Burn in Hell." Better yet, they had a PA system set up where they could broadcast their hate to everyone under the guise of trying to save our souls. The sad part was they had a little three year-old girl holding up one of the signs. This really proved that hate is taught at home, because this little girl had no idea what the sign said or meant.

All the politicians on the talk shows keep saying the Christians are being persecuted for their religious beliefs, but these holy rollers proved the fact that there is Christian persecution going on, because if you don't agree with their beliefs then they are going to abuse and condemn you. What they don't realize is how bad they really look spouting the hate. We don't show up at their events and spout hate at them for their beliefs.

"Little boy dressed as a girl, don't you know you are hurting God by your abhorrent behavior?" the minister said through the PA.

I really wasn't sure whom he was talking to, so I pointed to myself, to which he replied, "Yes, you in the dress. God didn't intend for you to wear women's clothing. You need to turn to God and ask for his forgiveness," the bigot yelled.

My only response was, "I did invoke God's name last night as my boyfriend was shoving his nine inch cock up my ass. Oh God. Oh God," as I gyrated my ass back and forth, but the float kept moving so I didn't get a chance to hear his response. Plus he had already moved onto his next target in the parade.

"I thought you didn't have a boyfriend," Marty said.

"I don't. It was the first thing that popped into my head. They sound as bad as my mother," I said.

"For me it's my father. He hasn't come to grips with me being gay yet, so it makes it difficult to go home and visit," he said.

"I'm sorry to hear that."

"It's all good. I still love him, and I realize it may just take some time for things to change," he said.

"That's a great attitude. I need to keep that in mind when I deal with my mother," I said.

Germaine was keeping up pace and passing out fans as he went. Every person he gave a fan to stayed in the procession and walked behind him. My little fan boys were doing their job as they would shove a fan in their Speedos for someone in the crowd to come and pull out. It was weird seeing my face sticking out of someone's crack. At least it was a great picture of me so I didn't mind.

It was nice having people scream my name and running up to the float to have their picture taken with me. "I loved your show," I heard from several people, which was even better since it was a labor of love. I even had a couple of people bring me Jell-O shots for the ride. It was an incredibly festive ride with lots of positive energy flowing both ways.

It was great having Marty with me. He didn't mind if I hugged on him and squeezed him tight. He was just a really nice guy and he smelled great. Just like the beach.

The girls were all civil on the float. I think that's because each of us had our own cheering section along the route with friends popping up everywhere.

As the parade progressed, I noticed there was my fan brigade all following behind Germaine, fanning their selves with my face. After a while, the fan brigade started spreading out, and before I knew it, they had surrounded Athena's car. I glanced at her, and she did not look too happy. The parade route was full of stops and starts for the entire two hours, and every time her car stopped, the fan brigade stopped with her and stayed exactly where they were.

Finally, Athena had enough. "Giles, stop this car right now!" she screamed.

"Miss Athena, please remember where you are. There are cameras everywhere," Giles said.

"I don't give a fuck," she snapped back. "Listen up, all you ass fucks. I suggest you get the hell away from my car before I step off and kick your ass. Don't think that I won't do it."

I leaned down to Germaine and asked, "Who are all these people?"

"They are friends of Kit and Biff. It is good to have friends in the A Gays," he said. "They sent an email out to their list of friends asking them to run interference on Athena, since she is your biggest competition."

As much as I loathed them, I thought it was pretty generous of them to do that for me. I looked back to see

Athena trying to grab fans out of the fan brigades' hands. It became a game of keep away with Athena in the middle, not able to reach the fans raised high over the boys' heads. I watched her jump in her heels and scream at the top of her lungs, but the group wasn't fazed. The best part was watching everyone film it on their cell phones. I could hardly wait to see these videos posted.

"Who is that?" Marty asked.

"That is just my biggest competition for the crown," I said.

"Why do you want the crown?" he asked.

"I don't know anymore," I admitted. "It started because it looked pretty, and it was a way to meet people. Then I realized I could do something good for other people. I committed to the contest, and I will see it to the end. I would rather see your end," I said.

"Baby, you can see that anytime. I would rather show you the front sometime. Where is your phone?" he asked.

I pulled my cell out of my purse, popped in the password to open it up, and handed it to him. The next thing I knew he put it in picture mode, pulled open his Speedos, and took a picture of his dick. Then he dialed a number. "That is my cell number. Save it when you get a chance." He then handed me back the phone, turned, and started gyrating to the music again.

I got so distracted that I forgot about the drama with Athena. I looked and she was back in the car as the parade was moving along. She looked extremely disheveled as she was trying to relax in the backseat. Fortunately for, her the fan brigade dispersed as we came closer to the viewing stand as the crew started passing out fans to everyone they could. Marty snuggled up to me as we waved to the viewing stand. I could see Kit and Biff about half way up, and they were waving back.

This is what Pride should be about. A community coming together to celebrate our differences, but all committed to making the community stronger. It included the roller-skater boys, the lesbians, the marching band and flag corps, the politicians, the transgender community, the bears, the muscle boys, the athletes, the volunteers, and just everyone. There were people, flags, and floats as far as I could see up and down Peachtree Street.

The float rolled over the new rainbow crosswalks at the corner of Tenth Street and Piedmont. Here was where the crowd was the largest and the most festive. They all screamed and cheered as the floats went by as the music filled the streets. The cocktails had been flowing and a large group of the sweaty men here all had their shirts off. It was a pretty sight to see.

The time had come for us to exit the float, since we were at the end of the parade. Marni was there waiting for us with the ladder to exit down. "It was great riding with you," I said to Marty.

"You've got my number. Give me a call sometime," he said as he hugged me goodbye. It was wonderful watching his tight ass walk away with the rest of the Speedo boys.

"Germaine, you must be exhausted. I can't thank you enough for walking the route and passing out the fans."

"At least the wagon got lighter as the parade route went along," he said.

I hugged him and we started walking back up the hill of Tenth Street. We needed to get to his car so that we could get home. My feet were killing me, and I needed to get out of this dress and into some boy clothes.

Half-way up Tenth Street, we ran into Biff and Kit. "Great performance today on the float," Kit said. "But you do not need to be seen hugging on that trailer trash who was on the float with you. We need to find you a boyfriend to improve your image."

"He was nice," I said.

"That is beside the point," Biff said. "If you want to become an A Gay, you need to be seen hanging out in the company of quality people. That is not quality. The people we were sitting with in the viewing stand are quality people.

They are the decision makers in this city, and you need to meet them."

"Boys, thank you so much for your support. We are both pretty beat, so we are heading home," Germaine said.

"Not yet," Kit said. "You need to make an appearance at Toby and Keith's party. It's only up the block at Myrtle Street. We want to introduce you since you are the up and coming star."

"Come on, sweetie. We'll stop in and have a drink. Then we can head home," Germaine almost pleaded.

"Just one," I said.

We marched up the street, turned left on Myrtle, and we were there. The house had a gracious front porch that was draped in a ton of men. The minute we came up the front walk, I could hear people calling out my name. It was a very nice welcome. We left the wagon parked on the front lawn and Germaine held my hand as he helped me up the front steps. I could hear Biff and Kit telling everyone who I was. I think I was their talking point for the party.

As we entered the great hall, you could see the bar set up in the kitchen. We made a beeline straight for the bar and the hot bartender, who was formally dressed with a pressed white shirt, black pants, a bow tie, and a vest.

"What may I serve you?" he asked.

"A screwdriver for the lady, and I will have a Manhattan," Germaine ordered.

"Coming up, sir. Would the lady have a choice of vodka?" he asked me.

"I would like Deep Eddy," I said. Deep Eddy vodka was the sponsor for one of the benefits where I performed, and it didn't give me a headache the next day. Always a plus when you're drinking.

He poured our cocktails into real glasses and served them to us with a cocktail napkin. I hadn't seen anything this formal in my life except on TV. I could get used to this.

"Enjoy," he said.

We strolled around the party as Kit and Biff introduced

me to everyone. It was a little awkward that they didn't introduce Germaine, but I made sure everyone knew he was my friend. I felt like I was pressing hands and kissing babies. I should have been running for an office, but I was running to be Miss Club Cabaret.

We stayed longer than I wanted to, but we finally made our escape. I was beat as we headed up the block to the car. All I wanted was a shower and my warm bed. We turned the corner at Piedmont and headed up to Twelfth Street. I looked ahead and I could see Marjorie and the boys laughing and walking up the street on the other side. I missed them, but they were no longer part of my life. We turned up Twelfth and loaded the wagon into the car. Home James was all I wanted.

# CHAPTER 52

Athena's Miss Firecracker Pageant on July 4th was one of her big fundraisers. It was being held at a private home off of Elizabeth Anne Street with a pool, which was a perfect setting for the glitz and glamour she promised.

Germaine said he would tag along with me, but for this event, I chose to go incognito as myself so as not to draw attention from the girls who were competing for the title. I didn't think it would be fair to show up in drag to a drag pageant that I wasn't in. We had a free weekend away from Kit and Biff, as they were on their way to Fire Island, no doubt to screw their brains out. They kept encouraging me to have a slut phase, which I didn't think I was ready for. I was having a hard time finding just one person to have a slut phase with. I had texted Marty after the parade, but so far nothing back yet. Oh well. On to the next one, whenever that would come around.

We headed up Sheridan, but when we got to Elizabeth Anne, the cul-de-sac was already jammed with cars, which forced us to park in the parking lot of the closed camera store and walk the block and a half back to the house. I just couldn't believe there were that many people here for this. She must have been making a killing off of this fundraiser. I knew she was charging the girls $50 to enter the pageant and they had six contestants. The cover charge at the door was $10. I was afraid to see how many people she had here. I had to remember it was a competition, and we were all raising money for our charities.

We strolled up to the side gate, which was the entrance to the pageant, and paid our entry fee like everyone else. The setting was gorgeous with the landscaped backyard and expansive patio surrounding the kidney-shaped pool. There were half-naked men soaking in the last rays of light, lying around the patio sipping cocktails. As it turned out, Athena and her supporters had gotten several margarita slushy machines to provide for the guests, which made the mood very festive.

The dressing room for the show was the two-car garage, which was to the right of the pool. It had a door that came right out to the patio by the pool, which made it easy to enter and exit the performing area. They had even built a runway over the pool to the other side so the girls could work the entire crowd. There was a DJ booth, a great sound system, and even a spotlight, since the show didn't start until it was getting dark which wouldn't be until around 9:00. This production was very well thought out.

We worked our way up the stairs of the two-tier deck so that we could get our free cocktails. From up here, we had a great view of the whole party. It was really starting to pack out. I was hoping the deck was built to support this much weight. I could see it on the news now. "Drag queens killed by collapsing deck. News at 11." Once upstairs, I ran into Mary Jane out of drag. She came out to check the competition, which she usually didn't do, but it was great to see her.

"You usually don't come to these things. What brought you out tonight?"

"One of my friends, Heather Lockless, is competing in the pageant. He doesn't take this too seriously, so that's why he wanted to do this show. He figured he'd get a few laughs out of it. Oh, and take a look at this."

With that, she pulled out a flyer and handed it to me. One of the contestants had printed up flyers and passed them out to everyone she knew. In big headlines, it said

"Free Alcohol,"

"This is why it's so packed," Mary Jane said. "Otherwise it wouldn't be so nuts."

"Does Athena know about this?"

"If she didn't, I'm sure she knows by now. From what I have been able to learn, she's holed up in the garage with the contestants still putting on her face. I hope they are surgically sewing on a new one because the one she has looks like she got hit in the face with a sack of oranges."

We all laughed.

"Time to relax," Mary Jane said as she pulled out a joint and lit it up. "Do you want a hit?"

"No thanks. Every time I drink and smoke pot, it makes me puke. I'll stick with the free drinks. Germaine, would you like a hit?"

"Yes, please. I thought you would never ask," he said.

So all three of us had great spots along the railing watching everything unfold below us.

"Are you Desire and Mary Jane?" a very thin twink asked.

"Why, yes we are," Mary Jane said.

"May I get you two a cocktail? I've enjoyed both your shows and want to say I appreciate all you do for the charities."

"You are welcome," I said. "I would love a screwdriver, and for Mary Jane, a margarita please."

"Yes ma'am," he said as he made his way over to the bar.

"When did I slip into the ma'am territory?" I asked Mary Jane.

"Don't worry, honey. To him, everyone is a ma'am. You look fabulous just the way you are."

We still hadn't seen Athena yet, but I did see Dixie Monroe pop up all of a sudden and with a photographer in tow. She was in full high-whore drag, which she could do even thought this wasn't one of her events. We watched her as she went from one hot man to the next. She would sit down with them for a minute, and then her photographer would pull out a clip board with something on it for them to sign. Once they all signed, Dixie and the photographer corralled them all together and started posing them in different positions around the party. He would then snap a ton of shots of the men individually and then in pairs. It was all very erotic as they were posed pressing their bodies as close together as possible with only their thin swimsuits protecting their penises from rubbing together. I had no idea what she was doing.

Mary Jane texted one of her friends on the patio level and asked them to find out what was going on. We watched as he went over to a cluster of the models and asked what they were taking the pictures for. He chatted with them briefly, then we saw him text. Within a second, we heard the ding on Mary Jane's phone. She read us the text.

"Shooting for a calendar that will be a wallpaper for the computer. She is selling them to raise funds for her charity. That's a big no no against the rules."

I agreed, but since we didn't like either Dixie or Athena, we didn't say or do anything. The photo session dragged on as the photographer got creative with the positioning of the models and pulled out some props. He had a shamrock for March and a Santa hat for December. They were going about their business until we all heard the garage door slam open.

Athena stood there in her regal Fourth-of-July themed-dress with a headdress that appeared to be three feet tall. She stopped and posed so that everyone could see her before she slowly started walking to the runway over the pool. She moved very elegantly. As the light struck her headdress, it sent sparkles all around the party. All hell didn't break loose until she set foot on the other side of the pool.

"You fucking cunt!" she yelled.

Dixie, who wasn't paying any attention to Athena, turned her head very slowly and replied, "I knew you were coming by the earth tremors I felt. They were so heavy they caused me to orgasm."

"What the hell are you doing here, you bitch?" Athena

said surprisingly calmly. I thought her head would have exploded by now. "The rules state that no contestant can work another contestant's event, and that's exactly what you are doing."

"The rules?" Dixie said. "When the hell do you play by the rules? You truly didn't do that in any pageant we were in. You screwed so many of the judges, I thought you would have left a snail trail behind you for weeks or your intestines would have fallen out right there on the stage."

"At least I didn't look like afterbirth on the stage."

"I have to thank you for putting the red spots on my evening gown where my vagina was. It looked like I had gotten my period. Luckily, one of the judges had a fetish for that and scored me higher than you."

"That's the only time you ever beat me in a category. I've got the crowns to prove it. And what have you got? You got the loser roses and the plaques that said you were first runner up. That is all you will ever be to me. The first place loser and my lackey. You aren't even worth being my lap dog, you bitch."

Dixie sat there for about one second looking over at Athena. She stood up very slowly and composed herself. By this time, every eye in the place was staring at the two of them, but it was all choreographed to a thumping beat, which was very strange. She walked straight up to Athena and never said a word. Next thing we saw was Dixie's right palm slapping Athena across the face, causing her head to snap. Needless to say, Athena wasn't expecting it from the look on her face. Before you knew it, she slapped Dixie right back, snapping her head back. Dixie recovered and threw another slap striking Athena across the face again. Athena returned the favor slapping Dixie across the face.

Dixie finally clenched her fists and let out a primal scream as she lunged at Athena, catching her off guard as they both tumbled back onto the runway. It looked like two rats fighting over a day-old biscuit as they rolled back and forth up and down the runway with wigs and shoes flying everywhere. Athena's headdress slowly floated to the bottom of the pool as Dixie's wig ended up floating like a dead rat. All you could hear was muffled grunts and they rolled and rolled.

Eventually, members from each fan club came up and pulled the two apart. There was no Marni here to stop this show. Dixie's photographer was helping her off the ground and started dusting her off. Athena was able to regain her composure as she got back to her feet. "Please remove this trash," she said as she pointed to Dixie.

"You don't have to remove me. We are leaving," Dixie said as she grabbed her purse and hobbled out on her one good shoe. Her photographer reached down and grabbed the floating wig, which left a trail of water droplets as they headed out the gate.

The crowd stood there silent until Athena yelled, "Haven't you ever seen a wounded duck waddle around?" Everyone laughed and the moment of drama had passed. Athena went back into the garage dressing room to clean up and the DJ announced over the beats that show time was in five minutes. Not bad for ten bucks. A wrestling match and a drag show.

Once the show started, it moved along swiftly and professionally for a backyard show. It was full of glitz and glamour as promised. It was very interesting to watch because I had never seen any of the contestants perform anywhere before. Mary Jane said that this was most of the girls' first time ever competing for a title and that they usually just did drag for fun.

Her friend, Heather Lockless, did great in presentation, but then it came time for talent. Heather was a skinny girl who put in some padding to give her some curves, so she looked great. But she decided to do a song that wasn't that well-known-"Put Your Hands On Me," by Sinead O'Connor. Most people knew Sinead from her Prince cover of "Nothing Compares 2 U," but after that, they had no idea of what her music sounded like. Heather got out there and really worked the runway and patio, but she just didn't generate many tips. In this pageant, you got bonus points based on your tips, and since it was a fundraiser, it really helped Athena out for the contest. The crowd clap at the end was more of a golf clap instead of a roar. I remember that feeling from my first couple of performances and how that feeling passed as I got a little more practice.

The pageant finished up with the evening gown portion. The gowns were beautiful. I wouldn't have minded having a couple of them for my wardrobe since I thought I could do them some justice.

The places were announced and Heather Lockless finished in the middle of the pack. "Not bad for a first time out," Mary Jane said. "Enjoy the rest of the holiday. I'm out." Mary Jane gave Germaine and me hugs and headed down to congratulate her friend.

"This was very interesting," Germaine said.

"What do you mean?"

"There was nobody here I knew. We must have been at the wrong party."

"At least you had a good time. That's what's important," I said. "Time to go home."

As we headed to the car, we could hear the fireworks from Westfield Mall going off in the background.

# CHAPTER 53

Kit and Biff kept true to their threat to fix me up on a date. It was a blind date. I had never gone on a blind date before, so I wasn't sure what to expect. Biff gave me Robert's number and I called him up. He was very nice and polite on the phone and we agreed to meet for dinner and drinks and see how the night would progress from there.

"Robert is a very nice boy and he comes from money," Germaine said. "His family is very connected in banking up in Tennessee."

"Are you sure he is right for me? It sounds like we have nothing in common."

"Just remember to be yourself and have a good time. It's just dinner. If you have a great time, even better, but if you don't, then you have only lost an evening of your time. It's not like you are interviewing to be the boyfriend of someone who isn't very well off."

"How do I look?"

"You look splendid. I see everything I picked out fits you to a 'T.'"

He was right. He had picked out my entire outfit even down to the shoes, which were a little more formal than I usually was. Robert suggested meeting at Franco's, an Italian restaurant on Cheshire Bridge Road. "I like Italian," he said. The food was excellent so it should be a good time. I just needed to remember to be myself.

"Just remember to not get anything on your shirt,"

Germaine said as I headed out the door. I was already nervous and didn't need the extra pressure of getting stains all over my clothes. I think Germaine even had my dress shirt pressed and starched, which chafed my neck a little.

It was a quick drive over to the restaurant and there was ample parking. Robert had said he would meet me out front, and when I turned the corner of the building, I could see a very handsome gentleman at the entrance. He fit the description - medium build, sandy hair, little taller than me, and really well put together. I headed his way and before I could say anything, he said, "Tyler?"

"Yes, it's a pleasure meeting you," as I shook his hand. He had a very firm grip and his skin felt very soft. He smelled fantastic.

"I made a reservation for us and got a table on the patio. Is that good with you?" he asked.

The patio was covered and glassed off. There was even a window unit A/C, so the room was quite cool even though it was the middle of July. It was very romantic with black table clothes, white linen napkins, candles on every table and soft Italian music in the background. The waiter led us over to a table. Robert, being the gentleman he was, pulled out my chair for me. So far bonus points for him.

"Would either of you care for something from the bar?" the waiter asked.

"May we see the wine list, please?" Robert asked.

The waiter gave him the list. Robert quickly perused the list and made the decision for both of us. "Two glasses of your Cakebread Chardonnay, please."

"Good choice. I'll be right back with your drinks.

"I hope I wasn't too forward," Robert said. "I thought a little wine would relax us both."

"You are being a perfect gentleman. I have to admit I am a little nervous since I've never been on a blind date before."

"Don't worry. I've had several blind dates, and they can be a lot of fun. Why aren't you dating anyone?"

I thought that was a little forward since we had just met,

but I decided to give him an answer. "I just haven't met the right person yet. It's hard with working and doing the contest to really meet anyone. Most of the people I meet know me as Desiree and have no idea who Tyler is. Plus, have you ever tried to get a date when you're in drag?"

The heads at the table next to us quickly spun around.

"So you are Desiree," the gentleman said. "I enjoyed the show very much. You have a great voice. I'm trying to get more friends to come to the next one. Keep up the good work."

"That is very sweet of you," I said. "Please have your friends come. It is for a good cause."

"That was a little rude," Robert said.

"It is fine. I appreciate that people get what the show is about. That is the greatest compliment I could get."

"So back to me now. Where were we at? Oh yes, I can honestly say I do not know how me doing drag would go. I've never done drag. Not even for Halloween," he said.

Since he asked I, figured it would be a fair question back, "Why are you still single?"

"I work a lot, and I like to travel, and just haven't found anyone that I feel compatible with. Friends tell me that I'm a little too picky. I just tell them I know what I am looking for."

"And what are you looking for?"

"Someone I can have a conversation with. There are too many men out there who only want to fuck. I like sex as much as the next person, but I want someone who is intelligent, funny, and creative. That's why Biff thought we would be a great fit. He told me how much of your time and energy you poured into your show. I really need to come and check it out."

"You need to. Just let me know the date, and I can put you on the guest list."

"It's nice to know someone in such a high place. I will definitely come and check it out."

The waiter returned with our wine and a special shot.

"This drink is for you from the boys in the corner. When they heard it was you, they wanted to let you know how much they enjoyed the show. It is a shot of cowboy cocksucker."

"Tell them thank you very much." I downed the shot and waved thank you.

"I see you really are a popular girl," Robert said.

"I didn't think people would recognize me this much out of drag."

"Neither did me."

We both took a sip of our wine, and Robert took the opportunity to order some Calamari Fritti, which I had never had before. "What is calamari?"

"It is deep fried squid cut up. Be adventurous and try something new. It tastes a lot better than it sounds. It is one of my favorite items here. I promise you will love it. Some other great items here are the Veal Parmigiana, the shrimp in wine sauce, the Italian crab cakes, and the chicken with capers."

The conversation continued to flow at a rapid pace, but most of it was coming from Robert. I think I had heard his entire life story before the appetizer arrived. It was hard to get a word in edge-wise. I was hoping he was as nervous as I was and maybe that was why his mouth was running a mile a minute.

Our waiter served the calamari with the marinara on the side. It looked good. I'd always enjoyed fried food, so hopefully this would be no different. I took my fork and scooped a couple of pieces off the plate and took the spoon and piled some marina on top. I tried to stab the calamari with my fork, but it seemed a little rubbery, which I wasn't expecting. I tried it again and succeeded on my second attempt. I could feel Robert's eyes on me as I lifted the fork. I put the piece into my mouth, and at first, all I could taste was the marina, which was very good, but when I bit down all I could feel was something rubbery in my mouth. I felt like someone was playing a trick on me. I tried chewing it some more, but it wasn't getting any better. I finally gave up and spit it back out onto my fork. This was not my most ladylike moment.

"Didn't like it? For some it is an acquired taste. I'm sure it tastes different from the fries and onion rings you are used to."

I wasn't quite sure how to take that comment, so I decided to let it slide by. "I think it is a texture thing. I don't like mushrooms either, but that has a lot to do with them being kind of rubbery also."

"I love mushrooms. Especially stuffed mushrooms. You don't know what you are missing."

The rest of our food was excellent so this was a good choice. Robert even surprised me by picking up the tab.

"I have some friends who are having a get together, and I would love to take you over there and introduce you. Nothing big. Would you be interested?"

"That would be lovely." It was early so I might as well enjoy my time off.

"They live just down the street. You can either ride with me or follow me over there. Your choice."

"I better follow you in case you want to stay out past my bedtime."

"Don't worry. I wouldn't let you stay out past your bedtime. My bedtime is probably earlier than yours."

He was driving a Lincoln MKZ hybrid, which meant nothing to me when he described his car, so he finally said to follow his silver car. So I hopped into my car and followed him from the parking lot. He wasn't kidding because his friend's home was just down the street on Welbourne. There were more cars here than I was expecting for a small get together. I just parked at the end of the line of cars along the curb, hopped out of the car, and walked up the block to where Robert was waiting for me in front of a very sprawling contemporary. I didn't see Robert's car so I wasn't sure where he ended up parking.

"You think this is impressive, wait till you see the inside."

He held my hand as we headed up the walk way and into the party. This small gathering turned out to be over a hundred people. "I thought you said this was nothing big."

"This isn't anything big. His last party was over two hundred people. Come on, I want to introduce you to some people." Again, he took me by the hand as we mingled among the crowd.

"Artimis, this is my friend, Tyler. You might know him better as Desiree from 'Bombshell,'" he said.

"That was you in the show? I saw it and thought it was brilliant. Robert, you finally brought someone not as boring as yourself. Tell me, Tyler, how do you get yourself prepared to sing live? It is just so different from what the other girls are doing out there. Where are my manners? Let me get you a cocktail."

Artimis had the server bring over a tray of drinks, one of which one was a screwdriver, so I was very happy as we settled into his overstuffed couches. On one side of me I had Artimis, and on the other was Robert who decided to rest his hand on my thigh.

"I have some vocal exercises that I run through before every show," I said. "I met with a vocal coach who gave me pointers on my voice and how to breathe while I sing. It really helps. She also put some of them on a CD so that I wouldn't forget them and could practice along with them."

"You sounded beautiful. The entire cast did. I enjoyed it so much that I'm sure I'll be coming back for a second helping," he said. "Robert, have you seen the show yet?"

"No, Artimis. I have not yet, but it is on my list."

"Not surprising, sweetie. You need to get out there and experience the culture this city offers," he said as he turned back to me. "I hate it when people say they are bored in this city. There is always so much to do and so much to see."

We sat there for a while as Artimis dished the dirt on many of the party-goers. "I think these people only hang with me because of my trust fund," he said. "It is the cross I bear, but there are a handful of people here who would come if I needed them and said bring a shovel with no questions asked. Come on, let me give you a tour of the house. My idiot contractor just finished all the renovations so this is the house warming party. Come on, Robert, you can come too."

Again, Robert grabbed my hand as Artimis led us from room to room, extolling the virtue of marble over granite and pointing out all the architectural details. I didn't mind Robert holding my hand. It was nice to feel wanted.

Along the way, I met so many people my head was spinning. Robert kept introducing me as his friend Desiree from "Bombshell," which was great because he was helping spread the word about my show. If all of his friends showed up, that would be one sellout with very little work involved.

Artimis led us to the back screened-in deck that overlooked his in-ground pool. There were people milling about as the servers circulated with drinks, making sure everyone's libation was overflowing. "It took me a year to get this house just right," he said. "The former owner had tried to do some things, but didn't succeed very well. Thank God they had the intelligence to not screw it up too badly."

Our conversation got interrupted by one of the servers who whispered something into Artimis' ear. "If you will excuse me there's a catering emergency in the kitchen. Darling, this is Tyler," Artimis said to the server. "He is a special guest here tonight so please get him another screwdriver and keep his drinks flowing all night. He deserves them for putting up with Robert. Enjoy yourselves. I'm sure I will see you later. Robert, this one's a keeper." Artimis winked at me and off he went.

I was starting to get a little chilly and overwhelmed by everyone around me. I think Robert sensed that as he put his arm around my shoulder. "Do you want to go to my place for a night cap?"

"Sure."

Robert led me through the party and we said our final goodbyes. I only got a chance to wave goodbye to Artimis, who looked deep in conversation but managed to wave back.

"Let me get my car, and I will follow you," I said once we were out front. "Where are you parked?"

All Robert did was point to the house next door. "I'm right there," he said pointing to his house, which was a two-story traditional with a garage. That's why I couldn't see his car.

I felt safe because if anything did happen, I could always run back over to the party plus in the front window I could see a small dog staring out at us. It started barking as we got closer to the door. "That's Eubie, my little child."

Robert opened the door and Eubie about wet himself. "He is very excitable, so I need to let him out before he gets any attention, otherwise he will wet the floor. Come on in and make yourself comfortable on the couch." Robert went to the back of the house and let the dog out. I got to sink into the comfy couch, which faced a mammoth flat screen. On the coffee table were some table books. I started thumbing through the one that had photographs of the naked male form. These men were sexy and beautiful. I knew my body would never be in as good a shape as theirs were.

"I see you have a good eye. They were all shot by a local photographer. What would you like?"

"A screwdriver please."

"Coming right up." And off he went to the kitchen. "Turn on the TV if you like. It's the small remote on the left."

I grabbed the remote and hit the power button. It drove me nuts when people had ten remotes for their TV, cable, and sound system. I just hoped I got the right one. The screen fired up, but instead of your regular programming it was an X-rated channel showing two naked men going at it. I was extremely surprised and dropped the remote onto the floor. When it hit the ground, the volume went up and all I could hear was the heated moans coming from the surround sound with the occasional "fuck me hard." I quickly grabbed the remote off the floor and started pushing buttons. Damn remotes.

"What's all the commotion out here?" Robert asked coming with two drinks in hand. "I didn't know it was that kind of an evening." He grabbed the remote and quickly muted the TV.

I think I was turning a bright shade of red as I could feel the heat radiating from my face. "I'm so sorry. I just turned it on and that's what was on."

"Don't worry, I was just enjoying some extracurricular activities earlier and didn't realize I had left the channel on," he said as he sat down beside me without turning the channel off. "Take a sip of your cocktail. I'm sure that will help calm you down."

I grabbed the screwdriver and chugged most of it down. I was kind of embarrassed, but I was also turned on by the video. Robert slid up closer beside me on the couch and started rubbing his hand on my thigh. Here was a rich hot guy hitting on me, and it was a huge turn on.

Robert turned and looked directly into my eyes. "Tyler, you are a very handsome man. I know it is only our first date, but I really want to kiss you."

I didn't waste any time as I leaned in and kissed him. He reached up and grabbed my head on both sides and pulled me to him for a real kiss. It was all lips and tongue and it made me stiff as a board. I reached down to feel Robert's package and it was at full attention. Robert hit the volume button and the room was filled again with the sound of sweaty men pounding each other's asses. He started unbuttoning my shirt slowly, one button at a time. Each time he popped a button, he would rub on my nipples, making me edge even more. He finally reached the last button and then gently pulled out my shirt, slowly slid it off my shoulders and dropped it to the floor.

I swung my legs over Robert so that I was sitting on him and facing him. I could feel his dick strain through his pants to reach my hole. I grabbed his head and slid my tongue into his waiting mouth. He tasted like candy and vodka. Robert reached down and started massaging my ass, which made me moan in his mouth. Robert smiled. I started unbuttoning his shirt, but I didn't do it slowly. I was very fast and proficient because I wanted to see the fur under his shirt. As I pulled the shirt away I could see the perfectly formed pecs with their perfect pink nipples covered in just the right amount of fur with a happy trail over his six pack heading straight to the Promised Land.

Robert reached down and undid my belt, popped the button on my pants, and began to pull down the zipper. He spread open my pants, revealing my straining cock, which needed release. He then slid his hands down the back of my pants and boxer briefs, working over the cheeks of my ass. I started to grind back and forth on his dick. I really got his comment from before that he liked sex as much as any other man.

He reached down and pulled out the coffee table drawer. In it were lube, condoms, and a variety of toys. You could tell this wasn't the first time this scenario played out on this couch. "I wasn't sure if you needed any toys to loosen you up."

"Let me loosen you up first," I said as I bent over to remove Robert's shoes one at a time. With them off, I undid his belt, popped the button on his pants, and pulled his zipper down revealing his cock-filled striped bikini underwear. I didn't stop there as I started pulling on his pant' legs to remove his pants. Robert was kind enough to arch his back, which made his pants slide off with ease. This man had an incredible body from his upper torso to his meaty thighs, all of which were covered in a very light, sandy, colored fur. I couldn't stop myself from rubbing my hands all over his body.

My hands worked their way back to the cock-filled bikini briefs and slid their way between his thighs and the material so I could pull them straight down. There were no complaints from Robert as he arched his back again as I pulled his briefs off and tossed them on the floor.

In front of me was his perfect-looking eight inch dick with a base of furry balls. "Can I take a picture of your dick?"

"Absolutely. I love it when someone sees perfection," he replied as he spread his legs wide apart so I could get the best shot of the shaft and balls.

I reached for my phone on the coffee table and snapped a couple of quick shots. I checked the photos to make sure they came out clear, and when I did, I noticed something but I wasn't sure what it was. There were some darker spots on his balls under the sandy colored fur. I bent my head down to take a closer look, and when I did, Robert grabbed my head, assuming I was getting ready to suck his dick.

"Oh yeah, baby, take my dick," he said as he positioned his cock in front of my mouth.

All I could say was, "Wait a minute, baby," as I looked into his sex face. There is something else I want to look at. His sex face turned into a confused face.

I got down on my knees and grabbed his cock with my hand and pulled it up so that his balls would stick out a little more. There wasn't a lot of light in the room, so I grabbed my phone and turned on the flashlight and brought it close to his balls.

"This isn't going to hurt, is it?"

"No, I'm just taking a closer look." When I brought the light closer to his balls, it was like a bunch of cockroaches running from the light, but these weren't roaches. They were crabs. I could see their little feet moving as they crawled in and around his pubic hair. His balls had a whole family living there. I don't know how he didn't feel it.

"Do your balls feel itchy?"

"A little now and then. Why do you ask?"

"Because you have crabs. I suggest you go out and get yourself some A-200 to get rid of your infestation." Once he heard, that he immediately deflated, which was fine because I already had deflated the minute I spotted the dark spots on my phone. I just hope none got on me.

I hopped up, zipped up, buttoned my pants, and tightened my belt. I grabbed my shirt from the floor, put it on, and buttoned it up.

"You're not going to tell anyone, are you?"

"Of course not. Your secret is safe with me," I said. "I got to go. It has been a very interesting evening. Have a good night."

I left him sitting on the couch, grabbing on his balls. The party next door was winding down, as there were fewer cars on the street. My only thought at this point was heading to the Publix and getting some A-200 for myself. I would rather be safe than sorry and make sure I killed anything I may have picked up from the Crab King. I guess this was why I had never been on a blind date before.

I got back to the apartment and of course his secret was not safe with me. I had to unload to Germaine the minute I walked through the door. I told him I didn't realize I could have had crabs twice tonight. We both laughed.

# CHAPTER 54

The hotel was busy as usual, but luckily Germaine and I were working the same shift at the front desk. This made time go by so much faster when I had him there to cut up with.

"I have to thank you," he said. "These past weeks I have met so many influential people and it is all because of you. I never would have had this opportunity if it weren't for you."

"Don't you mean Desiree?" I said. "Most of these events we are going to I'm done up in high-whore drag, but I'm not complaining. I have met so many people and it really has helped with my donations for the contest. As much as I hate saying it none of this would have happened without Biff and Kits' contacts. I just can't believe how many people they know."

"Isn't it amazing? I wanted to remind you that I'm going to the Fireman's Charity Ball tonight with Kit and Biff."

This was the first time that they actually invited Germaine without me. They even let him bring Miss Gigi with him. I was glad they were starting to pay more attention to him since he had busted his butt doing everything they had asked. Even better, I would have the apartment all to myself tonight, so I could have a marathon of "So You Think You Can Dance" and get caught up on all the episodes I missed.

While Germaine went to get coffee, I buried myself in some useless paperwork at the desk.

"Why, my sir, they must work you to death around here."

I looked up and staring me in the face was Thunderball. Her daddy, Spencer Jack, was holding her up at counter level. "What does a dog have to do to get a room around here?"

"You have to bark like a dog," I said. "It is so good to see you, Thunderball. And your daddy isn't so hard on the eyes either. How are you doing, Spencer? I didn't know you were coming in." I took a better look at Spencer and realized that he was pretty pale.

"Neither did me. I've been having more seizures lately, so they made me come up immediately for more testing. This time my mother is with me. I'm checking her into the connecting room next to mine."

"I am so sorry to hear that." It was sad seeing someone close to my own age with so many medical problems. "What can I do for you while you are here?"

"I don't know yet. I really enjoyed our drink last time, but I don't think I will be able to do that this time. We are heading over to the hospital almost immediately."

"Here are your room keys. Do you need any help getting upstairs?"

"No, there's mother now," he said as a woman came rolling into the lobby with one of the hotel carts with several pieces of luggage on it. "I'll stop by when we get back."

"Please do. I would love to spend some time with you while you're here if you feel up to it."

"Thank you so much. It gives me something to look forward to," he said. "Have to go." He went and met his mother and they both rolled the luggage cart over to the elevator. I watched until the elevator door closed. Little did I know that was the last time I was going to see Spencer. While at the hospital, he had another seizure, but this time he did not recover. Word spread around the hotel, and Sheila was the unlucky one to share the news with me.

I felt crushed. I wished I could reach out to Marjorie to let her know what happened. Spencer, was a great guy, and I had shared with Marjorie my fantasy life with Spencer from the picket fence to several Thunderballs roaming around the yard. So I decided to slip to the back to one of the computers and message her on Facebook. I knew it would message her instantly on her phone. I opened Facebook and did a search for Marjorie from my friends list. I hit enter, but nothing came back. I went to the full list, and realized she was no longer there. I typed her name in on the main search, and she did not come up. It took me a second to realize that she had unfriended me. This was the final blow to my day. I tried reaching out to Germaine, but my calls went straight to his voice mail since he had slipped out of work early to get ready for the charity ball. I really felt alone as I headed out the hotel door and drove myself home. I stopped and picked up some Taco Bell, which was comfort food for me. A Mexican pizza and a bean burrito.

I got to the apartment and it was     quiet      because Germaine had gone out for dinner with the boys before the charity ball. I turned on the TV and sat down to eat my dinner. I channel surfed, but nothing was pulling me out of this mood. I needed to feel wanted, so I might as well go online and get some attention.

I set the computer up on the bed and put on some very mellow music to try and get me into a better head space. I didn't even care what I was wearing as I finally flopped down and hit broadcast.

The usual folks popped up immediately and started chatting with me. This was the best ego booster you could get when people start telling you how beautiful, sexy, and hot you are.

Finally, my night got better when Leatherman sent me a private message.

Leatherman25: "Didn't know you were going to be on here tonight. Also your room has changed. Not the same background as before"

From this point on, I ignored all the other chats and just private messaged with Leatherman.

SpankyBtm: "Had a falling out with my previous roommate and had to get out of there so the new background. Getting settled into the new place. I think I could get used to it"

Letherman25: "Thought you and your husband were living together. Hope it all works out."

SpankyBtm: "We weren't getting along with that roommate so had to move. Didn't plan on being here but had a bad day"

Leatherman25: "Tell me about it"

SpankyBtm: "Had a very nice acquaintance pass away today and found out former roommate unfriended me on FB"

Leatherman25: "If I were there I would be giving you a great big hug"

SpankyBtm: "Just the thought of that gives me some comfort. Didn't mean to dump all this on you"

Leatherman25: "Baby that's what I am here for"

SpankyBtm: "That's all I needed to hear. Got to go to bed. Thanks for being you"

I turned off the computer and the lights. I tossed and turned and kept asking myself what I had done to be cut off from my former friends? I'm a nice guy, and I try to treat everyone with the respect they deserve. I don't think losing their friendships really hit me until today, and it really hurt.

"God, why is this happening to me?" I thought.

# CHAPTER 55

"Bombshell" was on hiatus while most of the cast rehearsed for their upcoming community playhouse production, so I needed to get some of the other fundraising ideas off the ground to bring in some money.

I had spoken to Sherell, the owner of Pop My Bubble Salon, and she and her staff were willing to donate their time to do a Hair-Cut-A-Thon, with all proceeds donated to my charity. We set it up for a Monday when the salon normally wasn't open. I had also asked them if they would be willing to do some haircuts for the homeless group that lived under the bridge on Monroe, and she was extremely gracious and immediately said yes.

It was time to get the marketing going. Germaine called Kit and Biff, who came over to discuss this fundraiser and some other options that they had in mind.

"We can use the homeless angle to get you some press in the gay rags," Kit said.

"Yes, since there is the human interest story, they should jump all over it. I will give the editors a personal call to ensure the coverage. Plus, several owe me favors for some ad revenue I sent their way," Biff said.

"I don't know if using the homeless people is the best marketing tactic for this," I said. "The salon and I are both doing it to help some people out who are down on their luck."

"And you should use that and be thankful you are not

down on your luck and like one of them," Kit said. "I thank God every day that I am not one of those poor creatures who come knocking at my car window every time I exit at the expressway. I know its hot outside, but I'm not opening my window and letting out my cold air and none of them are ever sexy looking. They look like they need a bath."

"Think of it this way, sweetie. By getting more press, you will be raising awareness of the plight of the homeless in the city. Maybe that will lead to people making a donation to help get these people off the streets," Biff said.

"You really think so?" I asked.

"Absolutely," Germaine chimed in. "You can't fix a problem if people don't know about it."

What they said sounded good, and I really just wanted to help them out. "You have my blessing. Please contact the gay rags and see what you can do." Plus, with them doing the promotions, it was one fewer thing that I had to deal with.

"I'm so glad you see it our way," Kit said. "We will get the phone tree activated and get the Facebook event up and running."

I was extremely shocked when I got a call from one of the magazines asking to set up an interview and photo shoot that same day. Of course, the photo shoot was for Desiree, which was a first for her, and it would be the first time a photo got published. This was going to put me in front of thousands of people. I guess it really was good to know people in high places.

Now that the promotions were set up, I needed to speak with Temple. At least I knew where I could find him on Saturday to see if he and the other homeless folks would even be interested in getting haircuts. He was at his usual corner at Monroe and Piedmont trying to collect money.

"Good afternoon, Temple," I said as I approached.

"Good afternoon, fine sir. How are you doing today?"

"Very well. I'm not sure if you remember me from before, but I wanted to ask you a question."

"Sir, I always remember individuals who are kind and

generous to me. You were the gentleman who gave me his lunch and some money to make sure I would eat. I greatly appreciated that."

"Yes, that was me, and thanks for remembering me. I wanted to ask you a question. I am organizing a Haircut-a-thon, and I wanted to see if you and some of your friends would be interested in getting a free haircut. I know it is not much, but I wanted to make the offer to you. It would just be just down the block right over there," I said as I pointed to the salon. "A couple of Mondays from now at 4 P.M."

"I would be glad to take you up on that sir, and I'm sure there are several others who will be interested. How can I reach you to let you know? I don't have a phone."

"I'll be glad to come back here next Saturday to check."

"That is a plan sir. I will see you next Saturday."

With that worked out, the next step was to get ready for the photo shoot. Biff, Kit, and Germaine spent what seemed like hours looking at all my outfits and wigs to determine which would be the best for the photo shoot. Everything was happening pretty quickly, so there really wasn't time to go get anything new. They decided on a short sequined dress that I didn't wear that often, which was good because they didn't want people recognizing the outfit in the photos. They also picked the wig and the shoes to go with it. I was happy with their choices because it was less for me to think about. Maybe this was a good thing with them being around. I got to use my brain less.

We all went to the photographer's studio with me already done up in my makeup. The boys carried in everything that I needed and were all there to help me get dressed. The reporter was meeting us at the studio to ask some questions for the article which was just going to be a one page spread in the magazine with a photo and a write-up about the charity.

The photographer was extremely hot. He was playing dance music in the background, which gave the room a great energy. After a final hair and makeup check with the boys, I was ready to pose. I had never taken any professional photos, so I was relying on the photographer for directions, which he was great at. I would arch my back or stretch my neck anytime he asked, but the boys were getting a little impatient and started barking out their own poses. Luckily, cooler heads prevailed and the photographer took control of the shoot again.

While all this was happening, the writer was shooting out questions for me about why I was doing this and what else I was doing. I would answer, and immediately, Kit would clarify my statement. I thought I was pretty clear, but what Kit was explaining was even more detailed than I could ever be. One of the questions did intrigue me. The writer asked if I had ever written anything else before besides "Bombshell."

I had to think about it, but one thing did pop into my head. "When I was in about 6th grade, a friend and I thought we could write a hit song, so we started pounding out things on the upright piano at my house. I even remember the title - 'Venus and Mars Rising.' It was probably terrible, but when you're eleven everything sounds great."

Once the shots were taken we all stood at the computer screen to choose the right shot. There were several I was happy with, but those didn't meet the boys' criteria, so they chose another shot that they felt best captured my essence, as they put it. Much to my surprise, the photographer and writer both agreed with them. I couldn't wait to see it in print.

The article ran the following week. The picture really looked great. I decided to grab five copies of the magazine from the rack just to keep. I thought for a minute of sending one to my mother, but that thought was fleeting. I swear the minute the article hit the newsstands, my phone lit up like a Christmas tree. I had tons of people calling me and texting me to tell me how great the picture looked. I also had people asking if they could donate clothes for the homeless and other toiletries. But the best surprise was Stephanie from Bonk, who called to say she would donate bagged meals for the homeless who show up. That was even better because I really want to make sure they didn't go hungry. And while I had Stephanie on the phone, I asked if we could do a dining night out and beer bust at the restaurant. She jumped on that right away and gave the green light.

It's funny that it took this fundraiser and the boys' help to actually get me into the magazines, since none of them ever did anything about "Bombshell." Realistically, it was the boys' help that got me the notice. I guess it was good to know the people with power and money. Money and power seemed to be making my life easier. I could really get used to this.

I met Temple as promised. He had a total of ten people who were coming in for their haircuts. "I do want you to know that there might be some photographers taking pictures for the magazines there."

"If you don't mind, sir, I do not think anyone in the group really wants to get their pictures taken. A lot of us are embarrassed to be in the situation we are in."

"I completely understand. I'll make sure that the photographers leave before your group arrives." He was quite relieved by that. There was no sense in making them feel uncomfortable when all we were trying to do was help them out.

Finally it was the day of the Haircut-a-thon, and from the Facebook event, it looked like there was going to be a great turnout. To avoid any issues at the salon, the Facebook event made it very clear that they were just getting haircuts. No color jobs and no eyebrow waxing. It would be nice to do all that, but since the stylists were all donating their time, we were trying to get through as many people as possible.

"Your outfit is already laid out on your bed," Germaine said. "With the event starting at 2, we need to be there no later than 1:15 to make sure everything is set up. Also, the event photographer will be there around 1:30."

"Thank you so much for your help on this. I couldn't have done it without all your help," I said as I gave

Germaine a hug. "About the photographer. We need to tell them that they cannot take any photos of the homeless people. They just don't feel comfortable having their pictures taken."

"Shouldn't be a problem. I'll make sure they are aware of that. Most of the shots are quick shots of people having fun and getting their hair done. That way it can show up in the Scene At section to give you another plug. That's why I chose that specific outfit for you to wear. It's an outfit that most people will not remember you wearing, and you don't want to be seen in the same outfit in these photos."

"I dropped off the plastic bin for any clothes that were donated at the salon yesterday on my way to work. That way Temple can take it and it will be protected from the weather," I said.

I got Desiree's pretty little ass together and Germaine chauffeured us over to the salon. When we got there, there were a few people milling about already with their donations in hand. Sherell was inside with the stylists getting the salon set up, so we joined her inside. Biff and Kit arrived shortly thereafter and brought the photographer with them. The photographer immediately went to work taking pictures of everyone in very candid poses. Sherell cranked up the music in the salon, and by the time we opened the door at 2, there was a line waiting with money in hand. Once the haircuts started, there was hair and scissors everywhere. The people were being processed as quickly as the staff could work. It did my heart good to see all the clothes that were donated. I figured what-ever wasn't needed, I could donate at Goodwill, which was next door.

By 4 P.M., we had processed everyone and Temple and his group arrived. "You look a little different," Temple said. "The outfit makes you look beautiful."

"You are so kind," I replied.

It was a rag tag bunch, but they were all smiling and extremely chatty with all the stylists. I did let Temple know that we had also collected clothes, and each person was able to find something that was needed from the bin. Between shoes, shirts and pants the bin was overflowing.

Stephanie arrived with several coolers of food to give to everyone as they left. This way, they had a good meal and a bottle of water. I could not thank her and the staff at Pop My Bubble enough for all their hard work to help those in need.

"Biff, Kit, and Germaine, I want to thank you personally. If it weren't for, you none of this would have happened. I owe you big time, so please let me know if there is anything I can do for you."

"Well, now that you mention it, there are a couple of events we need you to make an appearance at," Biff said.

"I am at your command."

# CHAPTER 56

"You need to go shopping," Biff said. "If you are going to be seen with us, you must be glamorous and shine."

"Yes, no more hand-me-downs from those junky thrift stores," Kit chimed in. "You can't be seen wearing the same outfits at these parties because there are photographers at all the events we go to, and we can't risk your picture showing up in the publications wearing the same dress. It will not do. Not do at all. Especially if you will be seen with us. We have a status to maintain."

"I understand, but I can't afford new outfits right now. I'm kind of on limited funds and can't afford to drop a bunch of money on new outfits."

"Then Germaine will pay for them," Biff said, pointing to Germaine.

"Yes, Germaine will pay for them," Kit echoed.

"I could never impose on Germaine like that," I said. "Plus, working at the hotel, we don't make that much money."

"Please don't say anything about money," Germaine pleaded.

"Honey, Germaine doesn't need the money from the hotel," Biff said.

"Yes, sweetie, he doesn't need the money from a job," Kit said.

"What do you mean?"

"Please don't," Germaine repeated.

"Germaine is loaded," Biff said very plainly.

"Germaine's grandparents were very wealthy and before they died they set up trust funds for their two grandchildren, Germaine and his sister Felicia. The only stipulation of the trust was that they had to maintain gainful employment until they reached the age of 58, which for Germaine is just around the corner. If they didn't work, then the other one would inherit the trust from their sibling," Kit said. "That is why you see that strange man at the hotel every now and then checking up on Germaine to make sure he is working."

"He was hired by his sister to keep an eye on him to make sure he is still working. What a fucking bitch, but you have to admit she has balls to stalk her own brother," Biff said. "There is no love lost there."

"Can we stop talking about money now?" Germaine asked. "My parents always taught me it was uncouth to speak about money."

"That's where they were wrong, and that is why you haven't made the break into the A society. All these pretentious bastards do is talk about their money. Who has it? Who lost it? Who's going where and who's buying what? It makes them feel important and it makes their dicks get hard," Kit said.

"How many times have we heard from a pompous ass that their Cole Hahn shoes cost $2000? It's like music to my ears, especially when I know that bastard bought them on sale for about half the price," Biff said. They both laughed.

"You sound like you hate all your friends," I said.

"Don't be silly, my child. I love every one of them as much as I love their bank accounts, and I believe the feeling is reciprocal," Kit said. "We wouldn't be hanging out with them unless they had a bank account."

"There is nothing worse than when someone loses all their money because they become a pariah on us all and are banished off to the Walmart's of the world," Biff said.

"I didn't realize you had money," I said to Germaine.

"I don't like to talk about it as much as these two. I want

people to like me for me versus for my money. I think that is why I have a hard time trusting people because if they know how much I'm worth, I'm never sure if they truly like me or are just after my money," Germaine said.

"Germaine, you need to loosen up and have some fun," Biff said. "Let's go shopping. I've lined up my personal shopper, Esteban, to take us through Regents Plaza and find you some new outfits."

"I have never even set foot in Regents Plaza," I said.

"There's always a first time," Kit said.

So we all loaded into the car with Kit and Biff sitting in the back and being chauffeured around by Germaine and headed to Regents Plaza. Regents Plaza was the very high-end shopping mall in the city with everything from Versace to Vivienne Westwood and was located across from Westfield Mall, so it was shopping heaven.

Germaine pulled into the parking lot and headed straight for valet parking. "I'm glad you finally started using the valet," Biff said. "That's what they are there for, and we don't have time to waste circling this black top inferno."

We hopped out of the car and there was a very sharply dressed gentleman waiting for us. He had on a grey suit, a purple-checked, pressed, button-down shirt, and black shoes, which matched his slick, backed, black hair. His skin was olive-toned and he had just the slightest stubble on his chin. "Good morning Mr. Biff and Mr. Kit. It is wonderful seeing you today. Who are we shopping for today?" he asked.

"Esteban, this young gentleman is Tyler," Biff said.

"It is a pleasure to meet you," he said as he extended his hand. I took and shook his baby-smooth hand. It was like holding warm butter.

"And this is our other friend, Germaine," Kit said.

"Mr. Germaine, the pleasure is all mine," Esteban said. "Mr. Tyler what are your clothing requirements today? Slacks, shirts, resort wear?"

"No, Esteban, Mr. Tyler is better known as Miss Desiree, and she is in need of party outfits. I want every head to turn as she enters the room with us."

"Mr. Kit, every head already turns when you and Mr. Biff enter a room. Miss Desiree will only help shine the light on your pure perfection," Esteban said.

When I heard that, I think I vomited a little into my mouth, but I choked it back down. "Remember to play nice" was all I kept saying to myself.

We all followed Esteban down the marble staircase to the main floor of the shopping mall. I had never seen this much marble and wood work in any place except for a church, but this was so much more fancy.

This was a great place to people watch, as everyone was so beautiful. There were the leggy blondes and the well-quaffed male models who seemed to be everywhere, carrying all their purchases and glancing at each other as if to say "Great underwear ad." Everyone walked with a purpose. You didn't see any baby strollers anywhere, which I was so used to seeing in the malls that I went to. I also didn't see a normal food court with your usual pizza and burgers anywhere because here it was a French restaurant, salad bars, and sushi. I'm glad we ate before we got here.

The first store Esteban took us to was the H & M store. The only reason I recognized this store was because Madonna had been their fashion model for a time. We entered and were immediately swamped by the store staff all fawning over Esteban. He almost needed a stick to beat them off. "Good morning ladies. It's a pleasure to see you all, but my heart belongs to Jean." Just as he said this, a very petite brunette with curves in all the right places greeted Esteban with a very large Cheshire-cat smile.

"Why Esteban, my little darling, I didn't know you were coming by this morning, otherwise I would have worn something a little more revealing," she said.

"It was a change of plans, darling. I need you to help me find party dresses for Miss Desiree here," he said pointing to me.

She quickly sized me up. "We have some brand new

cocktail dresses in that will be perfect for the life of the party. Let me grab a couple. Please have a seat, and I'll have one of the other girls bring out the tea cart for your party."

"Gentlemen, please grab a seat on one of the leather couches," Esteban instructed. Everyone sank into the luxurious leather couches as the tea cart was rolled out in front of us with hot tea already poured and crumpets on a plate. "Desiree, I will need you over here. And please stay away from the crumpets. A minute on the lips, a year on the hips."

I sat on the round ottoman by the mirrors and Jean came out with several cocktail dresses draped over her arms. "These are from the new fall collections. I think this will be perfect because every girl needs a black cocktail dress."

Esteban held the dress up, and for me, it was love at first site. It was fun and flirty and I could see myself turning some heads in that dress. "Try this on in the dressing room," he said as he handed the dress to me and pointed to the dressing room to the left of the mirrors.

I stepped into the dressing room and slipped out of my boy clothes and started sliding on the black dress. It felt like a glove the minute it went on and I couldn't wait to see it in the mirror. I stepped out and all the boys gasped, and from the look on their faces, I could tell this was a keeper. I stepped up on the platform in front of the mirrors and immediately began to twirl. The dress was a killer from every angle and was pure perfection. I wanted this dress, but then I looked at the price tag. It was $500. I couldn't see Germaine spending that much on a dress for me. From the look on my face, the boys sensed something was amiss.

"Sweetie don't worry, Germaine can afford it," Kit said.

"Yes, honey, it is yours if you want it," Germaine said.

I couldn't believe that they were being so nice to me that the tears began to well up in my eyes. I had never had anyone in my life treat me so well.

"And the best part is we need to accessorize it," Esteban said. "Take that one off and try these two on," he said as he handed me more clothes.

I went back into the dressing room and slipped out of the black beauty and put on the next dress. It was a red leather mini dress that was really form-fitting. As I stepped out of the dressing room, it got the immediate thumbs down from the boys, so back I went. I came out with the next dress and it got more of a mixed reaction. Some liked it and some didn't, which meant it wasn't going home with me. I also tried on a navy blue polka dot number that looked great on me and got the immediate thumbs up. I felt like Julia Roberts in "Pretty Woman," except for the whole hooker thing.

We checked out and Germaine had no problem laying down plastic to cover the $1,200 bill. "Germaine, I can't thank you enough for what you are doing for me."

"You're welcome, dear. I can't thank you enough for what you are doing for me," he said, but I really didn't understand what he meant.

Esteban led us to the next store, which was a shoe store called, Looibitan. Again, the staff was all over him the minute he walked into the store. "Girls, it's time to play my favorite game. I've got the number, now let me hear your answers."

The girls immediately said 98, 115 and 121. "Rosalyn, you win!" he said. "The number was 100." The other two girls sulked away sadly.

"What were the numbers for?" I asked.

"I make them tell me their weight and the person closest to the number in my head gets to wait on my customer or me. It's always a low number, which encourages them to keep their weight down. I don't like to see fat rolls coming out between shoe straps," he said. "We need something with a four to six inch heel in a size 10 that will complement these dresses."

She took a quick look at the dress colors and then she was off. She came back with several boxes in her hands with several styles. "Try these on," she said as she put a black patent leather pump with a six-inch heel in front of me. I took off my shoes and socks and Rosalyn handed me a pair of ankle-high nylons to put on so I could try on the shoes. I put on the heels and was off touring the store. They felt pretty good, and when I looked in the mirror, they really helped shape my calves.

"Work it, girl," Biff said.

"I really like these," I said. "They feel comfortable."

"They should, you little slut. Trying on women's clothes. You should be ashamed of yourself," said the obviously dried-up older woman trying on a pair of shoes next to the mirrors. "God didn't intend on you wearing those things."

I was completely taken aback. Next thing I knew, Rosalyn was jumping into action. "Ma'am we don't allow any customer in our store to speak like that to any of our clientele. I'm going to have to ask you to leave."

"I'm not going anywhere, missy," she said as she firmly planted her ass in the seat.

"Rosalyn, get her out of here. I spend more in this store in a month than she will get from social security for the rest of her life," Esteban said.

"How rude," the dried-up lady responded.

"What's rude is your lack of couth, "Esteban said." I should have my wife come down here and kick your ass."

Security arrived and escorted the dried-up prune out of the store.

"Thank you, Rosalyn. Now where were we?" he asked as he dove back into the shoe boxes.

I looked to Germaine and asked, "He has a wife?"

His only response was, "Don't ask."

There were several pairs that were beautiful and would really complete the outfits. The only thing missing was the jewelry, which was our next stop. The bling was blinding and it was all costume jewelry. I was kind of relieved because I didn't want to worry about having any of it stolen or losing it at one of the shows. These other drag queens were going to shit a brick when the saw my new outfits. It put all those rags that Athena had to shame. Fuck her.

The final total for our shopping spree was $4,000, which was more money than I could ever spend on a shopping spree unless I won the lottery. I couldn't believe how generous Germaine was being. Kit and Biff congratulated him for finally prying open his wallet.

"Desiree, you need to wear the black cocktail dress on Saturday because you are going to a benefit with us that begins at 8. Germaine and Miss Gigi will bring you, so please arrive on time."

"Yes, sir, I will be ready," I said. I was ready for my star to really become a rising star, and with these boys' help, that was going to happen." I could feel it in my boner.

# CHAPTER 57

The next fundraiser that the boys had me set up for was working one of the concession stands at Georgia A & M University's home football game. What most people don't know is that these schools have programs where charity groups can work the various booths at the home football games, and they get to keep 10% of the sales for the day. The school provides the food items, which include everything from candy to hot dogs and popcorn, and you provide the man power.

To run the booth, you needed twelve people to fill all the position. From what I was told, several of the volunteers in our booth had food and beverage experience, which was great, since I had all the experience from working in the hotel kitchen, so it should be a good fit.

I was going to be the inventory control person while Germaine was going to be the money man. We had to be at the stadium four hours before game time so that we could get the inventory and money counted and start cooking the food. It was not a glamorous gig, but at least we should make some good money since the game was sold out and Georgia A & M was hosting Notre Dame, who was currently ranked number eight in the country.

To get into the stadium, we had to go through the tunnel located at the north end of the stadium. The table check-in lady was very nice and made sure that our list was correct, since everyone else got to show up an hour later and we all had to go through the same check point. Things were great until we met the little Hitler-wannabe, short, anal security guard who was the controller at the gate wouldn't let us enter until we had our all access wrist bands on.

"Sirs I cannot let y'all enter," he said. "You must have the appropriate identification on your wrists before I can let you down the tunnel. Also, if you decide to step a single foot onto the playing field I will have to eject you from the stadium. Is that understood?"

"Yes, sir," I said as we put on our proper wrist identification bands and entered the tunnel.

"Why is it short people have a Napoleon complex?" Germaine asked.

"What is a Napoleon complex?" I asked.

"What did they teach you up in that little redneck Podunk town you grew up in?" he asked.

I thought it was best to just ignore the questions and then later Google what a Napoleon complex was.

We went to the cash room to get our inventory sheets and cash. It was a madhouse since this was the first game of the season and there was a burly off-duty police officer guarding the door. From what it looked like, there were thousands and thousands of dollars flowing through that room.

"Y'all ready for your first day?" Rebecca asked. Rebecca was the person in charge of the food concessions for the stadiums here on campus. She was a bubbly blonde with tits for days and a great personality, but at this moment, you could see she was stretched a little thin with everyone pulling for her attention.

"Boys, grab your booth binder and Mary Lynne will get your cash counted," she said. "Once that's done, head on out and get your booth ready."

The other benefit of coming to the cash room was seeing Wes, who was the inventory manager for the stadiums. He was a beautiful heather bear with a full beard and thick head of hair. There was no other way of describing him except for heather bear. A heather bear is a beautiful furry bear who is built like someone from the military with the attitude to go along with it. If he had told me to lick his boots, I would have gotten down right there and spit shined them with my tongue. Next thing I knew someone was pulling on my ear.

"Come on, Cinderfella. There will be time for fantasy later," Germaine said as he pulled me out the door.

We went to our booth, which was on the mid-level eastside of the stadium facing the student dorms. It was a great beginner booth for us with tight quarters for everyone to work in. We immediately started getting our inventory counted, cleaning the counters, and getting our soda cups ready for the masses. Since it was early in the morning there wasn't a lot of traffic on the street outside the stadium, but there were some eye candy students walking about who were already partying for the game. I'm pretty sure that as I looked across at the dorms, I could see through the fogged glass someone sit down to take a shit. I'm pretty sure that was a bathroom window across from us in the dorm, and it must have been someone taking their morning constitutional. All I could think was "gross."

As time passed, our man power started showing up, and boy was this a beautiful bunch of men. Each one was more handsome than the last person to show up, all uniformly dressed in khaki shorts, blue, tight t-shirts, tennis shoes, and A & M ball caps. We were told that if you wore a University of Georgia ball cap here it would be taken from your head and burned in the street. These people took their football seriously. By the time the last boy arrived, our booth looked like an ad for Abercrombie and Fitch.

Germaine introduced me to each one as they came in, but I forgot that person's name the minute the next boy came in. I could already tell this was going to be a great day. These guys truly took charge, and they got everything up and running in no matter of time. The hot dogs were cooking and the ice bins were full. You could tell that a lot of them did have kitchen experience because they were able to check the soda boxes to make sure they were all full and ready and that the CO tank was turned on to pressure up the fountain drink system. It was nice to sit back and let some other people do the things that I had to do before.

"So Desiree, we hear we get to see your show for free for helping out today," one of the boys said.

"It would be my pleasure to escort you to your seats at the show," I said. "As long as I got a face, you have a place to sit."

He laughed, which I was going for. Sometimes when I say that line, I get a strange look back from the boy. If you don't get that line then you are not playing with a full crayon box.

As the gates opened, the masses started strolling by our booth. The boys were right out front selling our wares. "Hot dogs, popcorn, ice cold drinks." They were also selling their wares as each boy on the front line oozed sex. As you looked at our lines of people, it was all women and gay men waiting to make a purchase from the cute cashier. I knew there would be eye candy here, but didn't realize that it would be in our booth. I was hoping to meet some young college guy with whom I could have a whirlwind relationship. I also didn't realize that there would be a lot of daddies here. There were just hot men everywhere you looked, and I felt like I was a walking erection. Thank God Germaine was there to throw the cold water in my face.

You would think that we would have had some time to watch at least some of the game, but no such luck. Once the game started, our booth kicked into high gear. We had constant lines of people waiting and no one could get through the hallways in front of our booth. It got so bad that we couldn't get a refill on some of the food items we needed. I called on the walkie-talkie for our supervisor, but all I was told was that they would be over soon. It really got to the point where we had to send out some of our back-line help to go get more ice. That alone was a nightmare, as the ice cooler was on the complete other end of the stadium on our level, but with so many people packed in, it made it extremely difficult to get anywhere.

Germaine kept pulling money from the cash registers so that we would be ready for the money drops. He kept telling me that we were doing really well. I hoped so, because with seven home games, it could add up to a lot of money. I needed to keep up the pace because I was sure Athena had had some more tricks up her sleeve to pull in more coins.

None of us could tell where we were in the game because the lines never went down. You could also tell that some of the patrons had brought their own alcohol into the stadium since they wanted their soda cups only filled up half way with soda. It was a rule of the NCAA that alcohol could not be sold in any stadium that was on school property, which disappointed some of the fans from out of town who were hoping to buy beer at the game.

Even with us being slammed, I never saw one of the boys sweat. I don't know if it was their genes or what, but Germaine and I were both sweating like pigs. I was running the backline and slinging the food orders as soon as they were called out by the cashiers. We had a great pace going and kept the lines moving unless one of the patrons decided to linger at the register to stare at the hot cashier. I really couldn't deny that we had a beautiful booth. I felt like the odd man out because all of these boys obviously spent a lot of time at the gym. I think I saw several numbers passed over the counter to the front-line cashiers. It just wasn't the college age kids either. The sexy daddies also were lining up to order from the front-line boys. It was fun to watch and try to learn from these boys what they did when they were hit on. They handled it beautifully, as none of them ever lost the smile on their face and they all said "thank you" with each compliment. They even gripped some of the patrons' hands and held them for a second. Only to be that pretty, but I knew deep in my heart that there was someone out there for me who was going to love me for me. Or at least I better keep that belief otherwise I would spiral into the deepest depths of despair.

Needless to say, we ran out of food before the game was over, We had no infill food coming because the stadium was just sold out everywhere, which meant we could start cleaning up the booth and get out of here at a decent time. All of the boys were working really hard to pick up the trash, clean the hot dog grill, put away the cups, and take the trash out. As I counted, I realized one of the boys was already gone. He must have had to leave early, which was okay since we were pretty much done.

As the boys finished cleaning, they left one by one. The game was over. Georgia A & M lost to the top-ranked Notre Dame, but it didn't matter because I didn't get to see the game anyway. It was time to take out the last bag of trash and put it in the back hallway behind the booth for the stadium clean-up crew to pick up. I dragged it out the door and rounded the corner to the hallway. It led to an electrical room. I swore I could see movement back there. I pulled out my phone and hit the flashlight app. To my surprise, it was the boy who left early making out with one of the sexy daddies, who was a six-foot sausage of man meat. The daddy looked at me and asked if I wanted to join them and the boy motioned me back. My heart leapt out of my chest at the opportunity. I had never been involved in a three-way and both of these men were extremely hot, so I thought about it for a second and started heading down the hall. All of a sudden, I felt a sharp pain in my ear as Germaine grabbed me from behind.

"Now, now," he said. "There will be time for that later. I want to get the hell out of here and soak my feet." So I acquiesced as he pulled me back up the hall. Maybe the next game would be my time.

We left the stadium and walked over the North Ave Bridge as we headed to the Marta Station. We made good money today, and within ten days I would be able to pick up the check from today. It felt good.

The train was full of drunk Georgia A&M fans, which

was okay because we were heading to The Den, a gay sports bar near the Lindbergh Marta Station, to get a few drinks of our own. We could sit and relax for a little bit watching the sports bears check out the other college games before heading back to the apartment. Germaine and I sat at the bar and ordered our first round.

As I surveyed the crowd, I noticed an extremely intoxicated North Carolina fan sucking face with anyone within arm's length. At first, I thought one of the men groping and kissing him was his boyfriend, but I was corrected on that by one of the other patrons who was staring at the activities. Next, Mr. North Carolina worked himself over to the next pair of men and began rubbing his hands on them and started pulling up one of the hot guys' shirts and started biting him on the nipple. In return he and his boyfriend responded by groping the drunk's ass and pulling up his shirt, revealing a chest covered in fur, which matched his beard. Next thing I knew, their hands were sliding down his pants, and from their responses, I was sure Mr. North Carolina was hard as they started grabbing his penis, showing the outline in his jeans. Eventually, he worked his way back to his other group and they slipped out. It tuned me on.

To my surprise, a hot red head sat next to me in his sport jersey and baseball cap. He introduced himself.

"Hi, my name is Francis. Enjoying the activity? I couldn't help see you starring at the show just like everyone else," he said.

"If I ever get that drunk, I would hope someone would put me in a cab and send me home," I said.

"How was the game today?" he asked.

I'm not sure how he knew I was at the game, but then it dawned on me. "It's the jersey," I said. "We were working in one of the booths raising money for my charity and really didn't get a chance to watch the game," I said.

"It was a great game up until the fourth quarter where Notre Dame just blew A&M out of the water," he said.

"I guess so," I said. "I'm actually not that big of a football fan."

"What charity are you raising money for," he asked.

"Atlanta Street Rescue, which helps gay homeless youth get off the street," I said.

"They are a great charity," he said. "We did a decorator show home last year where all the money raised went to them."

"So are you a designer?" I asked.

"Yes, I have my own interior design business. If you know anyone looking to redo their home, let me know." And with that he handed me his card. It read Francis Bass.

"Come on, princess. Time for us to go," Germaine said as he pulled on my jersey.

"But I like this boy," I said.

"You have his card. That's a start," Germaine said as he pulled on the jersey more. "This camper is tired and needs to soak his feet in the hydro spa. Come on, Mary. It is time to go."

"It was nice meeting you Francis. I'll give you a call. My name is Tyler."

"It was a pleasure meeting you, Tyler. I look forward to hearing from you," Francis said as I was unceremoniously pulled off my bar stool and led to the door.

"I like that man," I said. "And I think he liked me for me and not Desiree."

"There will be plenty of time for whatever you want to do with him later. I need to put these tired bones to bed," Germaine said as we rolled our tired selves into the car to head back to the apartment.

# CHAPTER 58

Kit and Biff decided it was time that I should try out for the "Guys As Dolls Show" reality TV show. It was a drag competition where you won a car and $20,000. The exposure would be priceless. Of course, the cost of any video production was going to be handled by Germaine.

Since the main cast had already been selected for this season, they decided to get me into the fan favorite category so that they could get enough of their friends to vote so that I could make it onto the show in that slot. It was worth a chance, and if they were going to give me the opportunity, I wasn't going to let it pass me by. Here was my chance to extend my brand past Atlanta and be recognized on a world stage, since every queen watched this show. I have looked at the winner's tour schedules, and they are all over the world. People even post videos of the winners online when they see them around the world, so it is great to see how the world reacts to these entertainers. I could already see myself competing and winning the title. Germaine always said to visualize your dreams so that you can turn them into a reality. This was my one chance for fame, and I was going to do everything they wanted to make this video brilliant.

Kit and Biff had already decided what I was going to wear for the video shoot, since they had gone out and purchased it with Germaine's credit cards. They also had a script written, since they said everything in reality TV is scripted anyway.

"You will need to rehearse these lines for the shoot. This is what is going to get you through the producers so that you can go into the fan favorite category," Biff said. "You should be able to memorize this since you did your whole show."

"That should be no problem," I said. "When will I get the script?"

"It is still being polished and should be ready by tomorrow. The deadline for all submissions is two weeks from today, so we don't have much time," Kit said. "We have the script out for final revisions by a playwright in town who will know just the right things for you to say."

"Shouldn't it be more natural?" I asked.

"Honey, they don't care if you are natural or not. They are looking for new and rising stars and that is who you are. If you can't believe that, then you aren't going to sell that in the video." Biff said. "And when I mean sell it, you better sell it."

"Don't worry, honey, I will help you get everything ready," Germaine said.

"Yes, Germaine will help you with the final touches," Kit said. "But we are calling the shots here. Do as we say and you will be a star."

With all this talk of being a star, my head started swooning. I have some notoriety in Atlanta, but I would love to be that big fish in a big pond. To see my name in lights and magazines would be amazing. How would people greet me? Who would I be able to meet? This is mind-blowing. I was already attending the right parties here by the A-Gays and couldn't wait to see what fame would bring me.

"We are using the stage at the club to video several of your segments. We also will shoot you in some more natural poses to edit in and use some of the footage from Pride as well," Kit said. "The video will then be edited down into a seamless transition of your beauty."

They laid out the schedule in front of me for the shooting. I was going to have to shift around some of my work schedule for the next three days to accommodate all the shooting.

The first thing we did was try on all the new dresses. I liked the new outfits because they made me feel like a beautiful woman, since these were a lot fishier than something I would normally wear. They even included a black gown for me to wear with a full-throated train on the bottom that was lined below and then had Toole over the top of that. I wasn't sure how I was going to be able to walk in that one, since everything that I had worn before was either shorter or much lighter material. The heels they had picked out for me to wear underneath were basic black leather with a three inch heal, so of course this was the first dress we tried on. It slipped on like a glove and fit me just right in all the curvy places, giving me a fabulous figure. The problem came when I started to walk around in the dress. The train and lining were so heavy that I was having a hard time pushing my legs through the material so I kept stepping on the hem.

"Don't you rip that dress," Biff said. "It is one of a kind and was hand made by several small Chinese women who hand-sewed on all those beads. This is the dress where you will sow the seeds."

"What do you mean 'sow the seeds'?" I asked.

"Sweetie, every drag queen has their own signature move," Kit said. "When you are performing in this dress, you will be doing a very dramatic song to fit the dress. Your arm movement for parts of this song will be this."

Kit then began to perform and his right arm motioned from the middle of his body in a straight line to his right as his body bent over slightly to the right. This caused his arm to angle down slightly. As he got his arm fully extended his palm opened up, and then his arm pulled back up and into his body very slowly.

"That is what you call sowing the seeds," he finished. "You are taking the seeds and throwing them into the crowd, and then pulling back to see what you have sown. Do you understand?"

"Yes, I think I do. It is like when Athena stands there and pulls the cabbage," I said.

"Exactly!" Biff said. "You were right, Germaine, this girl does have some brains after all."

"Now walk, bitch, like you are wearing that dress and it is not wearing you," Kit barked.

And I walked.

"Hold your back up straight," Kit said.

And I walked some more. At first, my heel was getting caught on the train, but the more I practiced, the more the dress moved with me and not against me. We started flowing together, and I was as graceful as a gazelle. It was as if I was Cinderella making her entrance at the ball, and everyone was staring at me.

"That's better, princess," Biff said. "Now out of that one and try on the next one."

We spent an hour trying on the other dresses and shoes that were purchased for me to see which ones they thought would make the best impression on the producers. We settled on three looks that they thought best represented me for the video shoot. I personally would have chosen one of the other dresses for one of my three looks, but they seemed to know what they were doing so I just shut up and let them drive this bus.

The script was emailed over later that day so that I had a chance to memorize what I needed to say. To me, it was kind of bland and what you would expect to hear me say, and I didn't think it really best represented me. I made some editing choices and forwarded the revised script back to Biff and Kit. I had no sooner sent the revisions than my phone lit up. Both Biff and Kit were calling me, and I was afraid to answer the phone. I let both of them go to voice mail. I would rather listen to what they had to say instead of being talked down to. I waited patiently as the voice message box on my phone registered two new messages.

The first was Biff. "How dare you make changes to the script? Don't you realize how much effort is going into making you a star? Don't you go pulling a diva move now, honey, before you are famous? You are not a crazy Mariah Carey yet." And with that, the phone slammed down.

The second was from Kit. "Darling, I don't mean to complain, but what the hell are you thinking? Are we not good enough to be working with you? You seriously hurt my feelings because I have spent hours working on getting this script produced you ungrateful little cunt."

"Wow" was all I could think. So I emailed them both back that I would go with the script as presented. I didn't want them to think that I was ungrateful for all their help. Of course, they both responded immediately to the email as if nothing had happened.

"See you tomorrow at the video shoot," Biff replied.

So it was time for the video shoot at the club. Germaine brought in Miss Gigi for my final make up touches. I learned how to do good make up, but Miss Gigi came in and whipped my face into a totally camera-ready diva face. I was glad she was here. It was the first chance I had to chat with her since she and Germaine went to the Fireman's Ball.

"How was your evening, sweetie? Did you get to put out any fires?" I asked.

"Oh my gosh, there were so many hoooooot men there. I had to keep pulling out my fan and cooling down my coochie," she said. "Everyone was so nice. I'm surprised Biff and Kit even let me go."

"Well they have to throw a bone once in a while at Germaine," I said.

"I know they are pretentious asses, but they are good for business. I had several people come up to me throughout the night complimenting me on the show. The people love you as Marilyn. It was good to be recognized for talent for once instead of being thought of as that crazy drag queen," she said.

"Those days are long gone behind you. How do you handle being around that many people with all the drinks flowing?"

"I learned a trick a little while ago. If the glass in your hand looks like you're drinking a cocktail then people automatically assume it is a cocktail. Little do they know it is nothing more than club soda over ice with a lime thrown in? They assume there is some vodka in there, and I let them think that. Plus, I make sure Germaine is the only one who brings me my drinks. He is such a sweet man. That way I can truly watch what I drink," she said.

"That's a great plan. The problem I have is all these men want to buy me shots, and those really put me under the table. I just don't know what to do about that." I said.

"You either need to learn to play with the big boys and down the shots or you need to figure out a way to discreetly dump the shot. Next time, cup the shot in your hand with your fingertips instead of drinking it. That way, you can pretend to down it with the group of drunks and make a face when you are finished, and as you bring your hand down, slowly tip the shot glass over, dumping the drink on the floor or under a table or into a planter. Everyone will look at the face you are making and not your hand dropping to the floor. Hope that helps," she finished.

"It really does. How do you deal with the really drunk men who just keep hitting on you and still want to drink?" I asked.

"Here is another trick. If Mr. Handsie is drunk already and still wants to drink, get them a drink, but only pour a little alcohol on top. That way, once they take the first sip, they will be able to taste the booze and assume there is more in the cocktail. At least you can slow the drunk down a bit," she said.

"Ladies, your time is up!" came the scream into the dressing room by Biff. "Time is money."

"Well back to the grind," Miss Gigi said.

"I'm glad we had a chance to get caught up," I said. "We need to do this on a regular basis."

"Yes, we do," she said.

"Move it! Move it! We are losing valuable time," Kit said.

So we both came out and took our positions. Me on stage and Miss Gigi ready with a powder puff behind the camera. The director was adjusting the final lighting so we were ready.

It was explained to me that when the director started his countdown, he would point to me when the action was to begin. We had music in the background, which helped put me at ease because I was a little nervous being in front of a camera for the first time. I kept saying to myself, "The camera is the lover you never had. Seduce him and make him your bitch." With that in mind, my lines flowed out of me so genuinely and graciously that I thought I was going to make myself cry.

"Cut!" the director yelled. "Desiree, you need to be more voluptuous. Arch your back a little and tilt your head to give me an interesting angle. You look a little flat."

So the music restarted and the countdown began. I arched my back and tilted my head to create a different silhouette. I felt like I was on "America's Next Top Model" as I stretched my neck and looked for my light.

"Cut. Good job. Onto the next shots. Please get Miss Desiree into her next outfit."

With that, I was whisked backstage, and Miss Gigi helped me into my next dress and heels.

"Thanks for all your help," I said. "You have been a great friend to me."

"Honey, if it weren't for you I would probably be washed up and in the gutter by now. This girl loved to party, but with 'Bombshell,' I was able to find my way again and without your idea of doing the show, none of that would have happened."

"You would have found your way eventually," I said. "It's hard to keep all your talent under wraps."

The rest of the video shoot flew by, and before I knew it, we were finished. The boys were looking at the playback of the video and everyone seemed very excited about what they were watching. Now it was time for them to get it edited down and sent in. I knew the wait for an answer was going to be unbearable, but everything good was worth waiting for.

# CHAPTER 59

Stephanie at Bonk was true to her word and let me do a Saturday beer bust and on top of that Bonk would donate back ten percent of the proceeds from the food served that day. The club was kind enough do donate one keg and then sell me a second one at half price so we could make some money.

I decided to do this event out of drag since it was warm outside and I didn't want my face to be melting everywhere. Germaine even came, but of course it was too hot outside for him, so he took a spot at the bar in the air conditioning. Lucky bastard.

How a beer bust works is patrons buy a red solo cup for $10 from my band of little helpers and they can have all the beer they want while they are having lunch or hanging out. Either I or one of the other guys would come around with pitchers and refill the glasses as they got emptied. There was also going to be a raffle during the day. All the prizes were donated, and by donated Germaine went out and bought some items at the instructions of Biff and Kit.

It was a beautiful day to be on the patio. DJ RonRon donated his time and talents to entertain us and the lunch crowd as they came strolling in to buy some of our solo cups. Our crew was ready to greet them, with Victor collecting the money, Shelly explaining what the beer bust was, and Troy being the pump boy. That boy was the town pump in more ways than one, but he was so hot it didn't matter. He was just so pretty to look at and he stroked the tap just right. After hearing the explanation of what a beer bust was several of the patrons ponied up and bought a cup.

Being a beautiful summer day and being this close to Piedmont Park we had a steady stream of customers coming in all afternoon. The music filled the patio over the din of the chatter as the patrons consumed more and more alcohol. It was time for the first announcement about the upcoming raffle and the fabulous prizes one could win. So I graciously took the mic from DJ RonRon and let people know why they were here.

"Good afternoon, everyone! My name is Tyler, but some of you may know me better as Desiree from the show 'Bombshell' from Club Cabaret. I want to thank everyone for coming out and helping raise money for Atlanta Street Rescue. For those of you not familiar with them, Atlanta Street Rescue works to get homeless gay youth off of the streets and provide a safe place for them to go. We will be coming around to sell raffle tickets, so please donate generously, and again thanks for coming out."

That wasn't too bad. I was getting more comfortable with speaking in public while not embodying Marilyn. I grabbed the bucket and the roll of raffle tickets and started working the crowd. I had taped the list of raffle prizes to the front of the bucket so it made it quite easy to show people what they could win for each raffle segment. The first round included a basket of hair care products, and looking around at some of the lesbians here, they definitely needed the help. Hadn't they ever heard of hot oil? There were also some gift certificates to Target and Starbucks which everyone could use. Tickets for the raffle were a dollar apiece or $5 got you twelve tickets. I had some takers, but it really was a chore going from table to table selling tickets when people weren't interested. I didn't know if it was me or the prizes that didn't appeal to the crowd, and then it finally dawned on me that it was a crowd of mostly women. I don't know if they had left the park after a softball game or what, but they filled up most of the tables. There was a smattering of gay boys here and there who were more than happy to buy some tickets.

"Darling, we loved your show," one of the groups said. "Where is your partner in crime on the show, Miss Gigi?" they asked.

"She had to work today, but she said she would try to sneak out a little early if she could," I said.

"I hope so," the table said. "She really made you shine with that play of hers."

That was an odd comment, but I just let it slide by. "She sends her regrets that she couldn't be here to see her fans," I said.

"Here's another $20 for your cause," the group said. "And send that hot pump boy over. Our solo cups are empty."

"Right away, gentleman," I said and went straight over to Troy and pointed to their table. The boys waved at Troy, who grabbed a full pitcher and went straight over to fill their cups.

It was harder selling the raffle tickets than I thought so I decided I needed to take a break and check on Germaine. Plus it gave me a chance to hit the restroom, since all of us were drinking to keep up with the crowd. I usually don't drink beer, but a cold beer on a hot day was hitting the spot.

But before I headed in I swore I saw "The Package" running by. It had been awhile since I had seen him. The restaurant wasn't that far down Piedmont from Marjorie's apartment, so it could have been him. I wondered how everyone was doing.

As I entered the restaurant, I noticed that Germaine had a crowd of boys around him. I wouldn't call them men, since it looked like a gaggle of twinks. I would deal with this after I hit the restroom because I wanted to make sure I still looked presentable and I didn't have anything stuck in my teeth. There is nothing worse than having something green stuck in your teeth and no one telling you about it. I checked myself out in the mirror and cupped a handful of cold water and splashed it on my face. There was nothing more refreshing than wiping the sweat off of your face and neck and cooling down. Nothing in my teeth and my hair was all in place. I was good to go.

I sauntered over to Germaine. As soon as I got there he waved the boys away.

"Come back in fifteen," he said to the gaggle, and they all shuffled away.

"What was all that about?" I asked.

"As I have been putting myself out there more lately, I've discovered that the young ones are attracted to me," he said. "It is quite flattering to have these boys approach me. For so long, I was so tired of being rejected that I stopped even trying."

"Honey, they are attracted to your money," I said "Not to be rude, but they are only looking for a sugar daddy."

"I know that. I may be older, but I have been around the block for a long time," he said. "I would like to bask in their attention for a while, even if they are only after one thing. I am not intending on becoming a sugar daddy anytime soon."

"How does Miss Gigi feel about all your new attention from the gaggle of twinks?"

"Of course she is jealous, but I'm not trying to do anything to encourage this."

"Well I suggest you quit buying drinks for these boys. The minute you cut off the alcohol, they will focus their attention somewhere else."

"Did it ever occur to you that they may be actually interested in me? I find it insulting that you think they are only attracted to me for my money. I think I am a catch, and one of these boys may deserve my attention sometime. Look, I'm tired of meeting someone and giving them my number and then never having the phone ring, or them giving me their number, never getting that returned text or call. It is excruciating waiting for someone to return my affection and having my heart broken. It is absolutely soul-crushing. You haven't really experienced this yet because you fail to realize when someone is sincerely interested in you and you go through life oblivious to the pain of other people. Maybe these boys are only after one thing, but at least they return my calls and texts."

"Oh my God. You are right, Germaine. I didn't mean to sound so petty. I'm sorry."

"And you always wondered why I am not on the dating apps. Well the reason I'm not is because I got tired of chatting with people only to get blocked when they found out I am HIV positive. I had to get a thick skin very early in order to deal with this. I am upfront with every one of these boys and they don't seem to mind."

"I never knew."

"I don't share this with many people because it really isn't any of their business, but it has made me lonelier and shut in than I should ever have been. It's like when you were on the apps and the minute you mentioned to these boys that you did drag you kept getting the cold shoulder. People were judging you without ever having even met you. It really takes you to a bad place. Remember telling me about the guy who wanted you to piss fuck him, and then once he found out, he said he wouldn't do anything with you if you did drag full time?"

"I hated that feeling because it made me feel bad for doing something that I enjoy doing and they didn't even care. I really am sorry."

"Apology accepted. Now you better get back out there. It looks like it is shift change on your tables," he said.

He was right. It was time for the table to turn. The lesbians were leaving and their tables were quickly being filled up by hot men. Now it was time to work the crowd more.

I got back to our beer station and had to help collect money and pass out the cups. Plus Troy's arm was getting tired from pumping up the tap to keep the pitchers full. It was time for him to take over collecting money. The men were more than happy to put $10 into his hand or his shorts pockets, and Troy was even happy to oblige.

"What is your name?" one of the patrons asked him.

"Troy," he said.

"Toy?" the patron said. "I like that. Toy, could you please fill my cup?"

And "Toy" was more than happy to fill the cup. "Here you go sir," he said.

"I would love to hear you call me sir in the bedroom," the patron said.

"That's a possibility. Buy some raffle tickets from me later, and I'll give you my number," Toy said.

"Just come on by, sexy man, and I'll buy whatever you are selling."

Right then and there, I realized that "Toy" was the secret weapon. He was a hot man whom everybody wanted to touch. He was the key to making money on the raffle.

"Troy, may I use your body?" I asked.

"How do you want to use my body?" Troy asked.

"Look, the raffle is sucking wind, and I need you to be my ticket bitch. What I want to do is offer tickets from your crotch to the floor for $10. We can make a lot more money for the charity that way than what I was selling them for earlier when the lesbian lunch brigade was here."

Without missing a beat, he took his shirt off and there was this God of a man standing there in his loose gym shorts and tennis shoes. "Let's go," he said.

I didn't want to waste this opportunity so I grabbed the bucket and tickets and off we went. We went straight to the last patron who said he would buy whatever Toy was selling.

"Gentleman, we are having a raffle, and tickets are $10 from Toy's crotch to the floor. You can even measure the tickets out yourself." Of course, several $10 bills came out from several of the men at the table.

"Sir, you get to go first," Troy said, and the gentleman came over and grabbed the end of the roll of tickets.

"Remember, it is from his crotch to the floor," I reminded him.

"But his gym shorts are blocking his crotch," Sir said.

"Here, this should help," Troy said. And with that, he took Sir's hand and stuck it up his shorts to the edge of his balls. At least he was wearing underwear.

"How much if we can take the tickets down the other leg?" Sir asked. "Twenty-five bucks for both legs," Troy said.

Sir immediately pulled out another $15 and started pulling the tickets up one leg and down the other leg. Of course he had to cup Troy's balls in the middle to make sure the tickets were reaching the crotch. And as promised, Troy gave him his number. The entire table pulled out $25 and the process was repeated over and over.

As we walked away from the table I had to ask, "Are you good with this?"

"Of course I am. I work at a strip club so this is nothing. You should see what I do for a private dance. I'm making you $5 more than I make a dance, and I have to do a lot less here to earn the money. We're all good," he finished.

"Thank you so much." Was all I could manage.

We worked the room over and the men were more than happy to give up their money for a free grope. At this point, Troy let them know where he worked. Smart man. That way he could build up his clientele at the club where he worked. There was a brain in that beautiful body. We turned the money over to Victor, and I could tell from the smile on his face that we were doing well.

We took a break from the raffle ticket sales, and it was time for me to refill the solo cups on the patio. It really was a beautiful crowd with lots of men here whom I would have loved to just throw myself at. It was probably the beer speaking, but I was getting frisky and way friendly. There was a cluster of hot men standing in a corner under the awning who kept needing a refill, and I was more than happy to chat with them.

"My name is Uribol," the one gentleman said.

"Urkel?" I said.

"No, Uribol. It's Russian," he said.

"I will call you sex kitten," I said.

"That works," Uribol said as he stroked my face.

"You can do that all day long," I said.

"These are my friends Hans, David, and Raul," Uribol said.

They all shook my hand and took a refill in their cups.

"Your pitcher's empty. Come and see us on your next round," Uribol said.

"You can count on it, sex kitten," I said.

I left and went back to the beer station feeling hot and bothered. This was fun and we were making some money. Germaine even came out with a couple of twinks in tow to see how things were going.

"I see you are working the crowd well," he said.

"Yes, there are some hot men here and my starfish hasn't been poked in forever." I said.

"You call it a starfish?" Germaine asked.

"Yes, because that's what it looks like. A perfect starfish."

"As long as it is not an angry starfish. Otherwise it would be red. And I'm sure it likes to go to Bangcock a lot," he said.

"Ha ha. It's been forever since this starfish found a butt pirate to plunder it."

"The day is young, my little one. We're off. I will see you later." Germaine and his two twinks headed down the street.

As I waved at Germaine and his posse, I was surprised to see "The Package." It was him earlier, and I guess it was his return route because he was stopped at the corner getting ready to run right by the restaurant. I had to say "hi," so I went out the gate and stood on the side walk. The light finally turned green, and he headed my way. It was great to see a smile spread across his face as he instantly recognized me. Before I could even get a word out, he came up and hugged me.

"How are you doing, baby boy?" he asked.

"I'm doing well. We're here raising money for my charity."

"You look great. Doing charity work suits you well," he said.

"So how is the old gang?" I asked.

"They are doing well," he said.

"When you see them all next, time please tell them I said 'hi'."

"I sure will. Great seeing you again," he said.

And with that, he was off and running up the street again. Even thought things ended up poorly, I did wonder how the gang was doing. I hated the way things ended because it made me sad.

It was time to make another round with the pitcher. There were a lot of solo cups that needed filling first before I made a special trip back to Uribol and his friends. Everyone was so friendly that I decided I definitely had to do another one of these. It was pretty easy money. I needed to thank Biff and Kit for providing the help. If it hadn't been for Troy's body, the raffle wouldn't have made as much money as it did.

I grabbed two pitchers and headed back to Uribol's group. "Here you go, sex kitten," I said as I filled Uribol's cup.

"Who was your hot friend?" Uribol asked.

"Just my old roommate's boyfriend. He's really a nice guy," I said.

"Too bad he doesn't play for our team," Uribol said.

I then poured beer for his friends as well. These boys could drink as Raul chugged the beer down and was ready for a refill.

"What is your name?" Raul asked.

"I'm Tyler."

"You look so defenseless carrying both those pitchers," Raul said as they crowded in. I could feel his hand start rubbing my crotch and my dick started getting hard immediately. I was enjoying the moment. Uribol unzipped my shorts and pulled out my dick.

"Very pretty," he said. He grabbed it for a couple of

313

strokes and then put it back in my shorts and zipped me up.

"I need to go service a couple more tables," I said as I started to move. "But I promise I'll be back."

"We'll be waiting," Raul said.

I felt like I was in high school walking through the halls with a hard on. I'm glad I was carrying two pitchers so I could at least attempt to hide it. The bad part was I was going to have to go to the restroom to adjust everything because he didn't get my dick back into my underwear. Luckily we were getting close to the end of the beer bust anyway, so now was the time to slip into the restroom.

It was mirror check time again. Nothing in the teeth and my hair was still in place. Splash a little water, dry, and I was ready to go back to the boys. Before I could finish, I thought I heard a loud clap of thunder. I exited the restroom and headed to the patio. People were scattering like roaches when they turned the bar lights on since the heavens had opened up and the rain came pouring down. The beer booth group was huddled up under an umbrella counting out the proceeds from the day. And of course, Uribol and his group of friends had scattered like the wind with the rain.

All that was left to do was to secure the money and get the patio cleaned up. DJ RonRon had already closed up shop, so I stepped over the puddles to hug him and thank him for all of his time. It was extremely generous of him to come and help out.

Troy had his shirt back on, and he looked like he was competing in a wet t-shirt contest, as he was soaked from top to bottom. I went up and hugged him and thanked him. I could feel his hot flesh even through the soaked t-shirt.

"You are welcome," he said. "Let me know if you ever do one of these again. I'd be more than happy to help out again."

"Would you ever consider helping me out on one of my performances?" I asked.

"Sure, as long as it doesn't conflict with my work schedule, but a lot of your shows are pretty early, which would work." He grabbed a pen and wrote his number onto a dry spot on my t-shirt. "See you later." And off he went in the rain without a care in the world. It would be great to have his attitude. I immediately grabbed my phone and added his number into my address book. I couldn't afford to lose it to the rain.

The day was over and Victor and Shelly left under the protection of their umbrellas. Someone had the smarts to watch the Weather Channel. I thanked Stephanie for the use of the restaurant, and she let me know I would have the check from their portion later in the week.

"You did well, Tyler," Stephanie said. "Now go home and put on some dry clothes. We hugged and I left feeling accomplished. It was a great feeling.

# CHAPTER 60

I was in a state of euphoria and horniness when I arrived back at the empty apartment. I figured since Germaine was out, now was as good a time as any to go online and make a little money. The beer was still making my head a little fuzzy, but my dick was up and ready for some attention. I made a screwdriver from our bar and headed down the hall to my bedroom.

I fired up the computer and hopped on the bed looking as cute as I could be in a t-shirt and a very revealing pair of underwear. My ass cheeks were barely covered. My drink was just out of camera range. I wanted to keep this buzz going as long as I could today.

The usuals popped up pretty quickly, which always gave me an ego boost. Germaine had helped me get the mic working so that I didn't' have to type anything back. All I had to do was just speak and everyone could hear me, which made this so much easier. The only thing was I would still have to type to respond to private messages, but lately those had been far and few between.

Sometimes it got tiring answering the same questions, "Are you a bottom?" and "Do you suck?" At least there were some new people on here stroking my ego, which made my spirits soar. I know I'm cute, and these strangers helped solidify that in my mind.

I reached over and took a big swig from the screwdriver. I was having fun chatting today. The viewers wanted to see more, so I decided to oblige them and took of my shirt. It wasn't my usual shy and demure show today. I looked straight into the camera and slowly started tugging on my shirt. It started to rise very slowly, and I gave a pouty face as I started lifting it over my head. Once off I held it up and let it drop to the floor on the side of the bed.

I was feeling a little frisky, so I lay on my back and began rubbing my nipples, which I never had done before. The viewers were sent into a frenzy of comments, and I was more than happy to lead them on. The tip counter was going up way faster than usual. I guess I should have been a little sluttier in the past because it probably would have let me hit my tip total faster. I took another swig of screwdriver and fished an ice cube out with my fingers and put it in my mouth to suck the vodka off of it. I then took the cube and rubbed it on my nipples, making them get rock hard immediately. I didn't even realize that my dick was already rock hard in the underwear and was pitching a tent. Several viewers asked me to shove the ice cube up my ass. I hadn't done anything like that in the past, but there was always a first time. I turned my ass to the camera and slid my underwear down my thighs, exposing my pretty pink starfish. I took another swig of screwdriver and fished out another cube, since the other one had melted. I pinched it between my fingers and slowly edged it to my hole.

Just then, the private message bell rang.

I leaned over to the computer to see who it was, and it was Leatherman. I opened the message.

Leatherman25: "baby boy you don't need to do that"

It was my white knight riding in on his white horse to save me.

SpankyBtm: "so glad to hear from you"

Leatherman25: "you are better than this"

SpankyBtm: "I was just having some fun"

Leatherman25: "it's all fun and games until someone takes a screen grab"

I hadn't thought of that. That was all I needed - pictures

of my ass all over the Internet. I was sure some of these girls in the competition would have been more than happy to print them out and share them with everyone. I took another swig.

SpankyBtm: "Thank you for bringing me to my senses"

I dropped the cube by the side of the bed. Of course, the other viewers went ballistic, but I didn't care. I was chatting with Leatherman and happy.

SpankyBtm: "Today I ran into a friend from the old days and it made me miss my old friends"

Leatherman25: "I'm sorry baby. Give it some time. It will get better"

SpankyBtm: "I haven't heard from you in a long time. What's been going on?"

For a while, there was no answer, so I had to go back to calming down my other viewers. To make them happy, I flashed them my ass again.

Leatherman25: "I've been watching but I didn't want to communicate since you have a husband. It wasn't good for me to focus all my attention on something that wasn't attainable"

I was really flattered that he had been watching me and had had that kind of interest me. I'm not sure if it was me or the vodka talking, but I decided to set the record straight so to say.

SpankyBtm: "I need to tell you something"

Leatherman25: "ok"

SpankyBtm: "You know the only reason I'm on here is to raise money for my charity right?"

Leatherman25: "yes go ahead"

SpankyBtm: "Well on here you need to encourage people's fantasy so that they tip more"

Leatherman25: "I'm sure that is true"

SpankyBtm: "the friend who set me up here told me to feed the fantasy"

Leatherman25: "how did you feed the fantasy?"

SpankyBtm: "he said to create a husband so that

everyone would think you were stepping out behind their back"

Leatherman25: "really?"

SpankyBtm: "yes"

Leatherman25: "so no husband"

SpankyBtm: "no. not even a long term date yet"

Leatherman25: "wow"

SpankyBtm: "it just feels so good to tell the truth"

I sat waiting, but no reply came.

SpankyBtm: "you still there?"

No reply.

SpankyBtm: "are you mad?"

Finally the private message bell chimed again. I swear it felt like an hour had gone by.

Leatherman25: "yes I'm mad"

SpankyBtm: "why?"

Leanterman25: "because everything I told you was the truth. My feelings, my desires. I laid it all out there for you and bared my soul thinking I was chatting with someone who could understand what I was saying but instead it was all a game"

SpankyBtm: "I'm so sorry. It was never a game"

Leatherman25: "I feel like I was just your cash register and you used me to ring up your totals"

SpankyBtm: "that couldn't be farther from the truth. I really enjoy our conversations and everything I shared with you was how I truly feel"

Leatherman25: "I don't know what to believe anymore"

SpankyBtm: "I'm telling you the truth. You meant more to me than you will ever know. I wasn't ever happy here unless I was chatting with you. I love hearing what is going on in your life and sharing my experiences with you"

Leatherman25: "I'm sorry I ever put any faith into you"

SpankyBtm: "please don't think that. I have a good heart and my intentions were never to mislead you"

I didn't hear anything back.

I felt extremely bad mentally and physically. My head was

spinning and my stomach was churning. I couldn't keep it down anymore and turned to the side of the bed and threw up. I kept throwing up until all I had left was the dry heaves. I looked around and finally realized the camera was still on. I pulled myself up and closed the lid of the computer. I looked back down at the puddle of muck on the floor, and finally dragged myself off the bed to the bathroom to grab a couple of towels to soak it up. Thank God the floors were hardwood. Otherwise I don't think that color would have been coming out of the carpeting. I staggered down the hall to the laundry, tossed the towels into the washing machine, and shut the lid. My head was still spinning, so I took a minute to regain my composure and supported myself by holding onto the wall. I pinballed down the hallway and collapsed back into the bed. What a lousy ending to a wonderful day.

# CHAPTER 61

It was the night of the next performance of "Bombshell," but it was a different atmosphere. We had gotten word that all three of the local rags were coming to take pictures tonight, so we were all primping to make the best impression. It turned into a competition to see who could land the most pictures in the trades when they came out the following week. I was in my prettiest walk-around outfit - the one with the sparkling crystals that glistened when the light hit them.

There was already a line of people waiting to get into the room even though the doors weren't scheduled to open for another hour. They were as festive as they could be with cocktails already in hand. Several of the cast members were walking up and down the line greeting everyone and thanking them for coming out and supporting the show. It was my time to walk the line and thank everyone. The doors opened, and when I stepped out, there were shouts of "Desiree" and the crowd gave me a round of applause. It was so nice to feel the love coming from the crowd. They were so complimentary. Several patrons let me know that this was their second or third time seeing the show. They thanked me for bringing the show to life. It was great explaining to them how the whole idea of the show came about from my little brain and ended up on paper. I loved to share the story.

The photographers were already there, going up and

down the line getting people to pose. Miss Gigi even came in drag tonight, which was unusual, because she normally showed up in boy clothes since she was mostly backstage all night long. I guess she wanted to be in the pictures as much as the rest of us, as we all posed with groups to get our pictures taken. There was even a little jostling among cast members to squeeze into as many shots as possible. It was all good-natured fun as we all tried to relax and get ready.

The doors finally opened and the crowd herded in as everyone shuffled for the close-up tables and chairs. Kit and Biff even hired two people who were positioned just inside the theatre doors to pass out the new programs that they had printed up, or should I say, Germaine had printed up. Yours truly was the featured performer with the largest picture and largest bio followed next by Miss Gigi. It was my crowning moment in life so far. Now if I could only win the crown at the end that would be the capper. A photographer even got a shot of me holding up my picture in the program.

It didn't take long for the room to become full. The cocktail waiters were already making bank as the crowd was in a tipping mood. It was time to get away from the adoring crowd and slip backstage to change into my first costume. I did enjoy the quiet moments backstage as we all started slipping into character. I had never experienced acting growing up, so it was amazing to discover this new creative outlet for my life. I looked into the mirror and the happiness was beaming from my face.

Next thing I knew, there was a knock on the dressing room door. "Sweetie, I think there is something you should see," said Marni as he handed me a copy of Buzz Atl, which had just hit the news-stands at the club moments before show time. On the cover was Miss Gigi in high whore drag with the caption, "Meet The Creative Mind Behind Bombshell," so I quickly flipped through the pages to the article. I didn't realize that they had even interviewed her about the show, as she had never mentioned any of it to me.

I started reading the interview, and the further I got into

it, the more I felt the anger build up in the pit of my stomach.

"Miss Gigi, how did you come up with the idea of turning a TV show into a stage musical?" the reporter asked.

"I just love the show and have completely worn out my DVD's watching it over and over. Then one night I had a clear vision as I was lip-synching along to Marilyn doing the songs from the show. I felt energized as if I were Marilyn and I could feel the power of the music compelling me to write down the vibrations as they left my body," she said. "One song led to another and the words just flowed. I felt like I was having a transcendental moment, and before I knew it, I had written almost the entire show down on paper. I had to stop and read it over because it poured out so quickly I wasn't sure if I had even written what was on the paper before me."

Of course she had to read it over because she never wrote any of it down. What a load of shit. If it hadn't been for me, she would have still been heading down that dark cavern to the trailer park where she belonged. Fucking trash, taking credit for my work. How could she stab me in the back like this?

I didn't realize Marni had stayed behind me to see what I would do. I'm sure he must have read the article before he gave it to me. As I started to rise from my chair I felt a hand on my shoulder keeping me down.

"I suggest you wait till after the show to have that discussion," he said. "There is a room full of people waiting to be entertained and that is exactly what you are going to do. You are a professional in every sense of the word, and I mean that with all my heart. You have come a long way, baby, since you first stumbled in here to sign up for the contest."

He never removed his hand, so I sat there. I felt the rage ebb as I stared at myself in the mirror. I could see the redness around the edges start to fade and my blood pressure started retreating. "You're right," I said. "These people came out for a good time and there is no sense in letting this ruin their fun. I will deal with this after the show."

"Good girl," Marni said.

The moment was broken as Scotty came over the PA in the dressing room, "Showtime in ten minutes. Places everyone."

"I'm fine. I will give the people what they came for. A great performance with the only drama being on the stage," I said. Marni left and I had a moment to contemplate everything. Why would Miss Gigi say those things? I needed to find out.

I took one more look at the make-up and hair and I was ready to go. I headed out the dressing room door onto the right wing of the stage. My other cast mates were already in position. We had a couple of minutes left before the overture started. Everyone was idly chatting. I had regained my composer and was even nice to Miss Gigi, who was backstage. I winked at the bitch.

To everyone's surprise, the curtains parted and Mr. Winston came through followed by a very tall gentleman in a suit and tie. We weren't expecting Mr. Winston tonight, so this couldn't be good.

"Desiree and Miss Gigi, I need to speak with you both. Marni I need you in on this conversation also," Mr. Winston said. "Everyone else, please give us some privacy." And with that, the rest of the cast slunk back out to the dressing room.

"I want all of you to meet Mr. Larson. He is the attorney for The Mindful Company on Broadway. Your little show was brought to his attention and he has something he needs to say to you," Mr. Winston finished.

"It recently came to our attention that your show 'Bombshell' is infringing on our copyright of the TV show 'Smash' and their show 'Bombshell,'" he said.

"When you say came to your attention, what do you mean?" Miss Gigi asked.

"We were sent a video from a Miss Athena Parthenos,"

Mr. Larson said.

"I'll kill that bitch," Miss Gigi said.

"That is not all of it," Mr. Winston interrupted. "Let him finish."

"Since your show is using characters that are copyright protected, I am giving you this injunction to stop your show from ever being performed again," he said as he presented the injunction to Mr. Winston. "That includes tonight's performance as well."

"Mr. Winston, this can't be happening," I said. "These shows are for charity. We aren't making any money off of them."

"We worked our asses off for this. The parts we created aren't even in the TV show," Miss Gigi said.

"You mean the parts I created aren't in the TV show," I said correcting her.

"What do you mean you created?" Miss Gigi said.

"You think you created this masterpiece? If it weren't for me you would be in the gutter probably choking on your own vomit or sucking a dick for $25 bucks so that you could get your next fix," I said.

"You stuck up cunt!" Miss Gigi said.

"Ladies, not in front of our guest," Marni said.

"Look I had the club lawyer look at it, and it is legit," Mr. Winston said. "If the club violates the injunction, then we are the ones who will get sued and not you, so the show is cancelled. I suggest you tell the audience and refund their money."

"I'm glad you see it our way," Mr. Larson said. "Thank you for your cooperation. I will let my employers know that this will not be a problem to them anymore." He shook Mr. Winston's hand and then exited.

"Mr. Winston, you can't do this to us," I said.

"Desiree, there is nothing I can do. The fine if you violate the injunction is $100,000 for every time the show is performed. I don't think you have that kind of cash lying around and neither do I. Insurance doesn't cover it either. So as of now, there is no more 'Bombshell.'"

"Mr. Winston," Miss Gigi pleaded. "We've worked so hard on this and the room is packed. Can't we just do the show tonight?"

"No means no. That's final. Marni, please let the audience know that the show has been cancelled," he finished.

"Sorry ladies. I have to break the news to the crowd," Marni said. He parted the curtains and began his announcement. "Due to some unforeseen circumstances, tonight's performance of 'Bombshell' has been cancelled and will not be rescheduled. You can get your ticket refund at the box office window. We are sorry for any inconvenience this has caused." And with that announcement, a round of boos echoed throughout the crowd. "Now, now," Marni said. "Please head out to the front bar and the club will provide you with a free cocktail."

As soon as Marni made that announcement, the room vacated as fast as they could to get some free alcohol.

I was left there on the stage in shell shock. Germaine had taken Miss Gigi back to the dressing room to comfort her and Kit and Biff gave me an "if looks could kill" stare as they exited the doors. Marni left with Mr. Winston, I'm sure to discuss what their next move was.

I was alone and this time I really felt it. I had no one here to comfort me. Everyone I had started this journey with was nowhere to be seen. The only sound in the room was the bar staff putting away everything and Scotty shutting down the DJ booth. I felt like I could cry because everything I had worked for was taken away from me with a simple piece of paper. It's funny because the show started as a piece of paper and was now brought down by a single piece of paper. Oh, the irony.

I turned to slink behind the curtain. As I turned my back I heard a single clap. It was followed by another clap and then another clap.

"Brava, darling. That was a fantastic show tonight."

I recognized that cackle of a voice. Shell shock turned to

anger as I turned and faced the rat amongst us. "Why you bitch."

"I told you I was going to win," Athena said. "Sorry I had to bring your little three-ring circus down."

"This was for charity. Why do you even care what we did?" I asked.

"Because I am the most popular entertainer here, and it is going to stay this way. There is no way that crown is going to rest on your nappy head. It will rest gracefully on my wig, where it was meant to be," Athena said.

"Do you even care what damage you caused?"

"No, I don't. Do you think we all do this for the charity? And again, the answer is no. We all do it so that we can feel pretty and get attention from people. This is high school, and I am the head mean girl. Get used to it," she said.

"It is so sad that you have to be like this. I've never done anything to you and neither have any of the hard-working cast members done anything to you," I said.

"Sweetie, I am only looking out for myself. I don't care what happens to your cast, or to you, for that matter. Your life is meaningless to me and you are of no consequence," she said.

"I'm sorry you feel that way. You must be one really damaged individual to be like this," I said and started to walk behind the curtain.

"Come back here! There is nothing wrong with me," she yelled. I tuned her out as I slipped back into the dressing room. All the other cast members had already departed, so I sat there by myself. The only sound I could hear was the dull thud of the dance floor or was it the throbbing in my head? How did everything go so wrong?

# CHAPTER 62

I woke up and rubbed my eyes. The world had not ended. I was alive to face another day. I pulled off the covers and my feet hit the floor as I stretched out my arms as far as I could. I needed to check the fallout from last night, so I decided to grab my computer and check out the message boards for "Bombshell" and check out the on-line columns for Buzz Atl.

It didn't take long to see all the shit that people were saying about the show and me. It was some pretty harsh criticism starting with "Desiree is a liar" to "Get that hillbilly back up to the mountains where she belongs." I guess everyone felt free to say what they wanted since the internet has made people invisible so that they can spout out any bit of trash they want to.

The comments kept coming onto the "Bombshell" Facebook page. It was just more hate after hate. I understand people were disappointed about not being able to see the show, but I was bearing the brunt of the comments, especially after Miss Gigi lied her way through the interview. It really hurt that people were accusing me of taking credit for something they thought I didn't do. It was really bad to see the comments where everyone felt sorry for Miss Gigi. "Miss Gigi we love you!" and "Your show is beautiful. Don't let that crazy Desiree try to take credit for your fabulous words." It got to a point that I couldn't look at Facebook anymore.

In Buzz Atl online, they do a picture display in the "Seen At" section. The headline was "Bombshell Lays Bomb" and it was a picture of me with several of the cast members in a very candid shot. Not very flattering. To make it even worse, they didn't get me from my good side.

I felt bad for all the people who had put in all that hard work on the show that had now been turned into a punch line. The good thing for most of the cast was that they could fall back into their community theater. I didn't have another outlet. My only real outlet now was to do some more drag shows and make a push for the finish. I'd made a valiant effort so far, so there was no sense stopping that now. I'd got the Georgia A&M games yet to bring in some more money, so things could still go ahead.

I hadn't even thought about my phone until now. I had turned it off last night when I went to bed because I didn't want to be disturbed. I reached over and hit the power button. As it slowly opened up, it was time to take a leak. As I entered the hallway, I heard some noise coming from the kitchen. I figured it must have been Germaine making his coffee with the TV on. I turned the corner and there was Germaine in his bathrobe snuggling with one of his little twink boys who was only wearing his Andrew Christian underwear. At that moment, I finally realized I was only in my underwear, so I was a little self-conscious even though I had a much better body than the little twink.

"I thought you had to be at work this morning?" I asked.

"I got my shift covered so that I could visit with this nice young man," Germaine said. "Timmy, this is Tyler."

"Hey," Timmy said.

"Hey. I need to go put some clothes on," I said as I exited the kitchen and went back down the hall.

By this time, my phone had come to life and the text bell had been ringing and ringing. I quickly scanned to see whom the texts were from before I opened any of them. To my surprise, most of them were from the other contestants.

The first one I opened was from Precious. "Girl you were

screwed by that bitch! Luvd your show and luv u!" She really was a class act and proved that you could be competitive, but still respect everybody.

The next one I opened was from Mary Jane. "Sweetie you put something special together. Don't listen to the haters. Those of us who really know you know it was you who did all the work. You are the heart of that show." Wow again more support from my competition. I guess I really had become friends with some of the girls whom I got to know better.

Miranda was very kind in her text. "Thanks for being the doll you are. You make me smile and probably don't even know it. It's hard to crack this exterior." Once you got to know her, she really was a softy at heart.

Marni even sent a text. "Baby girl you have blossomed so much that this is only going to be a stepping stone in your career. I can see you doing great things in the future." That was probably the nicest thing anyone had ever said to me. I knew compliments are few and far between, so I needed to do the correct thing and respond back.

"Thank you for your mentoring. Without your support I wouldn't even still be in the competition. Love Desiree," I texted. I really did appreciate all the support and attention Marni had given me to make me become a better performer. And the nice thing was he didn't want to get into my pants. He was helping me because he was a generous and kind person. Why couldn't there be more people like him out there?

So I was feeling more positive, and even though the show wasn't going to continue at least I could still go on. At that moment, I felt like Celine Dion belting out the theme from "Titanic."

All that positivity was cut short when I saw the text from Biff. All it read was, "We are coming over." I hated it when he was cryptic because that meant all he was going to do was yell at me and go on a tirade about something I hadn't done or something that I shouldn't have done. I could never win with him. Sucked.

The time waiting for those two to come over always seemed like an eternity, so with Germaine entertaining, I thought I would just take my shower and get dressed. I had the day off from work, so I was in no real hurry to get anything done. I slipped into my bathroom, turned on the bath faucets, and pulled the diverter so that the water flowed out of the shower-head. I loved the feel of the steam as it descended from over the shower curtain. I slipped off my underwear, slid the curtain open a bit, and hopped into the shower. I just stood there with the water from the shower head soaking my entire body. The heat felt great as I felt my muscles begin to loosen up and release the stress from last night. I didn't move, as I let the water and steam do their work. I felt it in every crack of my body as my mind went to that total relaxation place. My mood elevated as I realized it was not the end of the world. So what? The show got shut down. I created something based off of someone else's work, so imagine what I could do if I put my mind to it. This wasn't the end, but just the beginning.

I opened my eyes with a new sense of positivity and was ready to face the day. I quickly washed my hair, grabbed the soap, and lathered up my dirty body. It was always a pain getting the make-up off, especially the eye-liner. I was sure I looked like a raccoon at times. I rinsed off and turned off the water. It was quiet again. I slid the curtain back, grabbed my fluffy towel, and started to rub my body dry. I finally realized that there was a little chill in the air. I guess I shouldn't have been surprised since it was fall.

I dressed, I was surprised that the boys weren't here yet. I checked my phone and there was the new command. Biff texted, "Meet us at my place." I was in trouble for sure.

I texted back, "Be right there."

Biff lived in a concierge building where you had to be buzzed into the parking area and then buzzed into the front door. I felt like I was going to be stripped searched every time I went in there. I swear, the concierge looked down on me like I was a piece of white trash that happened to be blown into the lobby by the prevailing winds.

I pushed the button to get into the parking gate. "Welcome to the Belmont. How may I help you?" came the voice of the concierge through the call box.

"I'm here to see Biff Davis," I said.

"I will see if Mr. Davis is taking visitors. Please wait," the concierge said.

It felt like an eternity every time he did this. "Mr. Davis will see you. Please pull your car into the parking area and take a visitor spot." With that, the gate opened and the guard arm went up. I drove up the drive and headed to the visitor parking area. The residents parked underneath the building in their reserved spaces and their entry was gate controlled, but each owner had a clicker to open their gate.

I parked and walked over to the building call box and pushed the concierge numbers. "Welcome to the Belmont. How may I help you?"

"Tyler to see Mr. Davis." With that, the buzzer sounded and the door lock opened. I pushed open the heavy wood door with the stained-glass inserts and headed into the lobby. I already could feel the stare coming at me from the concierge desk. "Oh, it's you again," he said. "Please fill out the guest registry. Will I have to get the parking lot cleaned again where your car dripped oil all over last time you were here?"

"No. For your information, I had that problem taken care of," I responded.

"Glad to hear it. Let me call Mr. Davis and let him know you are here." And with that he called Biff again. "Very good, sir, I will send him up. You may go up, Mr. Tyler. Please use the second elevator." He acted as if I was being released from jail.

I pushed the twenty-fifth floor button and the door closed and I was zipping on my way to a confrontation. I should have quit while I was ahead and left. The elevator slowed down as my ears popped going up this far in the tower. The door opened and Biff's penthouse was down the hall on the left. I felt like my feet were stuck in mud as I trudged down the hall and approached the door. I gathered up the courage and finally knocked on the door. Biff was there immediately to open it up.

"Why come in, Tyler. It is so good to see you," he said. He was too happy. I wondered if he had run over a small child that morning. Kit was already there waiting for me as well and he looked a little chipper himself.

"Can I get you something to drink?" Biff asked.

"No, I'm fine, but thanks for asking. Why was I summoned here?" I had to ask. I wanted to know what the crime was and what the punishment would be so that I could get out of here and get back to my normal life.

"Why are you in such a rush?" Kit asked.

"I've got things I need to get done today," I said.

"Well according to your calendar, there is nothing you have to get done today," Kit said. I had forgotten that they had an itinerary of my work and my planned events so that they could plan other things for me to do.

"Well the reason we called you here is to let you know that we did hear from the 'Guys As Dolls Show.' This letter arrived this morning, and we wanted to share the news with you as soon as we heard."

"That's excellent," I said. At least now I knew why they called me over. My heart was racing because I could use some good news today after the disaster of last night.

"Let me pull it out and read it to you," Biff said.

"Dear Desiree, Thank you for your submission video. As you know, we receive hundreds of videos from worthy performers across the country who are competing for one of the ten audience choice competition slots. After the talent committee previewed your video, it was decided that you did not make it into our audience choice category. We appreciate your submission and hope you audition in the future. Sincerely, Shandi Reommelle."

"Isn't that just fabulous news?" Kit said.

"After that debacle last night, this is just the best thing that could happen," Biff said.

"How can you say that this is the best thing that can happen? This is horrible," I said.

"Horrible for you, but wonderful for us," Kit said. "What it means is that we don't have to ever deal with you again."

"Your rising star has now turned into a falling star and we are done with you," Biff said. "Now turn your little tail around and walk your tiny non-star ass out our door."

"How can you be so mean?" I asked. "All I ever did was do what you told me to do."

"Well obviously what you did wasn't right," Kit said. "Now it's time to fly away, little rotten cocoon."

"And do not darken our door again," Biff said. "Shoo, fly, shoo."

I felt the anger well up in my body. I kept telling myself not to say it, but it just came out. "You two are the most pompous ass fucks I have ever met in my entire life. The only reason people kiss your ass is because you have money. If you were broke you would be too fat fucks who would have to be turning tricks in a dark hallway sucking people's dicks off through the glory hole because no one would ever touch your shriveled up sacks in a million years."

Biff took about one second to reply. "Look, you little white trash hillbilly, all our friends have money and so do we. You are nothing but a little blip on our road map that was a bad detour. I will walk out my condo door, hop in my Mercedes, and head to the club where I will have cocktails that you can't afford to purchase with my friends at the bar. You, on the other hand, will return to your little hovel where you will fade into total anonymity eating your ramen noodles and mac and cheese. Once you walk out that door, I will never think about you again."

"That's where you are wrong," I said. "Not only will I win the competition, but I'm going to make you eat your words."

I walked out and slammed the door. I headed down the hall and pushed the elevator button. I couldn't wait for it to get here because now I could truly relax. I was free from the evil queens.

# CHAPTER 63

The next event I had to make an appearance at was the Channeling Funds For A Change Campaign's annual bowling fundraiser. I had never bowled, so I was going to be there to mingle with the crowd and help keep them entertained. It would be fun and there were always a bunch of hot men there with money. Maybe I could get some of them to support me since the evil queen train was over.

The bowling alley was in Midtown, so it wasn't a far drive from the apartment. Germaine had other things to do that day so I was on my own. The organizer was a man named Chet, with whom I had only spoken on the phone. He wanted me there an hour early so that I could help check people in. Each participant paid $50 to bowl three games and they got their shoe rental included. From what he told me the event was sold out, so it should be a good crowd.

I arrived the hour early and the folks at the counter directed me to Chet. He was probably in his late forties with some grayish, thinning hair and glasses, and he had the best smile. He made me feel very welcomed.

"Hello, Desiree! I am so glad that you could join us today. I'm going to have you help with the check in. You will be sitting at this table. Everyone is in alphabetical order by last name. When they get here, all you need to do is have them sign next to their name. Very easy peasy," he said. "And if you get thirsty or hungry, we have drinks and a buffet set up in the game room. And please feel free to mingle among the participants. I'm sure they would love to meet you."

That was very nice. I rambled over to the game room and saw that they had a bar set up with a very cute bartender waiting to be helpful. There was also a buffet, but not a normal bowling food buffet. Where were the hot dogs, pizza, chips, dips, and chicken wings? Instead, it was a spread of kale salad, salmon, pot stickers, and fancy finger sandwiches that looked like they had cucumbers in them. This didn't say bowling alley, but I guess they knew their crowd.

I moseyed up to the bar and ordered a screwdriver.

"My pleasure, my dear. Any preference on vodka?" he asked.

"Whatever you think will be great. I'm Desiree," I said as I stuck out my hand to shake his.

"I'm Wallace. It is a pleasure meeting you," he said as he took my hand and kissed it.

What a gentleman! If this is any indication of how the day was going to go, I was in heaven.

So it came time to check everyone in, and I was positioned in the middle of two other CFFACC volunteers who seemed to know a bunch of the people. It seemed like there were a lot of people who had booked groups of their friends to bowl with, so after they checked in, they strolled over to their assigned lanes. You could see them hug and kiss as someone new arrived. I liked to people watch. I didn't recognize any of these people who were here. I went to a lot of events, but I didn't know where these people were from because they were never at the other fundraisers. It was very odd. Where were my people?

Finally, some of the club folks came into bowl because the club was a sponsor of the event. I didn't know what being a sponsor for the event entailed, but two of the bartenders and two of the bar backs came out to bowl. It was nice to see a friendly face and get hugged.

Once check in was complete, the DJ fired up the music,

turning the bowling alley into a huge night club. The only thing missing was a fog machine. The boys and girls were running back and forth to the bar and the buffet and everyone was in a very festive mood. One of my other responsibilities, it turned out, was to announce the winner of the door prize drawing, which they were doing every fifteen minutes. They must have gotten a lot of sponsors because they had a slew of door prizes, including everything from haircuts, tanning sessions, restaurant gift cards, and bar tabs. I wish I could have been in the drawings because I could have used some of these prizes.

So between drawings, I introduced myself to the different bowlers and let them know about my charity. The first pair of lanes was made up of all beautiful men who were in their mid-thirties and looked like clones of one another. They all had short hair that made them look like they went to the same hair salon on the same day and wore matching pink t-shirts with the slogan "If You Can Read This You Are Too Close" and blue jeans.

"Hello gentlemen, my name is Desiree, and I'm volunteering here today. I hope you are all having a great time so far."

You would have thought I had just opened up my panties and took a shit on the floor from the looks I got back from them. I swear they all managed to stare at me at once and then immediately turned their backs on me. It got extremely cold in here.

"Well, have a good one," I said as I headed to the next pair of lanes. This one was full of lesbians who ranged from a lipstick to a truck driver. The reception here was a little better, with one of the women donating $20 to my charity. It was nice to be acknowledged by them. We don't get a lot of lesbians at our drag shows so it was a great chance to spread the word to them about my charity.

Chet came over and tapped me on the shoulder. It was time to do one of the door prize drawings, so he handed me the microphone. "Hey everyone! It's time to pull out your door prize tickets for our first drawing of the day! This one is a $100 bar tab to The Forrest," I said. Chet then raised the bucket up with the tickets for me to pull out a winner. I dug deep and pulled out a ticket. "Everyone check your tickets. It's an eye-shadow blue ticket number 222369. Woo hoo! 69!" I chuckled into the mic. To my disgust, it was one of the clone boys who had the winning ticket raised over his head as he sashayed his way to the front counter. He stuck out the ticket and the numbers matched. "What is your name?" I asked.

"It's Arlo," he said.

"Everyone, let's congratulate Arlo," I announced to the crowd. "Keep your tickets handy because we will be doing another drawing shortly."

"It took me awhile to recognize you, but you were that crazy bitch claiming to have written 'Bombshell,'" Arlo said. "Miss Gigi is a friend of mine, and I can't believe you tried to steal her work."

"That's not true," I said as I tried to defend myself.

"Don't go there, missy. She told me the whole story. Shame on you," Arlo said as he walked away not giving me an opportunity to even discuss it with him. This day was quickly circling the bowl.

I made a beeline for the bar, and I must have looked like a wreck because Wallace had a cocktail waiting for me when I got there. "Baby, what's wrong?" he asked.

"This is a rough crowd," I said. "I'm just volunteering, but these are a bunch of bitches."

He looked around to make sure no one was listening in, "Can I let you in on a little secret?" he whispered.

"Yes, please," I said.

"The only reason I work this gig is because it pays stupid money, and the reason it pays stupid money is that no one wants to work with these bitches. These are the most pretentious fuckers I've ever met. The staff here at the bowling alley hates the crowd, but they are in business of making money just like me," he finished. "Don't take anything personally, they say."

"Thank you. I thought I was just going crazy. How should I deal with them?"

"Just give them a rash of shit back. You are only a volunteer, so no one is going to care what you do. I can't because I'm being paid to be here," he said.

"I think I will do that." I chugged my drink and had him fill me back up. He also made us a Kamikaze shot that we both swigged down. Nothing like a little courage to get your bitch mouth going.

I went back out with a new attitude and a smile on my face. I was going to talk to these people even if they didn't want me to. I went straight up to the next pair of lanes and introduced myself. One of the boys decided to sass off right away.

"I saw your show a couple of weeks ago and you were flat on some notes," he said.

"Well at least I can correct my notes next time I sing, but I don't think you will ever be able to save that flat ass of yours. It looks like it actually curves inward like your butthole was sucking your ass in." His friends all laughed.

"I'm Desiree, everyone, and I'm raising money for Atlanta Street Rescue if you care to make a donation." One of the guys pulled out his wallet and gave me $20. His little friend was still burning a bright shade of red as he slunk into his seat and sipped on his cocktail.

Thank God the next pair of lanes were the guys from the club. I could relax for a minute and cut up with them before I moved onto the next group. "Darling, we know how you feel. These people suuuuuuucccckkk!" one bartender said.

"The only reason we come here is for the free food and drinks. It's very rare that we get someone to wait on us, so we are going to take advantage of that," the other bartender said.

"Can I get a group hug?" I asked, and of course they all came in and wrapped their love around me. At least the day wasn't a total wash out, as I got to grab their asses. They loved the attention, and I loved giving it to them.

"Sweetie, the reason we love you is because of your positive energy. You are always up and fun at the club, and we love you for it," the bartender said.

"Thank you very much. That makes my day," I said.

Off I went because it was time for another drawing. "Hey boys and girls, this time we are giving away five free haircuts from another sponsor, Pop My Bubble Salon, and from the looks of some of your hair, it is just in time." Chet brought up the bucket, and this time, he pulled out a ticket. "Another eye-shadow blue ticket 245615. If this is your ticket, bring it up to the counter to pick up your prize."

Of course, the winner was another of the clone boys. I didn't know how they could be so lucky with all these other people here.

"Hey girl, here's the ticket," he said. The numbers matched so Chet gave him the gift certificates for the free haircuts.

"You know missy, you might want to use some of these gift certificates to get your wigs done. They are looking mighty tired," he said.

"That's okay," I said. "Because at least my wigs are all one color. It looks like you missed that back grey patch when you tried to do the bottle job at home. They need to call you Pinto since you have so many spots."

"How rude," he said as he stomped away.

"You need to be nice to the patrons," Chet said. "They have helped raise some good money for a good cause."

"Yes, Chet, I understand, but I'm not going to put up with their lack of manners. Just because they have some money doesn't mean that they have to treat everyone like crap. One of the things my mama taught me was to respect myself, and too bad these bitches never were taught the same lesson."

Back to the bar I went just so I could cool off. Wallace saw me coming and had my drink waiting for me. I grabbed it and chugged it down. He immediately filled me up with another. "Thank you. At least there are some well-mannered people here."

"You're welcome," Wallace said.

I looked at the clock on my phone, and luckily I didn't have much more time here to deal with this bunch. I finished my rounds of trying to mingle with the patrons who really didn't care if I was there or not. I'm used to getting some abuse from the girls in the competition, but I know that is usually meant with a little bit of love. These people were just rude.

"Hey skankarella!" I heard yelled my way. I turned to look, and a skinny twink boy was heading my way. "You should be ashamed of yourself for misrepresenting someone else's work as your own. I'm proud to call Miss Gigi a friend, and it is so sad to see you stab her in the back on your pitiful attempt to get attention and claim all the glory," he said.

"Honey, the only glory I'm looking for is the hole I'm going to shove my dick through with you on the other side to suck it dry. You need to wash the dirt of your knees, you dirty little cunt. Now go away and grab a burger you skinny railed bitch."

What I didn't realize that Chet had been standing behind me when I went off on this boy. "Desiree, I'm going to have to ask you to leave," he said.

"That's fine," I said. "I don't want to be around this bunch of assholes any longer. Let me just grab my purse from the front counter."

I sauntered over to the front counter, and instead of grabbing my purse, I grabbed the microphone. "Hey, boys and girls, it has been my pleasure to meet the most soulless people in the city of Atlanta. I have to leave now because the smell of you rotting from the inside out is making me sick to my stomach. Have a great day." I handed the microphone to Chet, who had turned white as a ghost, which was probably hard to do for him since he was the whitest man on earth already. I looked around and everyone was staring at me as I grabbed my purse.

Finally, the silence was broken as the bartenders and bar backs from the club all shouted in unison, "We love you Desiree!"

I strutted for the door and waved to Wallace at the bar, who was giving me the thumbs up. Desiree out, bitches.

# CHAPTER 64

So the next football game was coming up, and I needed to get people lined up to help with the booth. How hard could this be? You got to watch a bunch of hot, butch men parading themselves back and forth in front of the booth all day long. Lots of eye candy everywhere you looked.

I grabbed my phone and started dialing the people I had met through the club and who had come to my shows previously. I was sure some of them would be willing to help out.

My task was turning out to be harder than I thought. I left a lot of voice-mails, and the couple of people I did get a hold of were not interested in helping out. It was time to call in the cavalry, and Germaine was his name. I was hoping Germaine would have some free time since he was pretty preoccupied now with his twinks, was staying out late, and was having a lot of company over. I never knew who I was going to run into in the morning getting a coffee or in what state of dress they would be. I had seen so many pairs of boxer shorts lately that I could identify the twink just by the brand of boxers I found on the kitchen floor.

I dialed Germaine's number, and it went straight to voice mail. "Germaine, it is your favorite roommate. I need some help in getting people to man the booth for the next Georgia A&M game. Please let me know if you have anybody that can help out. Hugs."

Germaine was always predictable and he usually called

back within a couple of minutes. I knew he would have an idea of what to do.

I waited, but his return call never came. Now I was in panic mode. My phone was silent and none of the people I had left messages for even called me back.

How did I end up in this situation? I'm a nice guy, but I felt like a total pariah. I'd been shunned by everyone with whom I used to be friends and now the A Gay group has turned its back on me. I didn't realize how much I needed everyone, and not just for their help. They were my support and backbone that got me through everything, but I didn't realize it and let it slide through my fingers. I thought Atlanta was a friendly town, but it sure had given me the cold shoulder. I was at times like this that people turn to God, and I was not the exception to the rule.

"God, it's me. What have I done to piss you off? I try to be a good person and help all that I can. I know I don't go to church, but I truly believe in my heart that if you lead a good life, you will make it to the next level when you pass this great world even if you weren't at church every Sunday. I know you don't give people any more that they can handle, but I've had my fair share of it in life. Please give me some sign that things will be okay. Amen." My mother would have been so proud.

No answer immediately came, and I needed advice. The next person I called should have been the first person I called. "Marni, I need some advice. Are you available," I asked.

"Darling, anything for you. Meet me at the club in a half hour."

Marni would know what I should do. I was sure of that. I threw on some warm clothes and headed to the club. There was a chill in the air and the leaves made for a brilliant landscape. I loved Georgia at this time of the year because the humidity was gone and the scenery was incredibly beautiful. It made me miss the mountains because you could go to a mountain peak and just stare at the carpeted valley with all of its beauty and color everywhere. It really made me feel at ease.

I got to the club and Marni was already waiting for me at the bar with a screwdriver in hand for me.

"Rough day?" he asked.

"Yes. I don't know where everything went wrong. One minute I was on top of the world, and the next I couldn't get arrested if I tried."

"Welcome to the world of show business. One day, you're the belle of the ball, and the next, you are the tabloid headlines. The only thing worse is when they stop talking about you at all."

"That's what I'm afraid of."

"Don't be. You've worked too hard to get where you are. Don't let a lie ruin everything that you built up. All of us at the club know you were the brains and beauty behind your show."

"How do I fix it?"

"You work. You get out there and show these people that you won't be stopped. Look at all the entertainers who work here. They have busted their asses to get where they are and didn't let anyone tell them no. People don't tell you that being a professional entertainer is hard work. It's not just show up and entertain. You have to plan and practice and perfect your craft to make people like you. You have to put the show into the show."

"Where do I start?"

"Call one of your friends from the contest. Most of these girls love you and would do anything for you. Start there and get out there and show people that you are not afraid of a little bad press. Make them forget those stories and have them start telling your new story. Maybe this is your second coming?"

"I haven't come in a long time," I said and laughed.

"See, now you can see the humor in the situation, and with humor you can get through anything. You are a lot stronger than you believe you are."

# CHAPTER 65

I made the call to Mary Jane, who was more than willing to help me out. She was having a show that week and invited me to come and sing a couple of numbers live with her and the band. It was nice to have some support again. She really was a lovely person.

We got together to rehearse since Mary Jane was more of a rock chick than I could ever be. "Sweetie, you have to remember that some of the people with the best voices never make it big. Look at all those people on Broadway who are belting it out night after night without ever achieving world-wide fame. Do you know why they do it?" she asked.

"No, why do they do it?"

"Because they enjoy doing it. They are doing it because it makes them happy and not because they are seeking world fame and fortune. Yes, it is nice if that ever happens, but that is few and far between. And most of those people never make it big because they are not the pretty people whom everyone adores. Look at all the early videos on MTV. It killed the ugly person's careers in music. I do it because I want to make everyone happy. I like entertaining people and it brings me joy," she said. "I want you to do that with me and enjoy it as much as I do. Now we need to find some songs you can work with."

"I want to feel the music as much as you do."

"Well, let's find something that you feel comfortable

singing. How about 'Another Piece of My Heart' by Janis Joplin? I think you would do great with it."

"I'm not familiar with it, so let's hear it and see what we can do. If it is something you think will work, I'm sure it is something worth considering. I really want to break my mold and give the people something different."

"Janis it is, then. We just need to find you one other song that will click with the crowd. How about a little Pat Benatar?" she asked.

"You have to remember that I'm a little younger than you are and don't know many of the older artists."

"Older artists are just as relevant as they were back in the day. You need to get a musical education."

She went to her record collection. And when I say records, I mean records. She didn't have CD's or an iPod. Everything was alphabetized by artist's last name so she was able to locate everything quickly in one of her six Peaches Records crates. She found Pat Benatar and pulled out, one LP after the other, and examined the song list on the back. "The one thing you don't get to appreciate on a CD is the art work. When these records were done, so much more time was spent on the artwork for the cover, the back, and the LP sleeve. They really tried to sell a story. But now-a-days, it is just slap a picture on there and call it art. Oh my God, I sound like my mother. Here is a song I want you to listen to and tell me what you think. This was Pat's first big hit, and I think it would work for you. It's called 'Heartbreaker'."

She put the LP on the turntable. The first thing I noticed was the amount of energy in the song and the driving guitars. It moved you forward then you heard the voice of a dirty angel as she growled through the song. It was instant love, and I thought I could do it justice.

I started singing along with the chorus and Mary Jane knew at that moment that she had made the right decision.

"So Pat it is. The band hasn't played this one in forever, but it should come back quickly. Now let's get that Janis song."

"It's always good to expand your mind."

"Well, if you want to expand your mind, take a hit on this," she said as she pulled out a joint from her pocket and fired it up. "I need a smoke break."

She inhaled deeply and passed it to me. I'm not a big pot smoker, but since I hadn't been drinking yet, I took a couple hits off the joint. It made me relax a little, which was great, since I hadn't been able to find much peace lately. I passed it back to her as we both sank into her comfy sofa and let the music of Janis wash over us.

"Why haven't I heard this music before?" I asked.

"You didn't have that one friend around who could turn you onto some new music back in the day. Everyone needs a music geek in their life. I guess that is how I started out as a music geek. I loved discovering new music, and it was such fun back in the day to hang at the record store and talk to the staff to see what they were really into. I used to go to a place called the Head Shed, which sold music as well as paraphernalia. I think I discovered two of my true loves in one spot," she said. "They were always so nice to me since I was young when I started coming into the store. Every time I smell incense, it immediately takes me back to when I was thirteen years old. Those were the good old days."

"You're not that old."

"I know, but time flies by as you get older. It is hard to believe that crowning is just around the corner and that this process started months and months ago. To be honest, I don't really care who wins as long as it isn't Athena."

"I agree. I've had so much fun meeting everyone but she's been a total bitch to me the entire time," I said.

"Don't worry, she's been a bitch to everyone. That's just her. She didn't get enough love as a child."

"I was the opposite. I got smothered, but I didn't appreciate it like I should have. I guess if it didn't always come with a side of religion I would have been willing to accept it more."

"Honey, there are all kinds of love that are going to come

into your life in all different forms. You might not recognize it at first, so just let it wash all over you. Come on. Break is over. We need you to learn the lyrics so that we can get you with the band in a couple of days. The show is Saturday so we don't have much time."

"Holy crap," I thought. I haven't been in front of a big crowd since the debacle started, and I wasn't quite sure if I would be ready for it. So I listened to the music and wrote down the lyrics. It helped me to retain it better if I could visually see it. I just hoped I could keep up with the band.

Mary Jane said we were going to stick to the way Janis and Pat did the recording that I first heard. She was nice enough to load them into my iPod so that I could rehearse some more. That was the whole key for me, because when I did "Bombshell," I had already known all the music. Maybe I was just psyching myself out. This was only two songs, so I shouldn't be worried. At least I would be singing with Mary Jane, so I really needed to relax.

I also needed to figure out an outfit to wear. This was Mary Jane's show, so I didn't want to upstage her. There is nothing worse than when the secondary performer outshines the headliner, so I was going to blend in a little so that I didn't steal the spotlight. Since it was going to be in a bar I decided something mid-length and dark would be best. I could always accessorize a little to give it a little panache. Plus the heels were going to be five inches so that was enough showing off.

It was finally Saturday, and I was as ready as I was ever going to be. We had rehearsed a couple of times during the week, so I felt confident that it would be great. It was time to make my way over to Harriet's Club, where Mary Jane performed on a regular basis. It was a dive bar, but the patrons really loved Mary Jane and had always been supportive of anyone she brought out on stage with her. At least I wasn't trying to headline something right now because I didn't think I could fill a confessional with people wanting to come see me.

In the dressing room everyone was really relaxed. You could smell the pot cloud before you even saw it. There was a spread of pulled pork barbecue sliders with pickles and hot sauce for your liking along with Doritos and a small self-serve bar with a bucket of ice and a stack of red solo cups. I remember my momma calling red solo cups ruby red crystal to help me feel like we had something even though we were struggling at the time. She did try to make me feel secure even though she probably didn't know what was going to happen next. I need to thank her for that the next time I see her.

"Baby, are you ready for this?" Mary Jane asked.

"Yes, I am. And thanks for giving me the opportunity. A lot of people have turned their backs on me, but not in a good way," I said with a little nervous laugh.

"You have been before bigger crowds than this and you did great," she said. "Just remember they are all here to be entertained. We will do about a half hour before I call you up, so sit back and relax," she said.

"Already am," I said as I held up my red solo cup. Off they went, I could hear the music start bleeding through the walls. I was a little fidgety, but it was a good energy. I was looking forward to having some fun. I watched the clock and about twenty-five minutes in, I slipped out the dressing room door and stood by the side of the stage. Mary Jane and the band were killing it as usual.

She finished a cover of the Cars song, "Let's Go," and started my introduction.

"Alright, boys and girls, I want to bring up a good friend of mine to help me out on a couple of numbers. Many of you have seen her competing with me to be crowned the first Miss Club Cabaret, and through all this we have become good friends. Please welcome to the stage my friend, Desiree."

I started up the short riser of stairs to some applause and some boos, but all I could do was keep moving until I got to my mic stand. And to my surprise, Mary Jane had some

351

more to say.

"Hey, hey, hey. That's not how we behave here. Didn't your mother teach you some manners?" she said admonishing her own crowd. "When I bring someone up here, I expect you to treat them with respect. There have been many things said lately of this entertainer, but it has all been bullshit. Y'all need to quit believing everything you read on the Internet. I know for a fact that Desiree put all her energy into writing 'Bombshell' and she deserves your divided attention."

The crowd looked a little sheepish.

"We love you, Mary Jane," someone yelled.

"Thank you, baby. Now everyone please share your love for Miss Desiree," Mary Jane commanded.

This time the crowd went up and I felt much better. The band then went right into Janis, and the crowd knew it immediately. I grabbed the mic and did my best Janis howl, and we were off to the races. The crowd was singing right along with us, and I felt all their energy coming my way. It was great to sway and groove again on a stage and feel the music again. I had missed this.

The first number ended and the band went straight into "Heartbreaker." The crowd knew this one just as well and they were bouncing around and fist pumping. We just sang our hearts out, and I got almost every word right and hit every note right. It was a good night. The song ended and again the crowd was very generous with their round of applause.

"Everyone, Miss Desiree!" Mary Jane said as I waved my goodbye and headed off stage. I slipped along the club wall and grabbed a seat at the bar to watch the rest of their set.

I felt a tap on my shoulder and turned around to see a very sexy twink staring at me. "You were wonderful," he said. "And I never believed the stories about you. I saw 'Bombshell' and I knew that someone who was so passionate about her character and music had to have more invested in the show than just coming and reciting lines."

"That is the nicest thing that anyone has ever said to me." I said as I reached out to grab his hand. "What is your name?"

"I'm Caesar, and I'm glad I got a chance to meet you. I hope I can see you in some more things very soon," he said.

"I hope you will too," I said. He slipped back into the crowd. The rest of the evening, I had several other people come over and tell me how much they enjoyed "Bombshell." For once, nothing negative was thrown my way. It was good to know that there are some genuine people out there who can pay you a compliment instead of stabbing you in the back on the Internet.

Mary Jane's set was over and she joined me at the bar. She was patting herself dry with a towel.

"I sweat like a pig when I do these indoor gigs, especially with the lights," she said as she was running the towel up and down her arms. She even ran the towel over her hair, which turned out to be her real hair.

"It is my real hair," she said. "I like it long. Girl, I'm glad you came tonight. I hope this will put an end to all your gloom and doom. There are people out there who do love you."

"Thank you for making me realize that. We all get trapped in our own little bubble and this was the kick I needed to get my shit together."

"Are you ready to take Athena down now?"

"Definitely."

# CHAPTER 66

I awoke that morning feeling refreshed for the first time in a long time. After last night's performance, I felt more like myself and the drive had returned to win the contest. I realized that it was awfully quiet in the apartment, which was nice, since I rarely got any time to myself at home. Hopefully, Germaine was either at work or still out somewhere with the boy of the day.

I put on a bathrobe and leisurely strolled to the kitchen to get a cup of coffee and a cherry Danish. The sad part was that it had been so long for me that my cherry grew back and started shooting out pits.

I turned on the iPod player and a very sexy slow jam came on. I could feel the bass start to fill my body as I started to sway back and forth to the groove. I grabbed a broom and slowly glided around the apartment, dipping and twisting the broom as I moved along.

The moment was shattered, as there was a knock at the door. Who delivers packages this early? I put the broom down and sauntered to the door. A second knock rapped on the door before I had a chance to grab the knob. "I'm coming already."

I turned the knob and opened the door. To my astonishment Marjorie was standing there in a very cute outfit. "This is an unexpected surprise!"

"Hi Tyler. Is your phone not working?"

"I probably have it turned off. I was performing last night

and probably didn't turn it back on. Why do you ask?"

"Tyler, you should probably sit down."

"What happened?"

"It's your mom. She was at the Waffle House this morning with her neighbor Eugenia when she started acting strangely. They called an ambulance and took her to Clayton General. They think she had a stroke."

It took a second for what she said to sink in. I think part of it was the shock of seeing Marjorie for the first time in months and here at my apartment. "Is she alright?"

"I don't know. The hospital tried calling your cell several times, and then tried your home number from your mom's phone, which was my home number. I'm sorry to be the one to break it to you."

"Thank you very much. You didn't have to come over and tell me, and I greatly appreciate it. I need to head up there and see what's going on."

"I hope your mother is okay, and if you need anything please let me know." We hugged and said our goodbyes.

The door closed and I slunk into a chair. I sat there for a moment and began to cry. I had already lost one parent, and I couldn't stand the idea of losing my momma. We may have had our differences, but we had always loved each other even though her way was a little twisted. I grabbed a tissue, wiped my eyes, and blew my nose. I started shaking from my head to my toes. I really needed to get a grip. I was in no mental shape to make the drive, so I grabbed my phone and sure enough it was off. I turned it on and the messages poured in. I listened to several from the hospital and several from Marjorie. It just really drove home the point that I really could lose my momma.

I called Germaine to only get his voice-mail, so I left a message. I then sent him a 911 text, which was our major emergency signal, so he should have called me back immediately. I waited and waited, but the return call never came. I started to hit panic mode because I had to get up to Clayton. I finally heard the bell of a received text so a wave of relief washed over me. I picked up the phone and looked to see a text message from Germaine. I clicked on it and looked at it in shock. "I'm busy." That is all it read. No explanation, no caring, no nothing. My sense of self-worth bottomed out again because here was supposedly one of my best friends totally blowing me off without any explanation. I felt abandoned all over again. I had to stop torturing myself. I was not alone.

If Marjorie had come all the way over here to give me the information, then maybe there was some shred of our friendship left there. I didn't blame her for not speaking to me because I really had been a dick. Not a small dick, but a huge dick. The kind you see advertised for the giant dildos and not that fake schlong they had in "Boogie Nights."

It was time to swallow some more of my pride and make the call. I found Marjorie in my contacts and hit call. It rang one time.

"Hey boo. You alright?"

And that was all it took. I started crying and sobbing uncontrollably. I barely could get a word out of my mouth between the sobs.

"I'll be right there."

"Thank you," I stuttered and hung up.

There was no hesitation on her part. As I sat there, I realized I was still in my bathrobe. I needed to get presentable, but before I even finished that thought, there was a knock on the door.

I opened it to find Marjorie already here. "I couldn't go anywhere because I wanted to make sure you were alright," she said as she stretched out her arms to give me a great big hug. I didn't want the hug to end. "Do you want me to drive you up there?"

"Yes please," was all I could muster up.

"Go jump in the shower and put on some clothes. I hate to tell you boo, but you smell like an ashtray," she said.

"The life of a club kid," I said. "I'll process fast."

"You might want to pack an overnight bag as well," she

said. "Where is your baggage?"

"My baggage is all over my face," I said and managed to laugh.

"That's my boo. You could always make me laugh. Now get cleaned up," she ordered.

I jumped in the shower and took a lather-and-go shower. I rinsed every orifice and then stepped out onto the bath mat to dry off. The mirror was foggy and I could only make out a distorted image of myself as I dried off. I didn't want to look in the mirror because I didn't want to see how my face looked. I was a woman on the verge and needed to keep my nerves under control. I slipped on a fresh pair of underwear, wrapped myself in the towel, and went to my bedroom. To my surprise, Marjorie already had my bag packed and ready. She even pulled out a pair of jeans, a shirt, and my shoes to wear. She always knew what looked best on me. The only thing left to pack was my toiletries. All I had to do was throw them all into a bag, and I was ready to go.

I walked down the hall and I could hear talking. Germaine must have come home while I was cleaning up. I turned the corner and there was Chas sitting with Marjorie at the breakfast bar. "Howdy, stranger. How have you been?" he asked.

All I could do was run over and hug him. "I can't believe you are here," I said.

"Marjorie called and said it was an emergency. Plus, you need someone to drive your car up to Clayton if you are going to stay anytime, and I wanted to see the fall foliage, I hear it is really beautiful up there this time of year," he said.

I started to cry again. I couldn't believe that people cared about me enough to drop everything to help me out even though we parted not on the best of terms. I really dropped the ball on who my real friends were.

"Come on, Princess. I need your car keys so we can get rolling." Chas said.

"Here's a tissue. I don't need you dripping anything onto my seats," Marjorie said as she handed me a tissue.

"I would be more worried about what is dripping out of his pants then his nose," Chas said.

"Ha ha, bitch. I've missed you guys," I said.

"Come on. Time to roll," Marjorie insisted.

I grabbed my bags and tossed my car keys to Chas. We rolled the bags to the car, and I must say thank God to whoever put wheels on luggage because it was one of the best things that has every happened.

We got to the parking lot and Marjorie's Toyota was parked next to my blueberry. She popped the trunk and I loaded everything in. I was feeling anxious as I got into the car and strapped on my seatbelt. Marjorie sensing my uneasiness handed me a thermos. "Here, have a swig."

"I don't think I need any coffee. I'm already feeling pretty wired."

"Honey, it's not coffee. It will help you relax."

I smelled it and immediately knew it was my favorite drink. Nothing like a screwdriver to help you relax. "You know me so well."

"You're welcome. I figured it would help you settle down for the ride. I just hope we don't run into too much of the leafer traffic."

"It always sucks this time of year when the city folk invade the mountains to check out the color. It's great for the business, but it makes it impossible to get anywhere."

"You sound like your mom."

"Oh my God, you're right. At least I don't look like her in drag."

Traffic wasn't bad getting out of Atlanta, and Chas was right behind us.

"So how is 'The Package'?"

"He is doing fine. Things have really gotten good, and I wouldn't mind if he asked me to marry him."

"Can I be your maid of honor?"

"I wouldn't have it any other way. I just don't know when he is going to ask me, but I don't want to put any pressure there either because I don't want to scare him off."

"If living with me didn't scare him off, I think you will be alright."

"I hope so. He's a good guy. I did buy him some jockstraps to help hold his junk in while he runs. His balls are starting to hang a little low," she said and laughed.

"Really? I didn't think running could stretch your balls out."

"You would be surprised."

We chatted the entire ride up to the hospital and the time flew by. It was like old times, which I really missed. It also helped me take my mind off the situation even if it was for the briefest time.

Of course, as we got further into the mountains, the traffic filled up. The leaves were at their peak color and the scenery was breathtaking. I was always amazed at how the valleys looked like a multicolored rug from Pottery Barn. Just gorgeous.

I tapped my fingers on the hand rest and Marjorie could sense I was getting tense again.

"Sweetie, we will be there shortly," she said trying to comfort me. I just stared out the window for the last ten minutes of the ride.

We finally pulled into the hospital parking lot. I tried to regain as much composure as I could before we headed in.

"How do I look," I asked.

"Do you want the honest answer," Chas asked.

"Why not? It couldn't make the day any worse," I said.

"You look like a concerned son, and you couldn't be more beautiful," he said.

My heart melted. It was a real answer and wasn't dripping in sarcasm or hate that I was used to getting from the supposed A Gays.

Marjorie grabbed my hand and led me up to the ICU. Adding more shock to my day was Albert and Paul waiting for us outside my mother's room.

I burst out like a little baby again as I went to hug them both.

"We were up here already looking at the leaves," Paul said. "Then we got the call from Marjorie and knew we had to come over here."

"How are you holding up, sweetie?" Albert asked. "It's really good to see you, but I wish it were under different circumstances."

"Thank you both for coming. I want to say something to everyone. I totally fucked up our relationships, and I am so sorry. My stupid arrogance got in the way, and I destroyed everything we had, and for that, I am truly sorry," I said.

"No need to apologize, honey," Paul said. "You need to get in and see your mother now."

I pushed open the door and there was Eugenia by my mother's bedside. She came and gave me a hug. "Your mom is doing well, but she cannot speak currently and she is not moving," she said.

I looked at my momma and said, "Hi." I wasn't sure if it was her medications, but I swear I saw a spark of life in her eyes. I took her hand and squeezed. "I'm here for you," I said as a tear rolled down her cheek. "You remember everyone. They got me up here safely since I was a wreck." Everyone took turns saying some very nice things to my mother. I'm sure she appreciated it, but there was no telling how much she was comprehending. I just hoped they got her to the hospital in time, because every minute you can't get someone there to get their life saving drugs, the more the damage, and the longer the recovery.

"Can we say a prayer?" I asked the group. They all shook their heads yes.

"Dear God, please look down on your humble servant and grant her peace as she goes through this trying episode in her life. Please make sure that she knows she has a son who loves her very much and that she has many friends and family who are wishing for a speedy recovery. This we ask of you. Amen."

"Amen," everyone said.

"Visiting hours are over. I need you to shuffle along," the

nurse said. "Tyler, you can stay longer if you'd like."

"We are going to get something to eat before we head back to Atlanta. Do you want us to pick you up something," Marjorie asked.

"Yes, that would nice," I said. "Just something light because I really don't want anything heavy."

"We'll get you something to drink as well since they don't have many vending machines in this hospital," Marjorie said.

"Keep us updated won't you?" Chas asked.

"I promise," I said.

I hugged them all as they were heading out. I felt so much love coming back to me. It had been so long since I felt like this. It was a good moment in a messy situation. I watched as they all loaded into the elevator and disappeared. In that moment I went from pure joy to feeling all alone.

I spent some time by my mother's bedside while she slept. The nurses would come in at regular intervals to check her vital signs and make sure the drugs were dripping through the IVs. She looked peaceful as she was sleeping.

Eugenia and I met with the doctor, who informed us that she had had a mild stroke. They were going to monitor her and said we should go home and get some rest. They would call us if things changed. So it was time to head back to my old home. I still had the old house key on my key ring. There were a couple of other keys on there as well, I had no idea of what they were for, but the sad thing was I still kept them just in case I finally figured out what they were for. I think everyone does that because we don't want to toss them and realize that we need them.

The house had remained unchanged, as my mother was used to it and didn't want to change. A lot of it did remind her of my dad so she didn't want to lose touch with that feeling because, as she said, it felt like a warm blanket wrapped around her.

My room hadn't changed since the day I left, with the bed perfectly made, and all my mementoes in their same places. You could tell she had been in there to clean because there was not an ounce of dust to be found anywhere in the room. I sat on the bed and heard the old familiar squeak of the mattress springs. I bounced up and down a bit. The old memories washed over me as I sat there. It was hard to believe how fast things were happening.

I wandered around the house for what seemed like hours until my phone rang. It was the hospital calling. I hoped for the best but expected the worst.

It was Nurse Betty, who happened to be an old family friend. "Tyler, things are looking really good. She is responding extremely well to the medications and her vital signs are all very good. I'll give you an update before I go off my shift in the morning. I hope I won't be waking you up too early."

"Don't worry. I don't think I will get much sleep tonight. Thank you, Betty. I will speak with you in the morning."

At least one ray of sunshine finally broke through the clouds. Maybe God does answer prayers.

I found some leftovers in the fridge and made myself a very late dinner. It was time to get some sleep. People always say you can't ever go home, but this felt right.

The next couple of days was just good news after more good news. The stroke was mild and momma was getting stronger every day. The only complication was that she still could not speak, but they felt that would come back to her. After four days she was up and moving, and they felt she was ready to head home even though she wasn't speaking yet. I was amazed, but then again, my momma rarely ever got sick, so this shouldn't stop her. After a couple of days at home, her speech did return. It was timid at first, but day by day, it grew stronger as she started quoting the Bible again. This time the quotes were all positive and had nothing to do with damnation and hell. Maybe she was a changed woman.

The day finally came when I had to leave and head back to my life in Atlanta. It was nice to get away for a little bit. The boys and Marjorie had texted me every day to help keep me entertained while I was here, since there was not a lot to do around her when momma took her naps while she was rebuilding her strength.

My bags were packed and I squeaked the bed one more time just for the fun of it. Momma was waiting for me at the bottom of the stairs. "If you don't hurry you will get stuck in all that traffic in Atlanta," she yelled up at me.

"I'm coming, momma." I took one more glance around and it was time to return to the real world.

We hugged at the door. I knew she would be good, and all of her friends promised me that they would stop by and check on her. "I love you very much," she said.

"I love you too, momma." We hugged one more time, and then I was off in the blueberry.

# CHAPTER 67

The crowning show was Saturday, so all the contestants were making their final pushes to get ready. I was in pretty good shape as my team - yes, I had a team again - whipped me into shape for my final numbers of the competition.

We decided that I needed to sing one song live from "Bombshell" - "Let Me Be Your Star" - since the injunction said the musical couldn't be performed, but didn't say anything about singing a song. I would do it as the second number, which I was hoping would turn into a grab the cabbage song.

"I had bought this earlier for you, so I am glad you get a chance to wear it," Paul said as he pulled out a black dress bag from the closet. He gently placed it into my waiting arms. I placed it on the table and slowly pulled open the zipper and everyone stared in anticipation. As the bag opened I could see the coral blue bugle beads glisten in the light. I pulled the zipper faster as my heart raced.

It was a coral blue ocean in front of me, and as I held it up everyone oohed and aahed over it. The dress had a wide collar at the neck and flowed down the crack of my bosoms, expanding over the breasts, leaving my shoulders and arms exposed, and fell all the way to the floor.

"This will bring in the coins," Chas said.

"It is beautiful, Paul. I can't thank you enough," I said.

"I hoped you'd like it," was Paul's only response.

I held it up and looked in the mirror. My hair needed to

be pulled back into a bun and I needed some rhinestone bracelets to complete the look.

"Were you thinking about these?" Albert asked has he handed me two rhinestone bracelets.

"You know me so well," I said.

"And don't forget the teardrop earrings," Marjorie said as she held out her hands with two of the prettiest earrings I had ever seen.

"Thank you so much," I said.

"But you can't forget the first number either," Paul said as he held up a sparkly dance number with see through mesh in certain areas. "We were kind of thinking a non-traditional wig color for this dress would look great."

Chas pulled out a powder pink wig to go with this outfit. I tried on the wig, I liked the fact that it had bangs that framed my face. Now I just had to nail down the final number to fit the outfit.

The first song that popped into my head was Britney Spears's "Toxic." This outfit just screamed that into my head. So it was all decided, and just in time because the club was taking all the contestants out to dinner tonight as a way of saying "thank you" for all our hard work over all these months.

I got along with most of the girls during the competition with the exceptions of Dixie and Athena. They each took this competition to the nth degree as each was so hell bent on defeating the other one that they were not pleasant to be around, so to be trapped with them at dinner wasn't going to be fun.

I was going in boy drag to the dinner since it was a night off from the competition and I just wanted to wear something comfortable for once that didn't pinch and bind different body parts. I chose a pair of blue jeans and a light cotton sweater since there was a chill in the air tonight, though hopefully not at the table.

The club selected a restaurant in Midtown - Cam's - that was an old converted house, but the real reason I think they picked it was because it was within walking distance of the club. The restaurant had a gracious front wrap around deck and a lot of architectural accents. I entered from the deck into the very comfy bar area, which featured a lot of dark wood and a wall of bottles where Mr. Winston, Marni, and Kit N Kaboodle were already waiting with cocktails in hand. I didn't realize Mr. Winston was coming. I assumed everyone was going to be on their best behavior.

I sauntered over to the bar and greeted everyone with a very large smile. I was grateful to see them all.

"Don't blind me those pearly whites," Mr. Winston said.

"And feel free to order whatever you want tonight. The club is picking up the tab," Marni said.

"Hello, Miss Kaboodle. You are looking mighty cute. I don't think I have ever seen you just in boy clothes," I said.

"Why, thank you, kind sir. It is a rare sight. Don't tell anyone, because I don't want to lose my drag queen card," she said as she laughed.

The other girls started rolling in in their boy clothes as well, and we had a rolling good time chatting at the bar and getting caught up with one another. With all our fundraisers, we rarely got a chance to see anyone anymore.

Precious Oil arrived and she was hobbling around with one foot in an air cast. Before anyone could even ask she let it out. "I was entertaining a very nice gentleman the other evening when I decided to do a tipple axel when I should have done a triple Lutz. Next thing I knew, I was flying through the air where my foot landed on the dresser while the rest of me ended up pinched between the wall and said dresser," she said.

"Can you perform this weekend?" Marni asked.

"Hell yes! I wouldn't miss it for the world. I didn't do all this work to quit now," she said.

"That's the spirit," Mr. Winston said.

The mood was light and jovial until we all felt a cold chill as the deck doors opened and in stepped Athena and her ex-sidekick, Dixie, both dressed in high-whore drag. I just guessed everyone would be in boy clothes, but I was wrong.

"Hello, bitches!" Athena said. "I have another fundraiser I have to attend this evening so I can't stay here forever."

"And I have one more fundraiser scheduled later this evening so I will need to blow this popsicle stand as soon as dinner is over," Dixie said.

"I'm glad you could join us. Grab a drink," Mr. Winston said.

Luckily our table upstairs was ready, so we all proceeded up the winding staircase to the second story, which was all open now with a variety of seating areas. Some were larger and some were very private and romantic. If I ever got a date, this would be a great place to bring him to.

We all grabbed our seats and the appetizers were already waiting for us. It was a plethora of food on tapas plates ranging from chicken wings, olives, various cheeses, and hummus, and not being proud queens, we all started to dig in. I was even surprised to see Anna Mia eating. Normally a Tic-Tac put her over the edge, but here she was eating regular food. I had to ask. "Anna Mia, you have a good appetite tonight."

"There is nothing to help you fix your problems like a good psychologist and a dietitian. They taught me how to eat properly and figure out why my eating was so fucked up," she said. "The only problem is I'm starting to outgrow my dresses. I've got enough that will work this weekend, but I might need to make a dress run after the competition."

Everyone was very proud of her and gave her congratulations. All except Athena.

"So you're finally eating normally. Let's shout it from the mountains that food no longer grosses you out," she said.

And here I was feeling a sense of camaraderie from all the contestants that we hadn't really shared throughout the rest of the contest.

"Athena, who peed in your Cheerios?" Marni asked. "Can't you just enjoy a moment for once?"

"Yes, young lady. Have another cocktail, sit back and

relax," Mr. Winston said. He grabbed a knife and tapped on the water glass. Everyone turned their attention to Mr. Winston and actually paid attention.

"I want to say thank you for all you have done for your charities," he said. "Most people don't realize how much need there is out there in the communities because they are all isolated in their own worlds. The main reason I started this contest was to give back and bring attention to the various causes that still need our help. With the advancement of AIDS medications, the younger crowd thinks there is no reason to have safe sex anymore because they think of HIV and AIDS as treatable diseases. Those of us who have been around for a much longer time than most of you remember losing friend after friend. I do this to honor the people who have left us and moved onto a much better place and for those who will benefit from all your generosity. I want you all to know that you are artists in your own right and you have brought joy to this old heart. Raise your glasses. Here's to many more years!" he finished.

"Cheers," everyone said and took a swig from their respective glasses.

"Does he really think we are all artists?" I asked Marni.

"Yes, dear, he does. Mr. Winston is typically a man of few words, and what he says, he means."

"That's good to know," I said. It made me feel better.

"Well, girls, this has been lovely and fun, but I'm off like a prom dress," Athena said.

"But you haven't even eaten anything," Marni said.

"I'm watching my girlish figure, which some of these people at the table obviously aren't," she said as she stared at Anna Mia.

"Blow it out your pie hole," Anna said. "This chicken is delicious. It tastes like your ex-boyfriend's penis."

"Why you little bitch," Athena started before she got cut off by Mr. Winston.

"Now you all need to play nice, you hear?" he said. "Now is the time for celebration."

"I will be the one celebrating," Athena said as she stamped her way down the stair case.

"Thank God. She was getting on my nerves," Dixie said.

"How were you ever friends?" Miranda asked Dixie.

"I don't know. Everything was wonderful at first until the pageants started. Then she became a bitch that I couldn't stand to be around," she said.

"Well, as long as I've known her, she has always been a bitch," Mary Jane said. "But enough about her. I want more details from Precious about her trick. Let me guess, He was a big, white muscle boy with a great ass."

"You know me so well. Child, the things that boy could do with his tongue just had me screaming. I'm surprised my neighbors didn't come by to ask if anything was wrong," Precious said.

"Where do you meet all these men and what do I have to do to get someone to give me a tongue bath?" I asked.

"Sweetie, they are all around for the picking. You just need to pay more attention because, girl, you get cruised all the time and pay them no mind," Precious said.

"Yes, I agree honey. You are a cute boy, and once the competition is done, I'm sure you will have some time to shake your ass and start pulling in some tricks," Miranda said.

"I just don't notice anyone cruising me," I said.

"Girl! Open your eyes! They cruise you all the time. You are a sexy young thing that has people wetting their pants because they want to get into your pants. Capisce?" Precious said.

I didn't understand what "Capisce" was, so I just agreed. If my friends said people were cruising me, but I wasn't paying attention, then maybe I needed to open my eyes a little more. If I opened my eyes a little more, maybe I'd be able to open my ass a little more.

"The final show is Saturday, and I expect everyone to be on their best behavior," Mr. Winston said. "We have raised a lot of money, of which I am very proud, but the winning total won't be announced until we crown a winner. It has been an extremely successful fundraiser, well beyond what I expected. It will set a very high bar of what the next contestants will have to achieve to beat you bitches."

I was glad none of us knew the totals because that kept us in the dark and fed our drive to win. If you didn't know where you placed, then you always had the belief that you could still wear the crown. I didn't care where I was in the competition anymore. It was more about the journey of getting here and helping people out. I never would have met the homeless individuals who lived under the bridge on Piedmont if it weren't for my involvement in the fundraiser. I guess it has made me more consciously aware of the things I could do in the community to help it.

I didn't realize that Mr. Winston had asked me a question. I guess I was in my own world at this point.

"Tyler, so what have you learned from this experience?" he repeated.

"I've learned that the smallest action can have a huge effect on someone's life," I said.

And with that he said, "I wish you all well on Saturday, and enjoy the rest of the evening. I'm too old to stay out this late anymore. I'm looking forward to seeing what you do on Saturday."

Mr. Winston left our little group to chat and be as catty as we wanted to be for the rest of the evening. It was the evening I hoped would have happened much earlier in the competition, but better late than never.

# CHAPTER 68

My garment bags were packed and the wigs were in their box. I had my makeup case, shoe bag, and walk-about outfit already on, so I was as ready as I was ever going to be.

"Come on, my little butterfly," Marjorie said. "Time for you to spread your wings one more time."

"Yes, dear. I am ready and a little nervous." It had been an emotional journey and now it was coming to an end. Surprisingly, I would miss everyone, including Athena, because she pushed me to be a better performer even though she didn't go about it in the best way. "This is the last time we will be performing as a group, which will be weird."

"Don't worry. You will have plenty of other opportunities to perform with the girls," Marjorie said. "It isn't the end of everything, but just a new beginning. Whatever happens tonight I want you to know that you will always be my queen."

"Thank you so much. Tomorrow I will go back to being just a hotel employee."

"Don't think of it that way. Tomorrow will be the first day of the rest of your life and anything can happen. You also could be the homecoming queen, so you will have that to deal with for the next year."

"People don't realize that this was like having a second job. It was a lot of work, but I'm truly glad I did it."

"Come on, princess. Your chariot awaits," she said as we grabbed the bags and headed out the door.

We got to the club a little early. I was very surprised to see this many cars in the lot this early. I knew there weren't any events scheduled before the show, so I guessed people were getting here early so that they could grab a seat. At least this would give me some time to mingle with everyone and have a cocktail. Nothing like an orange shot of inspiration to deal with a bunch of hostile queens. At least the drama had died down for a little bit as everyone moved onto the next snipey bit of news.

The dressing room was starting to fill up as everyone slid into their dressing stations. Some of the girls had brought in some more hair and makeup people and dressers for this show. Well, not everyone. Just Dixie and Athena. It didn't shock me. Everyone else came with their usual helpers.

Marjorie and I got everything into its place and then slid out to the bar. As we opened the doors from the show room into the bar, there was a larger crowd than expected already drinking at the bar. We walked right up to the bar and the bartender poured me a double screwdriver. "This one's on me," he said. "I can't thank you enough for all the work you have done this year in helping the homeless kids. I used to be one of them, and I wished your charity had been around when I needed it. I'm just glad the lost kids have an option now."

"I didn't realize that," I said.

"It's not something that I share too often. It was rough, but I managed to come through it," he said.

"Thank you for the drink," I said.

There was a commotion at the door as Miss Gigi came strolling in trying to make as much noise as possible to suck all the attention out of the room. I hate to say it, but she did look gorgeous in her makeup and hair and her gown was stunning. All eyes had turned to her and she knew it. Could she be any more of an attention whore? I'm glad her racket was short lived as she headed off to the dressing room.

The crowd was jovial as they waited patiently for the doors to the show room to open an hour before curtain time. I did have a couple of patrons come up and tell me how much they enjoyed my performances over the competition, which did give me a boost.

We had no idea of what the other contestants had raised, but over the course of the competition I had raised a lot of money, so I felt like I had a chance to get the crown. I just hoped there were some bobby pins in the crown so that they could pin it to my wig when they put it on my head.

Marjorie had to tap me on the shoulder, "Did I lose you there for a minute?" she asked.

"Just visualizing," I said.

"Keep it all positive," she said.

The rest of the crew arrived. As they approached, I could tell Paul was holding something behind his back. He pulled out and presented me with a beautiful bouquet of daisies, which were my favorite flowers. They are just so bright and cheery.

"These are from all of us," he said.

"I can't thank you all enough," I said. "I know I went off the deep end for a while, but I am so glad you are back in my lives."

It became group hug time as they all closed in and embraced me in a circle.

Several of the other contestants were also mingling in the bar and chatting with their own support systems. I managed to meet most of the helpers over the course of the competition since we ended up bumping into each other backstage. It really was a great group of people who didn't get a lot of recognition for all that they did. These were the people in the trenches working to help raise money for the various charities. They were not the public faces of the charities, but they were just as important as the heads of the organization.

By this time, the crowd had formed a line at the show room doors so that they could grab a seat the minute the doors opened. From what I could tell, this was the largest crowd for any of the shows. I slid backstage to get into my dance outfit for "Toxic." I didn't want anyone to see my new outfits until I hit the stage. You could tell that the doors to the show room had finally opened as the volume level from the room rose dramatically.

You could feel the energy in the dressing room as the chatter and the laughter were going up. My flowers looked beautiful next to the mirror. Most of us bantered back and forth and were enjoying ourselves until Miss Gigi came over to my station. You could feel the room get a little quieter as she approached me.

"Hello," I said in my best ice bitch mode.

"Could we step outside and speak in private?"

"Why?"

"Because there are some things that I would like to tell you."

"I don't think that is a very good idea," Marjorie said.

"I agree with you, but I will give her two minutes outside," I said.

"Are you sure that is a good idea?" Marjorie asked.

"I'll be fine," I said. I followed Miss Gigi into one of the store rooms so we could speak in private. Before the door closed I took a look back to see Marjorie, Miranda and Mary Jane looking down the hall at us. When they saw I had caught them looking they all pretended to be doing something else. I turned back from their sheepish stares to face Miss Gigi. "So you have me here, what did you want to tell me?"

"First, I want to apologize for the way everything went down. I didn't mean to hurt you," she said.

"What do you mean you didn't mean to hurt me? How could you have not realized that what you said was going to destroy my name and that's all I've got," I said. "Why did you even do it? You've never given me your lame excuse for why you did it."

"That's what I'm trying to tell you," she said. "Once Germaine found his hidden power, I was no longer important to him. I felt everything I had built was slipping away from me."

"What was really slipping away from you? You had been going out with someone, and yes, maybe things were not working out. That's your life, not mine. You had all your community theater stuff that you were doing and enjoying," I said.

"But it wasn't enough for me. I loved the attention I got when we did the show together. People actually liked me for what I was doing," she said.

"Let me interrupt you here. People liked you because you were not a crazy psycho bitch anymore, and they finally got to see your creative side for once and actually took an interest in your life. I still don't understand what this has to do with me?" I asked.

"I was just emotional," she said.

"So is this all you have to say? If you're emotional, eat some chocolate or some cake. I don't really care what you stuff into your face. If that's it, then your two minutes are up. You publically humiliated me. Enjoy your life." I turned and walked away. I didn't have time to listen to anymore of her bullshit and there was no way I was accepting her lame apology.

I walked into the dressing room to find my crew waiting for me at my dressing station.

"How did it go?" Albert asked.

"You know. Once a crazy bitch always a crazy bitch," I said.

"Honey, this is your moment to really shine, so just let it slide off you like that jumbo dildo you have stashed away in the bedroom dresser," Chas said.

"How did you know?" I asked.

"Remember when I had to pack your bag for your trip to the mountains to take care of Momma? I'm very impressed," he finished.

I think I blushed, but you would never have seen it through the makeup.

"Why is everything about sex with you boys?" Marjorie

asked.

"You wouldn't understand," Chas said. "Unless you have a penis?"

"Did Germaine show up?" I asked.

"Sorry, sweetie, he hasn't," Marjorie said.

"His loss," I said.

Marni came rolling in with the "ten minutes till show time" announcement. "Ladies, I hope you are ready because we have a full house. I am so proud of all of you. Have a great show," he finished. He then came over to me. "You have a guest at the stage door who wants to come in. I don't know who it is, but he is hot."

"That's fine. Please send him in," I said.

"We are going to take our seats," Paul said.

"Break a leg," Albert said as they all hugged me on the way out.

All I could see coming at me was a large bouquet of flowers, which blocked the face of my mystery man. As he approached, all I could see were some extremely tight jeans showing off a nice package. He lowered the flowers. It was Tony from the Angel Flight benefit staring me in the face. "I would recognize that package anywhere. What a pleasant surprise," I said. "How did you remember to come out tonight?"

"I put the date into my calendar the night we met at Angelo's Hideaway. You were so kind to help me out that I wanted to return the favor and come out and support you," he said.

I put the flowers down on the table and hugged him very tightly. I just couldn't wait to get my arms around him again. He had on a leather vest, and this time, he had on a navy t-shirt with the sleeves rolled up that hid most of his hairy chest, but a fluff of hair still made it out over the collar. I could feel his heart beating as he pulled me closer. As he held me tight I could feel a thousand eyes in the dressing room burning holes through me. I'm sure they were all asking what this hot, sexy stud muffin was doing with me. I really didn't care because he was hugging me and not them.

The moment was broken when he asked me a question. "Why is my picture on your mirror?"

I turned to look at the mirror. There were several pictures on there, so I wasn't sure which one he was asking about. He pointed to the mystery man in the mask and mannequin tights from the Rexasaurass photo spread. "I was there for a benefit, and it was probably the only time I'd been there. You know, everyone gets their fifteen minutes of fame, and that was probably mine," he said.

I looked at the picture, and I didn't know what to say, so I moved in and stared a little closer.

"Oh my God, I didn't mess up your make-up, did I?" he asked. "You were looking so intently I thought I might have smeared something."

"Oh no, darling, everything is good. I didn't realize that was you in the picture. I'm not really sure how that picture ended up there. Maybe one of the other girls put it up there." I was too embarrassed to tell him that I was stalking the bar trying to find out who it was in the picture.

"I need to go out front. A couple of the guys came with me, and we are going to donate some money during your numbers," he said. He gave me a kiss on the cheek, and I could smell his cologne. It was the same one he was wearing the day we met. It set my senses on fire. As he turned, I finally saw the back of his vest, and it read "Leatherman 25."

My head started to spin. I don't know if it was the tight outfit or the rush of blood to my taped down penis that couldn't expand even if there was a hydraulic lift attached because of the many layers of sinchers and pinchers. I had to sit down.

"Are you alright girl?" Miranda asked.

"Just feeling a little flushed," I said and grabbed a fan. I could feel myself starting to perspire. I just hoped it didn't cause my make up to run. This was my dream man from the web, and he was here to see me. Did he even know it was me? He would have to I guess. Why else would he be here?

I snapped out of my dream world when I heard the overture begin which was followed by Kit N Kaboodle's number. From then on, she had the mic and the show was off and running.

A couple of the regular cast showgirls did a number before the first contestant came out to perform. "So tonight we are here to crown the first Miss Cabaret Club, and the winner will be the contestant who raised the most money for her charity over the course of the competition. Remember, all tips collected tonight will be added to their totals so please tip your favorite entertainers generously. The competition is very close, so every dollar counts." Kit said. "So without further ado, please welcome to the stage your first contestant, Ana Mia Drunkorexia!"

Ana Mia actually had curves tonight, which she had never had before on stage, and these were all real with no padding. Her time away had done her good. Instead of getting lilies from her fan base, she got red roses to show how much they loved her. It was inspiring to see the change in her played out on the stage as she went into "Beautiful" by Christina Aguilera.

The dollars just poured in, and I was getting a little worried that she might catch up to me. I wasn't sure if I was in first, but I had raised a lot of money. No one was sharing their dollar amount with the other contestants. The totals were a very highly guarded secret. I had to quit focusing on that, and just make sure I gave my best performance. One hundred percent was what I was expecting from myself.

She left the stage to a thunderous round of applause.

I stepped back a little further into the stage wing to gather my composure. A couple of the other contestants, Mary Jane and Athena, performed while I was rehearsing my dance routine in my head. All I really heard was a little banter between Kit and Athena, who sounded very composed for once. She didn't seem to have that angry edge tonight because she was focused on raising as much money as possible to pad her total. She was even charming. Damn her.

Miss Gigi was next. I didn't think she spotted me along the back wall where I was going to wait while she performed. She was introduced and off she went. She was doing one of her "bring down the house" numbers. When she was on, she was really good, and it seemed like she was hitting everything in the right spots tonight. I hated watching her impress the crowd. When you're mad at someone, all you want to do is see them fail, but this was her night. By the time she finished, she was bathed in sweat.

"Let's hear it for Miss Gigi," Kit N said. "She has a few words she wants to say." She passed the mic to Miss Gigi.

"I want to say congratulations to all the contestants who have worked so hard these months. Please give them a round of applause." With that, the audience cheered. "I want to recognize one of the contestants with whom I had the pleasure of working on the 'Bombshell' show, which many of you enjoyed. A lot of negative things have been said, and it is entirely my fault. Desiree didn't deserve all the abuse caused by me. In my struggle to get attention, I lied and said I wrote the show. I want to let you know that Desiree has been telling the truth and she was responsible for the show that many of you have seen. I want to make this public apology in the hopes that it will help ease the pain I have caused her. Have a good night everyone," she said as she handed the mic to Kit N.

"Well wasn't that special?" Kit N said. "Nothing like a little drama to make us all feel better about ourselves."

I was completely stunned as I stood in the wing. I never expected a public apology, but I was extremely grateful that she made one. I was hoping that all the crap that had been coming my way was going to disappear.

I didn't notice I had been introduced for my number until Dixie pushed me in the back, "Bitch, you scared to go out there?" she said.

The music for "Toxic" was already playing so I had to quickly get my shit together. I immediately hit the stage, and to my shock, the crowd came to their feet applauding. I was totally taken aback, since I had been the odd man out lately. I got into the groove and started shaking my ass and lip-syncing the words. The crowd was lined up to tip me, so I shook and grabbed, and shook and grabbed again. This was a fast number, so it was hard to just stand there and pull the cabbage, but I was determined to get every dollar I could. I was amazed that I had a line for the entire number. The last person to come and tip me was Tony. He had two hundred dollar bills to hand me. It was so beautiful, just like him, that it almost brought me to tears. By the end, I was a sweaty mess. I took my bow and exited the stage. In the wing Athena was waiting. "That's how it's done, Miss Thing," I said as I dumped the money into the bucket that one of Marni's little helpers was holding. It was a wad of cash. I'm glad they were there to take it and total it up. I didn't want to lose any of the dollars especially the ones that Tony had given me. What an incredibly generous thing to do.

Miss Gigi was waiting for me at my dressing station with a towel. "I figured you could use this," she said as she tossed me the towel. "I couldn't think of a better way to get you to really listen to my apology. I am very sorry for all the trouble I caused you," she said.

"Honey, I could never stay mad at you after that. It was much appreciated," I said as I leaned into hug her.

"I hope we can get back to where we were," she said.

"I think we can," I said. We all lose our way at some point, so I had to forgive her.

"Get a room," Marjorie said as she brought me another cocktail and came back to help me change into my next number. "I'm glad you two made up."

"Me too," Miss Gigi said. "Break a leg on your next number."

I needed to focus on the last number and do some vocal exercises before I went out and sang live. I hadn't had much time tonight with all the people being here early. It was very important to me that I got the number right. I wanted to go out with a bang. I thought once this show was over, it would be way too soon before I put a dress and heels on again.

Each contestant progressed through their numbers, and I could hear the applause all the way in the hall by the cooler, which was a great rehearsal space. I could hear myself sing here and know if I needed to change anything. My throat was thoroughly relaxed, and I could probably suck a mean dick right now, but that would have to wait.

I stood on the side and watched the banter back and forth between Dixie and Kit N. To me, Dixie was stretching too much to come off as authentic. You could tell she was faking it and so could the audience. It showed in how few tips she was getting on her number, which could hurt her final placement. I really didn't care.

Precious Oil was wonderful tonight and deserved all the praise that was getting heaped on her.

I enjoyed just being alone and watching from the wings. These girls really were talented, and I could see them going a long way with their craft if they wanted to pursue it after the competition.

But my quiet time came to an end when it was time for my final number. The DJ had special instructions to do a black out until I got to the mic. Once there, he started the track and a single spotlight illuminated my face as I started to sing live. The spotlight then widened, revealing my coral blue dream dress, and the crowd went wild. They lined up and I pulled the cabbage. It's always hard to see who's tipping you with the spotlight in your face, but I saw a lot of very familiar people coming up with dollar bills. I just kept singing my heart out and grabbing the dollars. Luckily there was a bucket right near, me so I could just open my hand and drop the dollars into the bucket. Finally, Tony came up as the last person in line. This time, my sweet man had three hundred dollar bills in his hand. He took my free hand and kissed it like a gentleman should and put the money into the bucket. Luckily I was near the end of the song, because I had a brief brain fart when it came to the lyrics, but I pulled them out of my ass somehow.

The number ended and the entire room was on their feet cheering and applauding. I was completely overwhelmed by their show of support that I started tearing up. I graciously curtsied and exited the stage. Most of the contestants were there to hug me the minute I got off stage and let me know how impressed they were. I thanked them all and reminded them that we are all artists out to change the world one show at a time. At that moment, I felt like I had found an extra family and all the pettiness and back biting was gone. A calm had come over me. Maybe this was inner peace?

The pomp and circumstance was over and now it was time to crown the first Miss Club Cabaret.

"Ladies and gentlemen, it is my great pleasure to bring back to the stage your contestants who have worked feverishly hard to entertain you and raise some money for some very worthwhile charities," she said. "Please welcome back to the stage Anna Mia Drunkorexia, Precious Oil, Miranda Lambadingdong, Desiree, Dixie Monroe, Mary Jane Bazooka, and last, but not certainly least, Athena Parthenos."

We had formed a straight line like at Miss America on the stage and were all holding hands and smiling. Athena looked like she had shoved her lips into the vat of Vaseline to keep that fake smile on. I swear there was a wad of oil in the corners of her mouth.

"Marni, please join me on stage with the envelopes," Kit N said.

Marni, all dapper in a tux now, looked like one of the accountants at the Oscar Awards holding the envelopes in his hand. "The order the contestants finished was determined by the amount of money they raised for their charities over the course of the competition, including all tip money from tonight," she said.

"In seventh place with a total of $3,250 is Anna Mia Drunkorexia." Anna stepped forward to accept her bouquet of flowers and then stepped back in line. "Just to let everyone know, Anna did an incredible job considering that her health prohibited her from competing for several months during the year. I must commend you."

"In sixth place with a total of $4,461 is Miranda Lambadingdong." Miranda let a bit old "Ye Haw" and took her bouquet of flowers and stepped back into line.

"In fifth place with a total of $4,869 is Dixie Monroe." Dixie looked like someone had sucker punched her in the gut as she accepted her flowers and stepped back into line.

"Better luck next year," Athena said from the front of the line.

"In fourth place with a total of $5,927 is Precious Oil." Precious, being the class act as always, stepped forward, threw a kiss, and thanked the crowd.

"In third place with a total of $10,111 is Mary Jane Bazooka."

Mary Jane stepped forward, "Thanks to everyone who came to the shows. I hope you had a rocking great time," she said and held her flowers high over her head.

Marni then had Athena and me step to the front of the stage. "Here are your two final contestants for Miss Club Cabaret. To say it was close was an understatement. The contestant in second place raised $12,539 and the winner raised $12,595. It all came down to the tips tonight to determine the winner."

I was stunned that I was standing there with Athena in the final two. Having Tony here turned out to be my good luck charm.

"Coming in second place is Desiree, which means our first Miss Club Cabaret is Athena Parthenos."

Athena pulled her hands away and they went straight to her face. All she could say was, "Yes. Yes. Yes." She then grabbed my hands and leaned in and whispered in my ear, "Suck it, bitch." She then kneeled down as the audience kept up their applause and Marni pinned the satellite sized crown to her head. Kit N placed the sash on her and handed her a bouquet of red roses. She immediately started mouthing "Thank you" to the audience and went into her Miss America wave. Her entourage came up on stage and started posing with her for pictures. She looked overjoyed and had a smile on her face from ear to ear. I was glad for her. She had wanted it more than I did, so I was glad she could enjoy the moment, even though she was an evil cunt.

My posse came up and all congratulated me for a job well done and hugged on me. We chatted briefly as my eyes kept darting over to Tony, who was patiently waiting for his chance with me. The gang sensed my distraction and said we would catch up later and left me alone.

Tony came strutting over. "Congratulations, baby. Sorry we didn't put you over the top," he said as he put his hands around my waist.

"Baby, you put me over the top in more ways than you can imagine. I am hoping that you are the Leatherman 25 whom I have been chatting with online."

"Yes, that is me,"

"What does the Leatherman 25 stand for?"

"When I was in high school, I lettered in baseball, so they retired my number, which was 25. So I had a letterman jacket with 25 on it, but then I came out and had a fascination with leather, so letterman became Leatherman 25."

"How did you know that was me you were chatting with online since you never saw me out of drag?"

"Your beautiful eyes."

"How could you tell from just my eyes?"

"I noticed on the night we met that you have a little bit of a brown spot on your left eye in your sea of blue. I recognized it instantly online."

"About the online stuff, I'm sorry that I wasn't more forthcoming upfront."

"Baby, don't worry about it. I'm a grown man, and I got my panties in a wad in a world of fantasy that I never should have. I had to get over myself because it was more important for me to be here for you."

That was the nicest thing that anyone had ever said to me, but there was still one important question that needed to be answered. "So I hope you are into boys and not just hitting on me because you like to get freaky with a drag queen?"

"I like boys, and I like you."

"Hold that thought, and let me go change," I said. I wanted to kiss him so bad, but I didn't want our first kiss to be smeared with make-up. I ran back to the dressing room and pulled out my box of baby wipes and had my face cleared off in record time. The posse was nice enough to have packed all the rest of my stuff, so the dress and all the other accoutrements were off and into their bags with post haste. I put on my boy clothes, checked myself in the mirror, smiled at myself, and went back into the room. Tony was standing there looking like an angel. I walked straight up to him, grabbed his thick black hair, and pulled his moist lips to mine. He grabbed me and pulled me as tight as he could. It was the most passionate kiss I had ever had in my short life, and hopefully there would be plenty more from where this came from. He finally gently grabbed my face and we stared into each other's eyes for what seemed like an eternity.

"Boys, I hate to interrupt your moment here," a strange voice said. Both of us turned to see a man in a pale yellow suit with extremely bushy hair and black-rimmed glasses standing there. "Miss Desiree, my name is Lester Chester, and I am the executive producer for the stage musical 'Bombshell.' There are a couple of things I would like to discuss with you."

"I'm sorry I sang the song tonight. I didn't realize that would violate the cease and desist order," I said.

"Heavens no! That's not why I'm here. I finally got a chance to see the video of your show that someone had submitted to us that led to the order, but I'm really here because I want to talk to you about some of your ideas for the show. You had some brilliant ideas that the writers I'm paying thousands of dollars to could never come up with. I want to talk to you about incorporating some into my show."

I think I let out a very high-pitched squeal. I looked at

Tony to see his reaction, but there was only a huge smile on his face. "I am so happy for you," he said.

"Yes, I would love to talk to you," I said.

He handed me his card and let me know he was in town until late Monday. "Have a great evening," he said. "Call me at my hotel first thing in the morning. The number is on the back of my card. I would like to set a meeting with you before I leave."

"Thank you, Mr. Chester. I'll call in the morning." I shook his hand and said good night.

I then grabbed Tony's hand and pulled him into the quiet wing of the stage. The house lights were up and music was playing, and all I could do was pull Tony tight. We started swaying to the music, and all I could say was, "Best night ever!"

# ABOUT THE AUTHOR

Berlinda Wall was born in Toledo, Ohio, which is a great place to be from. After surviving working in retail, Berlinda relocated to Atlanta in 1998. She quickly found herself involved with the local gay bowling community where she still participates in a league and helps on the local gay bowling tournament committee. She has been involved in volunteering for charities in the city and can be found performing at many benefits during the year. Berlinda also organizes her annual fundraiser, "Guys As Dolls Show," as a way of giving back to the community. You can communicate with Berlinda on Facebook at Berlinda Wall and Instagram at berlindawall.